Gender, Crime and Victimisation

Gender, Crime and Victimisation

Pamela Davies

Los Angeles | London | New Delhi
Singapore | Washington DC

First published 2011

SAGE Publications Ltd
1 Oliver's Yard
55 City Road
London EC1Y 1SP

SAGE Publications Inc.
2455 Teller Road
Thousand Oaks, California 91320

SAGE Publications India Pvt Ltd
B 1/I 1 Mohan Cooperative Industrial Area
Mathura Road
New Delhi 110 044

SAGE Publications Asia-Pacific Pte Ltd
33 Pekin Street #02-01
Far East Square
Singapore 048763

Library of Congress Control Number: 2010924434

British Library Cataloguing in Publication data

A catalogue record for this book is available from the British Library

ISBN 978-1-84787-027-8
ISBN 978-1-84787-028-5 (pbk)

Typeset by C&M Digitals (P) Ltd, Chennai, India
Printed by MPG Books Group, Bodmin, Cornwall
Printed on paper from sustainable resources

Contents

List of Figures

List of Tables

List of Boxes

Acknowledgements

I would like to thank several people who have encouraged me in the writing of this book. In particular, my colleague Peter Francis stands out for his unwavering support and for the valued wisdoms he has shared with me over the last 17 years. Hazel Croall, Barbara Hudson and Mary Mellor have also been inspirations to me and friends along the way. These and other colleagues, too numerous to mention, in criminology and sociology who must surely have been wondering what exactly I have been doing much of the time deserve to see a final product! I also owe a debt of gratitude to students who have debated many of the issues that appear throughout this book and who have done much to shape its content. Thanks are also due to the editorial team at Sage, Caroline Porter and Sarah-Jayne Boyd for their patience and support of this book.

Finally, thanks to my parents Joyce and Bill, my husband Damian and our children, Rory, Callum and Jonathan without whom I would never remain sane.

1

THE GENDER AGENDA TO CRIME AND VICTIMISATION

CONTENTS

GLOSSARY TERMS

Primary victimisation

Tertiary victimisation

Indirect victimisation

Victimology

Gender

Sex

Feminism

Crime victim

Masculinity

Gender-neutral

Gender-free

Gender myopia Gender-blindness

Gender-bias

Gender specificity

'Doing-gender'

Doing-difference'

CHAPTER AIMS

- Outline the parameters and the major frames of reference for the book
- Specify the aims and objectives of the book
- Establish the benchmarks for exploring gender, crime and victimisation
- Introduce the key research, theory and policy agendas

Introduction

Students of criminology and related disciplines can now be pointed towards a growing body of authoritative texts that feature the word 'gender' in their titles. Words in addition to gender such as *crime, criminal justice, violence* and *imprisonment* are connected in titles belonging to several of the more 'criminologically' focussed publications. The title and content of this book is therefore original and different from any of these in that it connects the word gender to both of the additional words, *crime* and *victimisation*. The latter constitute the two major frames of reference for this book's gendered journey.

Within one frame of reference, gender – *and crime* a detailed examination of gender patterns to offending and more broadly to the committing of crime are examined. How these patterns are variously established and represented, researched, explained, theorised and responded to by policy makers and criminal justice intervention methods are all examined through a gendered lens. Within the other frame of reference, gender – *and victimisation* is a detailed examination of gender patterns to victimisation including criminal victimisation, **primary, tertiary and indirect victimisation** and other forms of social harm. How these patternings of victimisations in society are variously established and represented, researched, explained, theorised and responded to by policy makers, criminal justice and other intervention strategies and support networks are simultaneously examined through a gendered lens. Using these two major frames of reference, which are given roughly equal weight, this book explores a comprehensive range of gender issues in the study of crime and victimisation.

The remainder of this introductory chapter outlines the scope, aims and objectives of this book. It includes a preliminary discussion on the gender agenda to crime and victimisation drawing on key developments within the discipline of criminology and its sub-discipline **victimology**. It justifies why gender is central to this book's content and it outlines a number of gendered themes and threads that are prioritised within its pages. It is initially important to clarify what is meant by **gender** as there is confusion evident in some criminological and victimological literature. This clarification of meaning is best achieved by reference to what gender does not mean as well as what it does mean.

The most appropriate way to explain how gender is commonly used throughout this book is to refer to it as a sociological term where there is specific distinction between sex and gender. The word gender is sometimes inappropriately used as a substitute for the word **sex** and this changes the original meaning. To clarify the sex/gender confusion Walklate's observation is useful: 'sex differences, i.e. differences that can be observed between the biological categories, male and female: they are not necessarily a product of gender. Gender differences are those that result from the socially ascribed roles of being male or being female, i.e. masculinity and femininity' (Walklate, 2004: 94).

When teaching these terms the following simple schema helps not only clarify but also complicate our understanding of gender:

SEX   GENDER

Male/Female   Masculine/Feminine

This simple schema raises oppositional associations of male/female and of masculine and feminine. These are often referred to as 'gender dichotomies' and a number of these are illustrated later in this introductory chapter.

Glossary

Above you will have noted how some words/terms/concepts – for example 'primary', 'tertiary' and 'indirect victimisation', 'victimology' and 'gender', have been highlighted in bold. When you see emboldened terms like this you should refer to the comprehensive glossary at the end of the book. There these terms are listed in alphabetical order and a succinct meaning of each is provided.

The scope of this book

This book will challenge and equip a range of readers including undergraduate, postgraduate, PhD students and other academic scholars and researchers as well as crime and justice sector workers, policy makers, crime journalists and other critical commentators to understand more comprehensively and to debate critically gender issues in the study of crime and victimisation. The book brings together research issues, theoretical developments and policy matters connected to the study of gender, crime and victimisation in a clearly signposted and uniquely structured way. It adopts a broadly historical approach to this project of combining academic and mediated knowledges and perspectives on the study of criminology with those of victimology. It draws particularly on the influences of **feminism** and on the author's experiences of teaching, researching and writing within the fields of crime and criminology and on the subject of the **crime victim** and victimology. A case study, entitled 'Women and Crime for Economic Gain', was concerned with critically examining women's motives for doing economic crime, forms a key point of reference, exemplification and illustration throughout this book. The aims of the particular research study which is referred to here as the main case study are briefly outlined later in this introductory chapter.

The broad aim of this book then, is to offer a detailed critical appreciation of how crime is a gendered phenomenon, how crime and risks to criminal victimisation and other forms of harm can be known about more fully and how gender impacts upon and influences the experiences and recovery from crime and victimisation in society. The book explores the changing understandings of femininity and **masculinity** through an examination of offending, the committing of crime more broadly and experiences of victimisation in society. It focuses on the importance of gender in part by drawing attention to areas of scholarship and practice where the woman and/or man in question is absent. Thus **gender neutrality** and **gender myopia** as well as **gender bias** are all considered within a broader appreciation of the social constructions of deviance, crime and offending, victimisation and social harm. This focus upon a gender/crime/victimisation nexus is original and this book represents one of the first efforts to do this. In this way the book will consolidate the knowledges that inform the gender agenda to crime and victimisation in society, yet it will explore more fully, explain, illustrate, exemplify, debate and critically analyse these knowledges, in its ambition to be innovative and forward looking with its arguments. As part of this task the book aims to explore and explain how a gendered approach variously informs understanding of each of the following –

- definitions of: deviance, crime, offending, criminal victimisation, social harm;
- patterns to: crime, types of crimes, offending, criminal victimisation and social harm;
- the above as socially and unequally distributed;
- processes of criminalisation and social control and their structural (gender) biases;
- visible and invisible: crimes, types of crimes, offending, criminal victimisation and social harm;
- the above as 'locationally' biased;
- fears, anxieties, worry and concern about: crimes, types of crimes, offending, criminal victimisation and social harm;
- risks to crime, criminal victimisation and social harm;
- the above as socially and unequally visited;
- crime prevention, community safety and control strategies and their structural (gender) biases;
- state, voluntary and other responses to populations experiencing criminal victimisation and social harm;
- familial, local, community, regional, national, international and global responses to crime, disorder, deviance and offending, criminal victimisation and social harm.

In order to ensure that all of the above are catered for within the pages of this book, a particular way of organising the contents has been devised. As you will have noted from the contents pages each chapter is clearly labelled. The contents allow us to explore:

- various mediated knowledges of the crime and victimisation problems in society;
- feminist influences and contributions to criminological and victimological ideologies, theoretical inquiry and policy making agendas;

- men's, and women's committing of volume crimes and violences;
- men's, and women's risks of experiencing of criminal victimisation and other harms;
- the feminist movement, state and voluntary sector responses to offending and the committing of crime;
- the feminist movement, state and voluntary sector responses to victimisation and harm in society.

The approach that is adopted throughout the book is one which is supported by a range of pedagogic features. These are explained in more detail later in this chapter. However, the main vehicle for exemplification and illustration is that of the case study. In the main this is used to demonstrate the practical element of key theoretical debates. One main case study is drawn upon – see below – and a whole variety of other mini-case studies are also offered to encourage the reader to engage in critical reflection of the issues under discussion and to facilitate this approach as an original method of research amongst potential researchers in this field. Alongside these illustrations the type of reflective critique that is offered incorporates the following:

1 a historical and contemporary approach to reviewing research and theoretical developments;
2 a historical and contemporary approach to reviewing policy and practice issues;
3 combining and contrasting perspectives on the study of criminology with those of victimology;
4 drawing especially on the influences of feminisms and the 'woman question' and later developments around masculinities and the 'man question';
5 drawing on the author's experiences of doing original fieldwork;
6 exemplification, illustration and evidencing all of the above.

The scope of the book is designed to help shape and construct a gender agenda for the future which is more fully appreciative and understanding of the nature, extent, distribution and experiences of crime and victimisation in society. It is simultaneously designed to facilitate the reader with material relevant to help inform scholarly and robust criminological and victimological opinion on the relative salience of gender. In terms of gender specific matters the key foci for the book are made explicit from the outset and for clarity they are simply listed below. The explanation and exemplification is left for us to explore in detail in Chapters 2–8.

Key foci for the book

- the framing of maleness and femaleness as related to knowledges about crime and victimisation in society;
- gender related ambiguities and conundrums about crime and victimisation;
- feminist inspired research and knowledges as a spur to improved gendered research and knowledges around crime and victimisation;

- to use the above to critique other scholarly and mediated knowledges as well as social and public policy around crime and victimisation;
- gender alongside other salient 'power' issues connected to crime and victimisation, in particular, the relevance of gender-class intersections;
- feminist, critical and masculinities scholarship abilities to confront current and emerging dilemmas and challenges around (gendered) offending, crime and victimisation.

The next section begins to address the fundamental question, 'Does gender deserve priority?' In the context of social division, multiple identities and the intersectionalities betwixt gender-class-race-age, is this book justified in prioritising gender as opposed to any other variable that might equally or more forcefully impact upon people's committing of crime and experiences of victimisation?

Crime, victimisation/social division nexus

Social divisions are social categories. Such categories can include race, gender, age, class, sexuality, disability, mental health and physical disability (Davies et al., 2007). Social categories are not static, but, rather, dynamic and change over time, space and place. As Best (2005: 324) states, 'Social categories are not simply given, they have to be established and maintained and the process through which they appear is known as *social division*'. They are situated historically, culturally, economically, and politically. From the outset it is important to acknowledge that the intersectionalties of class-race-age-gender or multiple inequalities (Daly, 1993) variously combine 'as intersecting, interlocking and contingent' (Daly, 1997: 33). Class, race, age, and gender are the major social inequalities in our society. To be poor, to be black, to be young and to be female, simultaneously represents different distinct social categories with combined significance and relation to relative disadvantage, exclusion, marginalisation and powerlessness (Davies et al., 2007). Gender is therefore only one of a number of processes or social variables – social class, age, gender and ethnicity – that are usually attributed to framing our experiences of criminal victimisation (Davies et al., 2007) and which get to the very 'nature and essence 'of things (Keat and Urry, 1975 cited in Mawby and Walklate, 1994: 18). Several contemporary theoretical, feminist inspired constructs, have been postulated (see Connell, 1987, 1995; Messerschmidt, 1993, 1994, 1995, 1997, 2004) which suggest that gender is sometimes highly salient in understanding both offending and victimisation. '**Doing-gender**', the theoretical formulation most extensively demonstrated by West and Zimmerman (1987) and West and Fenstermaker (1995) was later extended to 'doing race' and 'class' (Daly, 1993, 1997) so that a new understanding of 'difference' is that it is viewed as an ongoing interactional accomplishment. The focus on gender as something which is socially constructed sees gender as 'omnirelevant'. Moreover, it is something we are accountable for and any occasion offers the resources for doing it. Similarly **'doing-difference'** explains how gender, race and class operate simultaneously and like gender is a process. Race and class are similarly ongoing methodical and situated accomplishments (Lorber, 1994; Simpson and Elis, 1996; West and Fenstermaker, 1995; West and Zimmerman, 1987).

Gender salience?

Some gender and feminist scholars have focussed exclusively on the 'risk/ gender nexus', where 'gender and risk are interlinked and often mutually constitutive' (Hannah-Moffatt and O'Malley, 2007: 7) and yet they too are quick to acknowledge that identifying gendered risks is only part of the endeavour to capture the lived everyday realities of people's experiences of social harm and criminal victimisation. Gendered risks are integrally linked, simultaneously and interconnected to other inequalities and gender can be located within this broader matrix. Others have similarly grappled with intersections acknowledging that fundamental differences exist in the life experiences of women (Simpson and Elis, 1995; Simpson and Gibbs, 2006).

At the same time as the arguments in this book will be suggesting that a gendered approach is sometimes useful and helpful, it will also be suggesting it can be ambiguous and confusing and furthermore, it remains open on the question as to whether it is ever or always the key variable in understanding the relationship between gender, crime and victimisation. Others have briefly confronted this very question. Walklate (2003) for example, has asked whether there can be a feminist victimology. Central to this question she argues, are the tensions between conventional victimological concerns and a feminist-informed agenda. She swiftly poses the more gender-friendly question whether there can be a feminist informed victimology (2003: 38) and states:

> It is this kind of theoretical starting point, which neither treats gender as a variable nor locates it purely as a definitional category, which permits the inclusion of a critical edge of feminist work into victimology'. (2003: 41)

In relation to masculinities, elsewhere Walklate (2006) has queried when is it that being masculine is the key variable in understanding the relationship between men, crime and victimisation and when other variables might be more important. There are then some dissenting voices from highly gender sensitive scholars as to whether a culturalist-dominated gender studies continues to be useful (Hall and Winlow, 2003a, 2003b). The same authors have consistently asserted that men's and boy's violence is not best explained or likely to be reduced by focussing on the hegemonic masculinity thesis (Hall, 2002; Hall and Winlow, 2003a, 2003b). Some of these very issues are at the heart of discussions in Chapters 4 and 6 in particular.

Arguments in support of prioritising other key variables might be equally applicable to the study of victims and victimology. There is convincing evidence and debate for giving at least equal priority to age in explaining and understanding victimisation and social harm in society. In respect of the case study research example threaded throughout this text connected to women's motivations for committing economic crime, we might similarly question whether it is need and/or greed that is key to understanding the committing of economic crime by women (Davies, 2005) rather than their womanhood. There are then some minor signposts that indicate dissenting voices over whether gender ought to always be omnipresent. Is gender therefore a 'red herring' and a distracting cul-de-sac or precisely the opposite, a gateway to new revelations and knowledges? Here we justify and assume that gender matters, but that 'doing-gender' ought not to always and necessarily take precedence over economic and class explanations.

Nevertheless, from the outset, this book also focuses most explicitly on experiences, fears and perceptions of crime and victimisation through a gendered lens. At regular intervals class, race and age are also foregrounded as a reminder that readers are encouraged to think also about these interactions. As to whether or not it is justifiable to prioritise gender, readers are also encouraged to have an open mind on this question and to reserve their final opinion on it until after the final chapter. The arguments of the book are intended to be provocative and stimulating and to engage readers in serious consideration of whether and when gender matters most in understanding crime and the experience and recovery from victimisation.

A gender agenda?

The importance and significance of exploring structural variables in the study of crime and victimisation has long been recognised in the US and UK although some social inequalities and socio-structural factors have attracted greater attention than others. Class related demographics and influences were exposed as fundamentally important to sociological explanations of crime and deviance over several decades in the twentieth century. The Chicago ecologists and the work of Merton (1938, 1968), Shaw and McKay (1942), Cohen (1955) but also Mays (1954) and Morris (1957) in the UK were especially important. Compared with social class and associated theses such as strain, (Merton, 1938), sub-culture and status frustration (Cohen, 1955) economic marginalisation and explanations linked to opportunity (Cloward and Ohlin, 1960) and poverty however, gender (and race) has featured less and has a shorter historical pedigree in terms of contributing towards explaining crime and counting it as important to criminological wisdom. There are several reasons for giving primacy to gender, some of which are briefly noted at this juncture:

- Women and girls have been neglected and/or marginalised in criminological research theory and policy related matters.
- There is a need to:
  - 'redress the balance', add women in and set the record straighter/clarify the distortions, misrepresentations, dispel the myths, challenge assumptions;
  - articulate women's positions, and men's positions, give voice to these gendered positions and differently hierarchically positioned femininities and masculinities where some gendered positions are prioritised and promoted and others marginalised and downgraded;
  - reveal relatively invisible gendered knowledges;
  - demonstrate and explain why social control, policing, community safety responses don't always work to the best effect.

This list of reasons is far from comprehensive and is in no particular order but it does flag up some reasonably convincing justifications as a well as some thought provoking and challenging debates that warrant serious criminological and victimological consideration. In addition to these briefly stated justifications we can begin to add more detailed reasons. For example, despite a focus on men as criminals and boys as delinquents, sociological and other explanations for offending have failed to grasp the real significance and explanatory value of the differences in offending patterns between men and women and boys and girls. Men and boys became the subject matter for the study of crime and deviance and for criminology more generally. It was not until pioneering feminists trickled into criminological waters that the beginnings of a gendered understanding of crime and offending can be recognised.

The above has commenced the task of justifying why gender is foregrounded in this book. It is also important to signpost very early on, the huge impact that the second wave of feminism and the campaigning women's movement of the 1960s and 1970s had across social relations. Three waves of feminism are now discussed in the broad confines of a gender, crime and justice literature although the first two are most commonly recognised. The first wave has its roots in the Enlightenment of the eighteenth century, the social revolutions of the seventeenth and eighteenth centuries such as the English and French Revolutions and concerns over equality. Between 1848 and 1919 in the United States there was a strong focus on women's right to vote and campaigns for their suffrage (Morash, 2006). Similarly in Britain, 'suffragettes' famously demonstrated for the privilege of voting and were arrested and imprisoned in the early years of the twentieth century for their efforts which were finally successful when women over the age of 30 were given the right to vote in 1918. This birth of the feminist or women's movement was given further impetus in the 1960s and the emergence of the women's liberation movement in particular signalled the second wave of feminism. Signifying the more recent developments within feminist scholarship and activism, some of which are mentioned above (see *Crime, victimisation/social division nexus)* and notably since the 1980s, there is some discussion of these changes under the caption of the third wave of feminism. This book largely begins with the second wave feminist movement when a range of feminist oriented services and feminist inspired supportive provisions grew from widespread grass roots revelations of women's experiences of violence and abuse in the home by men. The latter issues are more fully explored in Chapters 7 and 8 whilst feminisms and their histories are discussed more thoroughly in Chapter 4.

In terms of a historical context then this book largely commenced from the platform that was most explicitly first established in the late 1960s/early 1970s. A period, as explored further in Chapter 5, now famous, at least through a gendered lens, as that of the 'feminist critique'. In bald terms this critique claimed that the study of crime and deviance – criminology – had been dominated by men, studying men from a male perspective, and women had been ignored. This platform signified one of the points of departure from the 'legacy of positivism'. This phrase, as with the 'feminist critique' is simply dropped into this introductory chapter as a significant feature and recurring notion and both are later explained and discussed in greater depth and detail. Much of the critique that informs the arguments of this book is challenging this legacy.

The remainder of this section introduces some key and recurring themes and threads that require some preliminary explanation and clarification. Several of these underlie and penetrate contemporary understandings of this subject area and are helpful in understanding some dominant and stubbornly steadfast legacies that are to be contended with when seeking a sophisticated understanding of gender, crime and victimisation in contemporary society.

Gender and gender dichotomies

Above, I referred to 'gender dichotomies' – oppositional associations of male/female and of masculine/feminine. There are a variety of traditional and common gender dichotomies some of which are illustrated in Table 1.1: Common dichotomies.

Table 1.1   Common dichotomies[1]

Woman (femininity)	Man (masculinity)
Family	Economy, work/business
Emotional	Rational
Ethic of care	Ethic of justice
Other/s	Self
Private	Public
Home	Workplace
Carer, nurturer	Provider
Passive	Active
Determined	Free will, deliberate
Subservient	Goal seeking, resistant
Selfless, altruistic	Selfish, purposeful
Passive, inert	Active, proactive
Conflict resolver	Aggressive, conflictual

There are a host of common gendered dichotomies and only some are illustrated above. The various ways in which gender, crime and victimisation are explored throughout this book see all of these binary divide dichotomies as hugely problematic. The arguments that will unfold will engage in a breaking down of these socially constructed distinctions which are sometimes taken to caricature-like ends (see Chapter 3). Traditional notions of gender identity, whereby feminine traits have been distinguished from masculine traits, are illustrated in Table 1.2: Traditional notions of gender identity, below.

Table 1.2   Traditional notions of gender identity

Feminine traits	Masculine traits
Submissive	Dominant
Dependent	Independent
Unintelligent and incapable	Intelligent and competent
Emotional	Rational
Receptive	Assertive
Intuitive	Analytical
Weak	Strong
Timid	Brave
Content	Ambitious
Passive	Active
Cooperative	Competitive
Sensitive	Insensitive
Sex object	Sexually aggressive
Attractive physical appearance	Attractive because of achievement

Source: Macionis and Plummer (1998)

---

[1]This table has been constructed drawing upon the work of several feminist scholars as follows: Folbre, 2001; Fox Keller, 1985; Gilligan, 1982; Harding, 1986; Jennings, 1993; Mellor, 1992, 1997; Miller, 2002; Walklate, 2001.

Many scholars have argued about the social construction of such dualisms, challenged their authenticity, their hierarchicalism, their judgementalism and their prescriptively gendered nature (Folbre, 2001; Fox Keller, 1985, Gilligan, 1982; Harding, 1987; Mellor, 1995; Miller, 2002; Nelson, 1996; Walklate, 2001). For example, in each of the Tables 1.1 and 1.2, the right hand column is typically associated with strength, rigidity and the positive – attributes that have become equal to masculinity, – whilst the left hand column is associated with weakness, softness and the negative – attributes that have become equal to femininity – and feminists including feminist criminologists who have confronted and challenged these social constructions and have suggested breaking down these divides and boundaries in diverse ways (Maher, 1997; Mellor, 1992, 1997; Miller, 2002). In support of furthering these endeavours, each of the following chapters in this book will variously address these socially constructed and gender-problematic dualisms as they connect to knowledges about crime and victimisation in society.

Much of this book, especially the early chapters, dwell on the influences of feminism (this point is more fully explained in Chapter 5) to explore how gender has transformed our understanding of many criminological subject areas. Indeed, a more specific and sustained focus on masculinities does not appear until the end of Chapter 5 and in Chapter 6. A balanced gender focus, where femininities and masculinities feature in equal measure would not be possible and to try to do so would not be reflective of the historical or contemporary unfolding of gendered knowledges. This introductory chapter has so far set out how the remainder of the book will encourage readers to understand and think critically about how and when gender matters in understanding: crime in society; crime prevention, regulation and control; the experience and recovery from criminal victimisation and other forms of social harm. It will now introduce one of the main illustrative vehicles that will be used as a reference point throughout.

Case study: women and crime for economic gain

The case study is an invaluable way of offering original, rich and detailed illustration and exemplification. Here are details on the aims and objectives of an original piece of research which forms the main case study of the book. The research was conducted by the author when investigating women's motives for committing economic crime. Linked to this case study, extensive examples, illustrations and evidence are presented to the reader. Materials connected to this case study form a backbone of original evidence, arguments and theorisations that unfurl throughout each and every chapter. In order to comprehend the slant the author has on many of the gendered themes and debates throughout this book, I provide some key details on this research below and the aims and objectives of the project which:

- explored existing evidence from official criminal statistics and also from observational, survey and secondary data sources the gender patterning of crime and women's economic crimes;
- investigated women's motives for committing different economic crimes through conducting interviews with offending women;
- examined the variety and extent of women's criminality;
- examined women's initial and post-hoc reasons and justifications for specific instances of criminality;
- examined women's means and methods of carrying out crimes;
- examined women's views of themselves as offenders;
- explored and compared in the light of the empirical data, existing theoretical connections and debates about women's experiences and motivations for committing economic crime.

The primary data was obtained from face-to-face, in-depth interviews with women who had been criminalised. Semi-structured interviews with women in prison and in the community focussed upon core areas connected to the points noted above. The analysis of the interview data identified key themes including those related to motivations, allusions to the economic, ways of representing the notion of the economic and degrees of rationalism. The research ultimately provided the theoretical basis for a more comprehensive explanatory framework of the behaviour of women who commit crime for economic gain. Most of the original illustrations and examples provided throughout this book are drawn from this research project. Thus the case study is referred to in each and every substantive chapter. Some chapters refer to the research methodology and in particular the experience of interviewing female offenders, whilst other chapters draw upon the case study to justify the arguments that coalesce around theoretical insights and arguments surrounding women's offending patterns and explanations for women's committing of economic crime in particular.

The structure and layout of this book

Some of the major, minor and emergent gendered themes (including some continuities and discontinuities) that run as threads throughout the text have been noted already in this introductory chapter. Chapter 2 explores past and present gender patternings to crime, and crime types, gender patterns to offending as well as the gender patterns to criminal victimisation and other forms of harm in society. This chapter focuses on two important questions about gender, crime and victimisation – the *levels* of crime and victimisation and the *correlates* of crime and victimisation. It begins to illustrate how a gendered scrutiny of crime and victimisation is achieved and ends in a summary of our gendered knowledges as amassed from a variety of different sources of information. Chapter 3 examines mediated gender, crime and victimisation. With much ground to cover, this chapter contextualises the importance of the media in representing crime and victimisation in society and in particular it focuses upon gendered representations and cultural constructions of crimes, criminals, offending and offenders as well as victims. It considers how news is constructed and how 'newsworthiness' and 'news values' help construct crime news agendas. Chapter 3 also illustrates how mediated and cultural constructions of the crime and victimisation problem have various structural and locational biases to them and points out the complexities, ambiguities, conundrums and paradoxes that are apparent in 'mediated knowledges' surrounding gender, crime and victimisation.

Chapter 4 specifically examines feminist ideologies to doing research on crime and victimisation. The first part of the chapter, as already noted above, comments on the inherent 'legacy of positivism' before focussing on feminist ideologies and their points of similarity as well as different feminist perspectives and feminisms and their points of divergence in the criminological and victimological research, theory and policy contexts. Through specific focus on 'rape knowledges' this chapter illustrates some simple to complex beliefs, understandings and contested knowledges about the crime of rape. The second part of Chapter 4 draws upon the main case study 'Women and Crime for Economic Gain' illustration in order to demonstrate some of the key hallmarks of valid and reflexively ethical (feminist) research practice. With a focus upon doing interviews with female offenders this illustration serves to highlight a number of important gender and other salient 'power' issues connected to doing criminological research.

Chapter 5 concerns itself with feminist and gendered perspectives in respect of explaining and theorising offending and victimisations. It examines the way in which women's conformity and women's criminality has been explored criminologically. It outlines the origins and development of feminist influences in criminology and albeit to a lesser extent, in victimology too. This chapter considers the backdrop to the feminist critique of criminology, the critique itself and its impact in terms of pioneering work and feminist influences in understanding crime and victimisation. The chapter continues to draw extensively upon the main case study 'Women and Crime for Economic Gain' in its effort to demonstrate key theoretical developments and debates. In doing so this chapter contains a summary critique of a selection of gender sensitive and not so sensitive explanations. In essence it suggests there is an 'explanatory gap' in feminist theorising. The chapter concludes by throwing down a gendered gauntlet to those engaged in criminological and victimological scholarship.

Chapter 6 is similarly concerned with feminist and gendered perspectives but this time in respect of fear and vulnerability to victimisation. It outlines gendered findings from the researching fear project whilst engaging in a feminist inspired and critical critique of survey derived knowledges on fear, risk and vulnerability. The chapter makes a point of providing examples and illustrations of hidden/invisible victimisations and outlines the gender patterning to them. It is at this point that a more intense focus on masculinities is offered and this includes a look at gender sensitive risk-taking. This chapter therefore operates at various levels in its efforts to bring a masculinities sensitive perspective to victim studies.

Chapter 7 is primarily concerned with how the criminal justice system responds to lawbreaking as seen from a gendered perspective. In the case study tradition that has been established throughout this book, this chapter achieves depth of analysis by especially focussing upon issues surrounding the harsh end of lawbreaking and penal policy. This chapter is therefore mainly confined to a discussion of imprisonment. Predominantly it dwells on women's imprisonment in debating responses to lawbreakers under the conceptual framework of gender-wise justice. After explaining the concepts that are drawn upon more fully, this chapter asks whether justice can be done through gender; and if ambitions to achieve sameness or 'gender equivalence' for lawbreakers facing the criminal justice system give way to 'gender difference' for lawbreakers. Chapter 8 scrutinises responses to victimisation through a gendered lens. In a similar vein to the critical commentary and reflections adopted in the previous chapters, Chapter 8 also engages in a gendered critique, this time, of responses to victimisation. It establishes how and why gender matters in responding to victimisation before embarking on an exploration of victims' needs as gendered needs. As in the previous chapter, here, too, the construct of 'gender equivalence' and 'gender difference' is called upon to ponder the relative merits of gender-wise and gender different responses to victimisation.

Chapter 9 is the final and concluding chapter that specifically focuses on the challenges to understanding crime and victimisation through gender. Crucially, this chapter returns to the fundamental question, 'Does gender deserve priority?' At this point once again we remind ourselves of the importance of the intersectionality of gender, class, race and age with the question of crime and victimisation. However, this chapter does much more than revisiting, reminding and consolidating. It pushes forward a number of challenges and forces a few more highly provocative questions directly relating to the main theme, gender, crime and victimisation but also more widely to victimology and criminology as the key discipline.

In addition to the recurrent themes and strong research, theory and policy threads introduced above, there are also several other features that are integral to the book as a whole and these are pedagogical. There is clear 'signposting' at chapter level and also within chapters. Chapter signposting includes similar features at the start of each chapter where:

- major sub-headings are listed including as standard chapter aims, introduction, key questions for each chapter, summary conclusion, study questions/activities, further reading;

- additionally, key terms/concepts are emboldened and explained in a glossary;
- at the end of this chapter and every other chapter you will find:
  - specific activities and/or thinking exercises;
  - suggestions for further reading.

Chapter 2 now focuses on gender patterns of crime and victimisation. It builds upon the introductory and precursory discussions raised in this first and introductory chapter.

STUDY QUESTIONS

At the start of this book readers are encouraged to ponder on some provocative questions listed under seven key areas:

1. Gender patterns to crime and victimisation
   - Are there any well established gender patterns to crime and victimisation in society which cannot be challenged by new knowledges?

2. Media representations and cultural constructions of masculinity and femininity
   - What do media and cultural constructions of crime, criminals and victims look like and how can they be challenged?

3. Feminist ideologies and research
   - How might you do gender sensitive research in your chosen area of study?

4. Gendered perspectives and theories for explaining offending
   - If crime is gendered, can it be universally explained?

5. Gendered fears of crime and vulnerabilities to victimisation
   - Why might an understanding of 'victimological otherness', combined with an understanding of masculinities, be useful in tackling crime and victimisation in society?

6. Gender sensitive responses to lawbreakers
   - Are lawbreakers victims or offenders?

7. Gender sensitive responses to victimisation
   - Whose responsibility is it to tackle victimisation and who can help and how in the recovery from it?

SUGGESTIONS FOR FURTHER READING

Daly, K. (1997) 'Different ways of conceptualising sex/gender in feminist theory and their implications for criminology', *Theoretical Criminology*, 1 (1).

Davies, P. (2007) 'Lessons from the gender agenda' in S. Walklate (ed.) *Handbook on Victims and Victimology*. Cullompton: Willan.

Walklate, S. (2004) *Gender, Crime and Criminal Justice*, second edition. Cullompton: Willan.

2

GENDER PATTERNS TO CRIME AND VICTIMISATION

GLOSSARY TERMS

Gender ratio   Victim survey

Gender gap

CHAPTER AIMS

- Specify and describe key sources from which knowledge about gender patterns is derived
- Outline and illustrate the benchmark gender patterns to: crime; crime types; offending; criminal victimisation and other forms of social harm
- Identify and illustrate the gender patterns to hidden crimes and victimisations
- Problematise criminological and victimological knowledges

Introduction

Chapter 1, outlined the parameters and major frames of reference for this book as a whole and stipulated that the two major frames of reference were those of gender and crime and gender and victimisation. Within these parameters the chapter then commenced the exploration of a range of gender matters relating to crime and victimisation. Chapter 2 will elaborate upon some of the obvious and less obvious manifestations of why gender matters in the contexts of crime and victimisation. It begins to illustrate how a gendered scrutiny of crime and victimisation is achieved and what it looks like. One frame of reference for this is the gender patterning to crime. This framing includes a detailed examination of gender patterns of crime and crime types. It considers various types of data to illustrate these gender patterns. A variety of different types of resources and sources of information are therefore used in order to demonstrate men's and boys' and women's and girls' participation in crime generally and in street crime, property crime and interpersonal crimes in particular. Whilst gender patterns are exemplified and illustrated, they are also problematised. The gender patterning to crimes that take place behind the closed domestic and boardroom doors as well as other relatively invisible/hidden crimes including corporate and white-collar crime and offending are also discussed.

A second frame of reference for the gendered scrutiny of crime and victimisation is the gender patterning to victimisation. Explored and illustrated within this framework is the gender patterning to victimisation including differences and similarities between and within gendered experiences. Various types of data which are illustrative of these patterns and experiences are examined. Within these two major frames of reference, the first three aims of this chapter which are to outline the benchmark gender patterns to: crime; crime types; offending; criminal victimisation and other forms of social harm; specify key sources from which knowledge about gender patterns is derived; identify the gender patterns to hidden crimes and victimisations, are achieved.

This chapter now proceeds to benchmark the gender patterns to crime and victimisation. It explores some official criminal statistics about levels of crime and types of criminal activity, including information available from the Ministry of Justice as regards the prison population, supplementary data from the British Crime Survey and other victimisation surveys. It offers critical commentary and, through a focus on hidden or 'invisible' crimes and victimisations, it opens up a range of evidence that might be used to explore a fuller picture of criminal and other forms of victimisation and harm.

Key questions for Chapter 2

- What is the nature of the relationship between gender and crime?
- What is the nature of the relationship between gender and victimisation?
- Is there a distinct gender pattern to all crime?
- Is there a distinct gender pattern to all victimisations?

- Is there a gender patterning to property crime?
- Is there a gender patterning to violent crime?
- Is there a gender pattern to hidden or 'invisible' crimes'?
- Are women more law-abiding than men?
- Are women becoming more criminal?
- Does crime data skew gender patterns to crime and victimisation?

For the most part this chapter concerns itself with two important questions about gender, crime and victimisation. First, it looks at the *level* of crime, and the *level* of victimisation. How many crimes occur each year? What is the rate of crime? How many victimisations occur each year? What is the rate of criminal victimisation? Are these levels increasing or decreasing over time? Second, the *correlates* of crime and victimisation? What crimes feature heavily? Who are the typical victims of crime? Do victim characteristics vary by crime and type? How is victimisation distributed across time and space?

Benchmarking gender patterns: sources of knowledge and wisdom

What then are the main ways of finding out about how much crime and victimisation there is? Who commits what types of crimes and who suffers? Below we consider some of the more obvious sources of information that are available to us including criminal statistics, Ministry of Justice National Offender Management Service (NOMS) data and victim surveys. We examine what these are and begin to show what each tells us as regards the gender patterns to crime, crime types, offending, offenders and criminal victimisations. We also begin to consider the omissions and gaps in this information highlighting *what* might be missing from the patterns revealed by such 'official' data. We also begin to examine *why* our knowledge about the gender patterning to crime and victimisation might be incomplete.

Criminal statistics

Smith (2005) has briefly summarised what recorded statistics on crime tell us. Following her approach, a brief summary still shows that recorded statistics present:

- a complex picture;
- crime as a 'male problem';
- women's crime as increasing in some categories of offences;

- youth (male) offending disproportionate;
- female crime less overall and less serious in nature;
- the numbers of men and women imprisoned as increasing;
- distinct male and female offending patterns.

The main distinction between men's and women's involvement in crime is revealed in the above summary. Crime is overwhelmingly a male activity. The concept of the **gender ratio** to crime is important for readers to grasp. This refers to the difference between the amount of crimes committed by men and those committed by women. Men, according to all measures of crime and offending, commit more crime than women and at all stages of the criminal justice process they are represented in greater numbers than women. For instance, we might find from criminal statistics that men commit 3 million offences of theft every year whereas women commit 1 million. Thus the ratio is 3:1. In the magistrates' courts, men and women appear at a ratio of 16:1. When making any comparison between men's and women's crimes, it is there-fore always wise to bear this different starting point in mind. It is also impor-tant to bear such gender ratios in mind when drawing attention to any apparent increases in the volume of crime committed by men and women. In percentage terms a small increase in the number of crimes committed by women can be made to look extraordinarily and sensationally high. This ratio reminds us to be wary of other comparative issues. For example, whilst thefts appear to be the crime type women commit most, it is important to remember that men still commit many more such crimes than women. These points are simply illus-trated in Figures 2.1 and 2.2.

The term **gender gap** as used in Figure 2.2 is also a useful term for readers to grasp. When referring to volumes of crime and victimisation and compari-sons between men and women on these counts, the concept of the 'gender

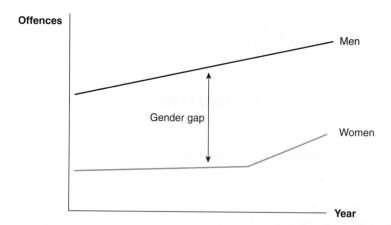

Figure 2.1   The gender gap

Figure 2.2 Men's and women's share of crime

gap' serves as a useful reminder of the different starting points mentioned above. The gender gap arises due to the gender ratio in the committing of crime. When students of crime and victimisation come to the problem of explaining why crime might happen or victimisation occurs, these are important concepts to remember. They remind us that a single explanation many not be universally applicable, that men may commit crime for different reasons from women. Moreover, in view of the further gender patterns to different crime types (see below), men and women may do different crimes for different reasons. These are issues that are returned to in greater depth in Chapter 5.

Criminal statistics also reveal distinctive patterns for men and women on:

- property crime;
- violent crime;
- indictable offence categories;
- reasons men and women are given custodial sentences;
- offences dealth with by the magistrates' courts for men and women;
- offences resulting in probation for men and women;
- offences resulting in imprisonment for men and women.

Ministry of Justice – national offender management service (NOMS)

In England and Wales, the Ministry of Justice was created in 2007. It is responsible for agreeing and publishing performance ratings of probation areas/trusts as well as ratings of prisons. The National Offender Management Service is responsible for the National Offender Management System (NOMS). It produces quarterly data driven performance assessments for each of the 42 probation areas. Performance is looked at across about 40 indicators which measure the work of the probation service under four key areas: public protection, offender management, interventions and organisational capability. This data is used to grade the probation areas into one of four bands from exceptional performance, rating 4, through to serious concerns, rating 1.

NOMS also produces quarterly data driven performance assessments for prison providers and here we provide a rather more detailed explanation of this particular data as a basis for a better understanding of gender issues explored in the context of lawbreakers who are imprisoned in Chapter 7. From the Ministry of Justice we are provided with weekly and monthly prison population and accommodation briefings which are available on-line. Some examples are reproduced below. In order to understand the data some definitions of terms are required. The briefings give figures, broken down by sex, on usable operational capacity. The definition of the operational capacity of a prison is the total number of prisoners that an establishment can hold taking into account control, security and the proper operation of the planned regime. This differs from the useable operational capacity of the estate which is the sum of all establishments' operational capacity less 2,000 places. This is known as the operating margin and reflects the constraints imposed by the need to provide separate accommodation for different classes of prisoner i.e. by sex, age, security category, conviction status, single cell risk assessment and also due to geographical distribution (Ministry of Justice, 2009). Population in prison includes those held in prisons in England and Wales, including those in the three immigration removal centres of Dover, Haslar and Lindholme. The sentenced population includes those sentenced to an immediate custodial sentence and fine defaulters. Adult prisoners are prisoners aged 21 years and over. Young adults are prisoners aged 18 to 20, but including 21-year-old prisoners who were aged 20 or under at conviction who have not been reclassified as part of the adult population. Population in custody now includes those held in prison establishments, police cells under Operation Safeguard, secure training centres (STCs) and secure children's homes (SCHs). All coverage is for England and Wales.

The prison population information is drawn from two prison sources. The first source is the routine provision by prison establishments of records of the numbers of persons held in custody at the end of each month, broadly subdivided according to age, sex, custody type and sentence length. The records are collated and processed centrally, to produce the main estimates of the population presented at the end of the month. The second source is the electronically held details for individual inmates such as date of birth, sex, religion, ethnic origin, custody type, offence and reception and discharge dates and, for sentenced prisoners, sentence length. These data are collected on a central computer database and are used to produce the analyses by offence group and individual year of age. They form the basis of detailed population breakdowns, supplementing the aggregates derived from the first source, to which they are scaled for consistency.

As noted above, the National Offender Management System (NOMS) Agency produces quarterly data driven performance assessments for each prison establishment. For both public and private prisons, the Prison Rating System (PRS) assesses 131 prisons (including 11 private prisons) by looking at performance as measured across 34 indicators. Similarly to the probation quarterly ratings, this data is used to grade prisons into one of four bands from exceptional performance (rating 4) through to serious concerns (rating 1).

Quarter 1, 2009/10 prison quarterly ratings showed:

- Exceptional performance (rating 4) – 12 establishments
- Good performance (rating 3) – 109 establishments
- Requiring development (rating 2) – 10 establishments

Again whilst this is interesting, the gender issues remain hidden from view here and it is the Ministry of Justice prison population and accommodation briefings and the monthly tables of the population in custody that show some of this information. As an example, see Figure 2.3: Prison population and accommodation briefing – 9 October 2009.

One way of beginning to make a statistical comparison of men's and women's imprisonment is to consult the Ministry of Justice Statistics Bulletins for any given month. For key points see www.justice.gov.uk/publications/populationincustody.htm. A snapshot can be gleaned from the 'Population in custody monthly tables'. For example in June 2009 England and Wales, these tables provide the following information.

The male prison population increased by 1 per cent (up 470) to 79,200 and the female prison population decreased 5 per cent (down 210) to 4,300 in June 2009 compared to June 2008. The tables give a breakdown of the population in custody by type of custody and sex and by offence for any given month of any given year. They can be re-worked and used to draw out key comparative information as shown in the examples in Tables 2.1, 2.2 and 2.3 (these comparative issues are considered in more detail in Chapter 7).

The information gleaned from official sources can be adapted to suit a gender based comparison which can then be used to draw out further points of comparison and difference. In terms of gender based comparisons there are both differences and similarities between the male population in prison by offence and the female population in prison by offence. Taking those given immediate custodial sentences in June 2009, most male prisoners were in prison for violence against the person whereas most female prisoners were in

Figure 2.3   Prison population and accommodation briefing – 9 October 2009

prison for drug offences. Comparing male and female prisoners in this way the order of offence categories is shown in Table 2.3.

There is little distinction between the rank order of offences for all male and all female prisoners broken down by age. All adult prisoners and all young adult prisoners follow a similar offence patterning. For both males and females the biggest difference is for those aged 15–17. For this age range, drug offences feature much lower in the rank order. For this age range females score highest

Table 2.1 Population in custody by type of custody and sex, June 2009

	Males	Females	Total
All population in custody, of which	79,481	4,406	83,887
Prisons	79,158	4,296	83,454
Police cells	0	0	0
SCHs	139	36	175
STCs	184	74	258
All population in prison, of which	79,158	4,296	83,454
Remand	12,617	839	13,456
Under sentence	65,092	3,396	68,488
Fine defaulter	99	14	113
Less than or equal to 6 months	4,658	458	5,115
Greater than 6 months to less than 12 months	2,271	193	2,465
12 months to less than 4 years	22,460	1,318	23,778
4 years or more (exc. indeterminate sentences)	23,458	1,039	24,497
Indeterminate sentences	12,146	374	12,520
Non-criminal prisoners	1,449	61	1,510
All adult population in prison, of which	67,705	3,872	71,577
Remand	10,105	727	10,832
Under sentence	56,263	3,087	59,350
Fine defaulter	95	13	108
Less than or equal to 6 months	3,610	386	3,995
Greater than 6 months to less than 12 months	1,687	173	1,861
12 months to less than 4 years	17,868	1,174	19,042
4 years or more (exc. indeterminate sentences)	21,579	984	22,563
Indeterminate sentences	11,424	357	11,781
Non-criminal prisoners	1,337	58	1,395
All 15–17-year-olds in prison, of which	2,048	54	2,102
Remand	531	12	543
Under sentence	1,517	42	1,559
Fine defaulter	0	0	0
Less than or equal to 6 months	324	13	337
Greater than 6 months to less than 12 months	204	6	209
12 months to less than 4 years	770	12	782
4 years or more (exc. indeterminate sentences)	156	5	161
Indeterminate sentences	65	5	70
Non-criminal prisoners	0	0	0
All young adults in prison, of which	9,405	370	9,775
Remand	1,981	100	2,081
Under sentence	7,312	267	7,579
Fine defaulter	4	1	5
Less than or equal to 6 months	724	59	783
Greater than 6 months to less than 12 months	381	14	395
12 months to less than 4 years	3,822	132	3,954
4 years or more (exc. indeterminate sentences)	1,723	50	1,773
Indeterminate sentences	657	12	669
Non-criminal prisoners	112	3	115

Table 2.2   Population in prison by offence – remand and immediate custodial sentence, June 2009

	Remand	Immediate custodial sentence
All prisoners	13,456	68,375
Violence against the person	3,444	19,950
Sexual offences	928	7,972
Robbery	1,431	9,049
Burglary	1,486	7,884
Theft and handling	931	3,382
Fraud and forgery	466	1,875
Drug offences	1,919	10,696
Motoring offences	129	1,149
Other offences	1,942	6,117
Offence not recorded	781	300
All male prisoners	12,617	64,993
Violence against the person	3,267	19,111
Sexual offences	913	7,918
Robbery	1,361	8,715
Burglary	1,437	7,678
Theft and handling	823	2,963
Fraud and forgery	410	1,628
Drug offences	1,787	9,803
Motoring offences	128	1,130
Other offences	1,796	5,758
Offence not recorded	695	288
All female prisoners	839	3,382
Violence against the person	177	840
Sexual offences	15	54
Robbery	70	334
Burglary	49	207
Theft and handling	108	418
Fraud and forgery	56	246
Drug offences	132	893
Motoring offences	1	19
Other offences	146	459
Offence not recorded	85	12

Table 2.3   Gender, offence and imprisonment

Rank order of population in prison by offence	Male	Female
1	Violence against the person	Drug offences
2	Drug offences	Violence against the person
3	Robbery	Theft and handling
4	Sexual offences	Other offences
5	Burglary	Robbery

for violence against the person (15) followed by robbery (10) whereas for males the highest ranked offence category is robbery (440) followed next by violence against the person (366).

The illustrations provided above related to the case study of populations in custody are a shorthand way of demonstrating that recorded statistics on crime do indeed present a complex picture. They do broadly confirm crime and offending as a 'male problem', that women's crime is increasing in some categories of offences, that youth (male) offending is disproportionate, that female crime is less overall and less serious in nature than men's, that the numbers of men and women imprisoned is increasing and that, finally, there are indeed distinct male and female offending patterns. Again the reader is encouraged to follow through some of the implications of these patterns derived from looking at levels and correlates of crime and to explore the dynamics and consequences of it throughout all of the following chapters. By remembering some of the key concepts drawn upon in the above section – most notably the concept of a gender ratio to crime and offending and the gender gap – you will be wise about this complex picture and the implications of relying too heavily upon criminal statistics and 'official' data'. The reader is reminded that we return to gender matters in prisons in Chapter 7. Now that we have looked at some of the obvious sources of information on crime and victimisation and shown how these can be unravelled to glean a gendered picture of crime patterns, we turn to alternative and complementary sources of information and **victim surveys**.

Victim surveys

Since the mid-1970s in the United States and the 1980s in Britain, the direct questioning of the victim has been central to the criminological and victimological enterprises and the victim survey has become of central importance to research into victims of crime. This is true for the positivist work of Hindelang et al. (1978) as it is for the radicalism offered by Jones et al. (1986). In part, victim surveys developed, as a result of recognised deficiencies in official crime statistics as valid measures of the extent of crime in society, with the growth of interest in victims of crime generally and concern about some victims in particular, as an impact of feminist research.

There are different ways of surveying victims. In the United Kingdom, local cross-sectional sample surveys are exemplified by research associated with radical left realist criminology (which in general terms is concerned with facing up to the reality of crime from a social democratic standpoint). Left realist surveys pay attention to the experiences of vulnerable groups within a particular locality (Davies et al., 2003). Appreciative surveys are another derivative. These are less concerned with seeking precision in estimates of victimisation in the community and more with the qualitative descriptions of the experience of crime from the victim's point of view. They may also seek to examine victims' experiences of being processed within the criminal justice system, for example by the police and in the courts. Appreciative victim studies are associated with victim support groups and with feminist approaches that have been especially concerned to explore women as victims of sexual crimes. Such studies can be drawn upon by social and political activities to reduce victimisation of vulnerable groups and to improve the treatment of victims in the criminal justice system (Davies et al., 2003). These are all matters that we shall return to in future chapters of this book.

Instead of solely relying on police data , victim surveys have become increasingly important sources of information and an alternative means of collecting data about crime, levels of crime and types of crime. Surveying victims is a flexible tool which has elicited much more information on victimisation. Survey data has provided detailed quantitative information on levels of crime and types of victimisation together with rich qualitative information. Surveys of victims have generated better estimates of the extent of crime and victimisation, details about the circumstances of the offence, relationships between victims, insight into victims' experiences, perceptions and worries about crime and their experiences of the various criminal justice agencies. Indeed victimisation surveys provide information about rates and trends, reasons for under-reporting, the correlates of victimisation, the risk of victimisation, the fear of crime and its relationship to the probability of victimisation, the experience of crime from the viewpoint of victims (men, women, older, younger, rich and poor and ethnic minority victims); and as noted above, the treatment of victims in the criminal justice system (Davies et al., 2007).

Perhaps the most well known and cited victim surveys are national trend sample surveys. This is typified in the United Kingdom by the British Crime Survey (BCS). The BCS measures crime in England and Wales and, being based on interviews, it includes crimes which are not reported to the police. Collecting information on victims of crime, the circumstances in which incidents occur and the behaviour of offenders in committing crime, it is an important source of information about levels of crime and public attitudes to crime as well as other criminal justice issues such as people's perceptions and attitudes to crime, anti-social behaviour, fear of crime and the criminal justice system, including the police and the courts.

The BCS selects a random sample of men and women of all ages (extended to children aged 10 to 15 since January 2009) and all backgrounds in order to reflect on the experiences and attitudes and concerns about crime of the whole population and therefore to represent the country as a whole. Since the first survey was carried out in 1982 there is now an extensive and rich database of information on levels, trends and attitudes to crime resulting from this type of survey based research. The BCS has paved the way for a number of additional surveys that are useful to criminological researchers. These include:

- The Northern Ireland Crime Survey
- Scottish and Justice Survey
- Offending, Crime and Justice Survey (OCJS)
- Commercial Victimisation Survey (CVS)

In the early 2000s the Home Office moved from only presenting the BCS and police recorded crime in separate reports to combining key findings of each (see for example Walker et al., 2006). Thus crime in England and Wales has for almost a decade now been annually reported upon in a complementary series that combines the reporting of police recorded crime and the British Crime Survey. Police recorded crime data reports on a financial year basis for example 2009/10 and 2010/11. Police recording practice is governed by the Home Office 'counting rules' and the National Crime Recording Standard (NCRS) as introduced in all police forces in April 2002 to make all crime recording more consistent.

However, in terms of doing criminological research through surveys and samples, can these techniques produce sufficiently valid, ethical, effective, rigorous and comprehensive data? The nature of the BCS and other victim-oriented surveys are such that they deal in sensitive issues. Respondents are asked to discuss harmful topics and experiences that they may not have disclosed previously, with strangers or via keying in data, albeit in a confidential manner. Can sensitive criminological research be conducted through surveys? Furthermore, one of the criticisms of the BCS has been that until very recently it has excluded those under the age of 16 and those living in institutions as well as the homeless all of whom might be deemed 'vulnerable populations'. Women and children suffering violence and abuse in their homes might warrant a similarly difficult group from which to establish truths about their experiences. There are then challenges to extracting accurate data. Deakin and Spencer (forthcoming) consider sensitive topics and criticisms of large scale surveys and illustrate these very issues by reference to the BCS. They go on to consider ways of generating ethically sound survey data on sensitive topics with hard to reach or vulnerable groups.

Problematising criminological and victimological wisdoms

The previous section looked at the most obvious and accessible ways of getting information on patterns to crime and victimisation. It showed how a gender based inquiry might start to develop yet drew attention to some of the difficulties in obtaining a full set of gender sensitive benchmarks. It broadly summarised the gendered picture in this respect. The next section of this chapter builds on both of these themes. It does so by focussing on the gendered picture, this time of victimisation in more detail, simultaneously considering these victimological wisdoms as problematic. It commences with an outline of what we know and do not know about men and women as victims and offers a useful template for considering some of the omissions and problems concerning gender patterns to crime and victimisation.

What we do and don't know about men and women as victims

The level of detail that has been amassed around gender and victimisation is illustrated in Figures 2.4 and 2.5. Box 2.1 provides information on men's and women's victimisation and summarises what we know about men and women as victims. Box 2.2 considers what we do not yet know about men and women as victims. For more in-depth critical commentary on much of this information and detail, the reader is guided to Chapter 6 of this volume.

BOX 2.1

WHAT WE KNOW ABOUT MEN AND WOMEN AS VICTIMS

WHAT WE KNOW

National and local survey data[1] shows:

- victimisation is generally higher for males than females. The exception to this pattern is rape;
- for some victimisations age combined with sex renders women more at risk;
- black males have the highest rate of violent victimisation and white females the lowest;
- single, divorced or separated women show higher rates of victimisation than those who are married or widowed;
- more detailed gendered knowledges are gained from specific case studies (see Szyockyi and Fox, 1996), local and subject specific surveys and empirical research (see Kelly and Radford, 1996; Lees, 1997) critical (Mooney, 2000, Walklate, 2000) and qualitative research (Chigwada-Bailey, 2003; Dobash and Dobash, 1979);

---

[1]Specific sources and references include: Budd and Mattinson, 2000; Crawford et al., 1990; Jones et al., 1986; Mirrlees-Black and Byron, 1999; Simmons and Dodd, 2003; Upson, 2004; Walby and Allen, 2004.

- risks to victimisation are gendered;
- divorced/single, poor women have higher risks;
- women are more vulnerable to domestic violence from current or former partners;
- women-on-women incidents are more common in acquaintance violence than in any other type;
- young homeless women are more likely to be sexually assaulted;
- female consumers are particularly at risk from some specific pharmaceutical products and services, household and cosmetic products, pressures to purchase substandard goods, assumptions of technical incompetence (Croall, 2007);
- women and men suffer from high levels of criminal victimisation;
- welfare workers, nurses, office managers (women) are three times more likely than 'average' to suffer from violence at work;
- female workers are particularly at risk from miscarriage and respiratory ailments, other illnesses and exploitation in certain industries (Croall, 2007);
- gender and age structure social experiences of fear of crime and victimisation;
- women are more worried and fearful about crime despite having lower chances of victimisation than men and young people;
- fear of sexual violence and harassment from men underpins women's greater fear;
- high impact of criminal victimisation on women;
- violence and sexual abuse are major reasons for young women running away from home;
- large numbers of crime committed by non-strangers against women are not reported to the police;
- levels of violence against women are far higher than the BCS and other national surveys show;
- different types of feminisms (liberal, radical, socialist and post-modern) have impacted upon our understanding and appreciation of women as victims (see Figure 4.1);
- Recent feminist concerns centre around:
- deconstructing women's irrational and rational fears of crime and victimisation (Stanko, 1987).
- Recent gender concerns centre around:
- the ways in which violence and abuse against men and boys has been marginalized within victimology;
- how masculinities theorising might help further understanding of men as perpetrators of crime and as victims of crime.
- Walklate (2004) has debated whether or not there can be a feminist victimology:
- the women's movement and the second wave of feminism had a significant political impact resulting in;
- women's refuge provision;
- Rape Crisis and Women's Aid;

(Continued)

(Continued)

- struggle for women's rights and;
- notion of 'survivorship';
- the voluntary sector has also been instrumental in supporting women victims of domestic and sexual abuse;
- women are often portrayed as particularly fearful of crime and victimisation as well as 'irrational' to due 'misplaced' fears of crime;
- the media reproduces women as vulnerable and reinforces and fuels women's fears of crime;
- the media portray men and young men in particular as criminally violent;
- fear and experience of crime and victimisation impacts upon women's lifestyles and day to day activities – thus in part – :
- women do control for themselves;
- women perceive and deal with risk via different types of coping strategies and constraints.

BOX 2.2

WHAT WE DON'T KNOW ABOUT MEN AND WOMEN AS VICTIMS

WHAT WE DON'T KNOW

- statistics on the nature, extent, impact and effects of victimisation upon individual women and upon different groups of women;
- much research remains partial and restricted to case studies and individual crime (see Croall, 2007 and Box 2.1).
- We have scant information and knowledge on the following:
- the real extent of crime committed by non-strangers and strangers against women;
- the impact of victimisation upon women suffering from violence at work;
- immigrant men's and women's experiences of victimisation;
- the effects and impact of different types of consumer crimes on young and elderly men and women;
- how global dimensions of white collar and corporate crime impact upon women as mothers, carers and workers;
- how men and women experience and survive disasters, human rights abuses and atrocities;
- how and why gender and age structure social experiences of fear of crime and victimisation.
- In terms of theoretical knowledge:

- there is a small but growing body of work seeking to theorise about the gendered nature of crime and victimisation, much focussing on masculinity and crime (see Connell, 1987, 1995; Groombridge, 2001; Jefferson, 2001–8; Messerschmidt, 1993–2008) and less that upon masculinity and victimisation (Walklate, 2007), other pockets of scholarship focus upon femininity and crime (see, for example, Joe-Laidler and Hunt, 2001; Miller, 1998). Walklate has asked if there can be a feminist victimology (Walklate, 2001, 2004).

Hidden crimes and victimisations

What has become clear so far is that there are some key places to look for information that can help with an inquiry seeking to establish gender patterns to crime and victimisation. What is also evident is that efforts to delineate gender patterns to crime and those to victimisation are fraught with problems no matter which source of information is used. So, although we have significant levels of detail, our criminological and victimological wisdoms are nevertheless, problematic and incomplete. Sometimes they throw up paradoxes and conundrums. Box 2.2 in particular clearly lists a number of gaps in our knowledge and some of the reasons for this are further examined in the following chapters. First however, hidden crimes are considered. Hidden or 'invisible crime' refers to:

- specific acts of crime which are not recorded in official crime statistics;
- categories of crime which are either not represented in official statistics or which are significantly under-recorded.

Previously with colleagues a template was offered as a heuristic device for helping understand why some crimes (and their victimisations) are less visible than others (Jupp et al., 2000). We called this the 'seven features of invisibility' and the rudiments of this template are illustrated in the seven features of invisibility below. The reader is encouraged to understand this template as a device for use throughout this book. It may help in understanding not only gender patterns to crime and victimisation but also our wider knowledge about gender, crime and victimisation.

The seven features of invisibility:

No:

- knowledge;
- statistics;
- theory;
- research;

- control;
- politics;
- panic.

No knowledge – there is little individual or public knowledge that the crime – and therefore the victimisation/s associated with the crime – has been committed.

No statistics – official crime statistics fail to record or classify the crime (see Tombs, 1999, 2000).

No theory – criminologists and others have neglected to explain the crime, its existence and its causes and invisible and hidden crimes lie relatively low on the criminological agenda.

No research – due to a combination of features (no knowledge, no statistics and no theory); practical problems (access) and political problems.

No control – there are no formal or systematic mechanisms for regulation, control and enforcement of such crimes and there are blurred boundaries between the legitimate and illegitimate.

No politics – they do not typically appear as a significant part of the political agenda. There is no real evidence of corporate business or white-collar misdemeanours (breaches of health and safety legislation) displacing street level crimes as a major public concern.

No panic – they are not constituted as moral panics and their perpetrators are not portrayed as folk devils; rather they are portrayed and represented as 'one-offs', scandals, sleaze with no identification of 'who'.

Summary conclusion

This chapter has continued to explore the threads commenced in Chapter 1. These were to examine the gender patterning to crime and victimisation in societies. It has begun to illustrate how a gendered scrutiny of crime and victimisation is achieved and what it looks like. This chapter has also concerned itself with two important questions about gender, crime and victimisation. It has explored the *levels* crime and victimisation, the *correlates* of crime and victimisation and has summarised our gendered knowledges as amassed from a variety of different sources of information. These sources of information have been outlined and examples and illustrations have been provided. However, in problematising some of the issues around finding information on levels and correlates of crime and victimisation it is clear there are two further important questions. The first concerns the *dynamics* of crime and victimisation. What is the nature of the relationship between a victim and their offender? Do victims contribute to their own victimisation? Do victims resist during occurrences of victimisation and with what results? The second relates to the *consequences* of criminal victimisation. How often do victims report their victimisations to the police? What is the extent of the injury suffered by victims of crime? What is the extent of economic loss? Within the pages of the following chapters these four important questions will continue to be addressed.

STUDY QUESTIONS/ACTIVITIES

Visit the science, research and statistics web pages and the Research Development and Statistics (RDS) website. Use these avenues to browse crime in England and Wales. Look at and compare findings from the BCS and police recorded crime.

- As considered through a gendered lens, what dimensions to the 'crime problem' are not captured in police statistics?
- Using gender as the test, examine how survey research lends itself towards the collection of both quantitative and qualitative data on crime and offending?
- Explore for yourself further what appreciative surveys and research involve. In particular, focus on oral or life history research, unstructured, free-format interviewing. Consider their usefulness in eliciting highly penetrative and gender-sensitive research findings.

SUGGESTIONS FOR FURTHER READING

Subject the first two of these suggested readings to a gendered scrutiny and then browse the contents of the third, an edited collection of cases studies.
Crime in England and Wales 2008/09 Volume 1 – Findings from the British Crime Survey and police recorded crime summary.
Regular statistics about sentencing and about offender management caseloads in England and Wales, describe the population in prison establishments, and the workload of the Probation Service. These statistics are available at:
www.justice.gov.uk/publications/statistics.htm
www.justice.gov.uk/publications/populationincustody.htm
Szyockyi, E. and Fox, J.G. (1996) *Corporate Victimisation of Women*. Boston: Northeastern University Press.

3

MEDIATED GENDER, CRIME AND VICTIMISATION

CONTENTS

GLOSSARY TERMS

Cultural Constructions   Stereotype

Folk devils   Newsworthiness

Ideal type   News values

Gender-blind   Signal crimes

Gender bias

CHAPTER AIMS

- Contextualise the importance and various significances of the media in representing crime and victimisation in society
- Outline gendered representations and cultural constructions of crimes, criminals, offending, offenders and victims

- Provide examples and illustrations of the framing of maleness and femaleness in crime and victimisation news discourse
- Exemplify and illustrate ambiguities and conundrums around women as serious and violent offenders
- Draw attention to the public and private locational biases to media representations of crime and victimisation in society
- Show how gendered knowledges connect with public/private locations for victimisation

Introduction

Chapter 2 considered some of the obvious sources of information that can be used to seek out information on gender patterns to crime and victimisation. It established what the over-riding patterns are and then looked at some more detailed information drawn from a complementary mix of quantitative and qualitative sources. There are, of course, other sources of information that are mediated and it is to some of the more blatant media representations of gender, crime and victimisation that we now turn. The significances of the media – particularly television and newspapers – in representing and shaping the construction of our social world have long been recognised. This chapter begins by contextualising the importance of the media in representing crime and victimisation in society, it stresses the various significances of such representations and in particular the gendered representations and cultural constructions of crimes, criminals, offending and offenders as well as victims. It considers how news is constructed and how 'newsworthiness' and 'news values' help construct crime news agendas. It demonstrates how gender, crime and victimisation are 'mediated' and how both simple and complex gendered discourses are evident and it does so through the use of various examples, illustrations and cases studies. Simply put, the most frequent frames of men in crime news discourse are as offender whilst one of the most frequent frames of women in crime news discourse is as victim. However, this chapter takes a critical look at crime news narratives in respect of gendered representations.

The chapter also illustrates how mediated and cultural constructions of the crime and victimisation problem have various structural and locational biases to them. Finally, in pushing forward gendered theorising, this chapter moves towards a conclusion that suggests that although gender clearly discernable in terms of patterns, representations, cultural constructions, theoretical and research agendas, policies and practices in respect of the crime and victimisation problem in society, these gendered knowledges are full of ambiguities, conundrums and paradoxes. This renders any singular gendered representation or generic cultural construction highly problematic. Gendered knowledges are therefore complex in all manner of ways. This chapter takes the broad topic of cultural constructions and the more specific focus on media representations that are connected to crime and victimisation, to explore and illustrate some of these simple and complex gendered themes.

Key questions for Chapter 3

- Why study gender, crime and victimisation as mediated?
- How does television and how do newspapers construct gendered crime news agendas?
- According to mediated representations, what does a gendered picture of the crime problem look like?
- According to criminological and victimological wisdoms, what does a gendered picture of the crime problem look like?
- According to mediated representations, what does a gendered picture of victimisation in society look like?
- According to criminological and victimological wisdoms, what does a gendered picture of victimisation in society look like?
- Who is readily ascribed victim status? Who is not?
- Can gender help us understand distinctions between media reporting of public and private violence?

Media representations of crime and victimisation

Some have argued that the media creates myths about crime, criminals and victims. Certainly it would seem at face value that crime news almost invariably over-represents violent and sexual crimes, while under-representing other forms of criminality. Popular attitudes towards, and understandings of, the crime problem are often constructed around stereotypical images of more serious crimes – the terrorist, the paedophile, the rapist or the armed robber for example. Since most of us have little direct knowledge or experience of criminally victimising others or being criminally victimised, our awareness is to a large extent derived from secondary sources. Gossip, hearsay, second- and third-hand storytelling, newspapers, magazines, television news, radio and various fictional accounts and presentations of crime in society fill in our knowledge gaps. Each of these media will often present an exaggerated picture of violence or deal with more newsworthy types of interpersonal violence. The term 'newsworthiness' encapsulates the perceived 'public appeal' or 'public interest' of any potential news story. We are offered, in effect, a skewed picture of the crime problem and a far from accurate or 'real' portrayal of the problem of crime and victimisation in society.

Arguments throughout this book are premised on the belief that the notion of a unitary or exclusive and simply defined crime and victimisation problem in society is fundamentally flawed. Part of the problem with such a notion is its self-fulfilling nature. Dominant mediated and popular political representations tend to convey just such clearly distilled visual and verbal lexical representations. This reductive picture provides and promotes stylised and often individualised por-traits of offenders and victims. It almost caricatures those who commit crime and engage in offensive behaviour as our criminal **folk devils** and criminogenic popula-tions. Similarly, it caricatures those who experience criminal victimisation and suffer from the activities of those criminogenic folk devils as '**ideal type**' victims. Offender status is readily conferred upon some and victim status is equally readily conferred upon others. Greer has recently articulated how 'ideal victims' and a 'hierarchy of victimisation' exist in the news media. Under such conceptualisa-tions of the crime and victimisation problem, offenders and victims are readily separated off from one another, made distinct and easily identifiable by a simple binary divide. In this complex to simple approach to reconstructing and represent-ing crime and victimisation, aided and abetted by mediated mechanisms, myths are constructed (note for example Jewkes (2005a) 'mythical monsters' and 'mad cows', see below) and dichotomies and divides are artificially constructed. Thus, if a media blanket does not literally create moral panics about crime and victimi-sation, they certainly help weave and knit, and ultimately reinforce and reproduce stereotypical and common sense wisdoms about crime and victimisation. These cultural and mediated representations and constructions are problematic victimo-logically and criminologically in several ways. They certainly have a specific gender bias to them whilst other demographic characteristics – class/race/age – clearly influence media interest in crime news stories (Greer, 2007).

The media impacts upon each of the following fundamental criminological and victimological questions:

- What constitutes the crime problem?
- What crimes are popularly considered the most heinous, damaging, harmful and serious?
- Who gets labelled as a criminal, classified as a perpetrator and treated as an offender?
- What counts as offensive and anti-social behaviour?
- What gets labelled, classified and treated as a victim?
- Who gets labelled, classified and treated as a victim?
- Where is dangerous and risky to go, be and live?

Doing and experiencing crime and victimisation: what and who?

A simple way of conceptualising these fundamental criminological and victi-mological problems is offered in Table 3.1. This table outlines what, typically,

Table 3.1   Doing and experiencing crime and victimisation: what and who?

What are crimes?	Who commits crime?	What/who is victimised?
Burglary	Burglars – jobless men	Homes
Robbery	Robbers and muggers –young, black men	Elderly, women
Theft	Of cars – young men and boys Of property – men and boys Shoplifters – women	Cars Property Shops
Violent crime – terrorism, assault, rape	Young men Terrorism – the disaffected, extremists Assault – men Rapists – men	Innocent people Women

popularly and mythologically, constitutes crimes, who commits crime and what/who is victimised.

This chapter is concerned with all of the above and with problematising this common-sense, overly simplistic, reductive and narrow set of representations. This is achieved by using a gendered telescopic lens. This particular perspective on the crime and victimisation problem allows us to demonstrate dominant gender patterns that are apparent in mediated representations of the crime and victimisation problem. In Chapter 2 we reflected on what we do and do not know about men's and women's victimisation and elsewhere I have also previously considered the questions and answers as presented in Box 3.1 (Davies, 2007b).

BOX 3.1

WHAT IS VICTIMISATION?

Q: What is victimisation?
A: Mugging, theft, disorder and violence, murder
Q: Where does victimisation happen?
A: On our streets, close to football stadiums and public city/town centre spaces – outside
Q: Who victimises?
A: Hooligans, youth
Q: Who is victimised?
A: The weak and vulnerable, the elderly and innocent people

The answers presented rely upon obvious manifestations, features and characteristics of victimisation and illustrate the legacy of positivist traditions in victimology. The latter is a theme which is explored in greater depth in Chapter 5.

However there is much misleading information and indeed missing data in these answers which denote only partial and limited knowledge about victimisation generally, and the gendered nature of victimisation in particular.

At face value the answers are **gender-blind** but on closer reading **gender bias** is implied. These common sense answers play down the fact that much crime and victimisation exists on a **gendered** terrain and that a rather different set of answers can be provided to the same set of questions. This more scholarly focus is informed by critical and feminist knowledges that demand an examination of public and private crimes and victimisations and that due consideration be given to the notion of gendered locations. This is further considered in the penultimate section of this chapter.

In the process of problematising the crime and victimisation and demonstrating dominant gender patterns that are apparent in mediated representations of the crime and victimisation, this chapter is beginning to demonstrate ambiguities, conundrums and paradoxes that reveal these patterns as only *dominant* gender patterns. The following section continues to explore and illustrate simple constructions, representations, definitions, wisdoms and knowledges of gender patterns to the crime and victimisation problem, all of which are thrown into sharp relief by mediated mechanisms and technologies. Yet, this first stage gendered analysis paves the way for a more detailed, critical and feminist inspired analysis. This layered and intersectional analysis will bring to the fore a much more complex and multi-faceted set of gender and other stratification issues. Thus several competing and overlapping social structural variables or 'intersectionalities', most notably class-race-age-gender, are considered as likely to impact variously upon the more genuine problems concerning crime and victimisation in any given historical period or temporal snapshot (Daly, 1993, 1997; Davies et al., 2007). These are more refined and nuanced representations and social-cultural constructions of the various crime and victimisation problems that achieve some occasional and limited criminological and victimological notice in popular representations.

In these popular representations, visible gendered representations of offenders and victims alike become *the* gendered representations. In the same way as visible representations that are mediated to us of crime in society become *the* crime problem in society (Muncie and McLaughlin, 2001), these representations become unitary, exclusive and dominant. At the risk of oversimplification, *the* crime problem becomes synonymous with *the* problem of (some types of) *men* in society. Visible gendered representations become stereotyped media caricatures. In this chapter we simply draw a parallel with the ways in which highly visible and commonsensical understandings (as opposed to good criminological sense understandings) of the problems of crime in society are (re) produced to us the mediated crime hungry audience. Most significantly what results in relation to the latter is that problems of crime in society – become *a* particular crime problem (with some crime types dominating and others being less visible). Most obviously, this particular crime problem is a problem of men (with women being less visible as offenders). Taking this line of argument one stage further, this particular crime problem, belonging most obviously to men, is a problem of some men in particular (with some men being less visible than others as offenders). This leaves us with the familiar mediated caricature of the youthful, hooded male (usually black) the embodiment of the crime problem in contemporary society (see the image below of white hooded males with the police community support officer in discussion on the street).

In mediated representations, young people, especially young men and boys, easily attract and are readily ascribed offender status yet have to work hard to achieve any kind of victim status (Brown, 1998; Muncie, 2004). Let us pause to remind ourselves of the gender/class/age/race nexus referred to in Chapter 1 as the social division nexus and above as interlinking social 'intersectionalities'.

BOX 3.2

STEREOTYPING

Taking the image below as the starting point, this image is a partial **stereotype**, partial in that the full blown stereotype would be a youthful, black, hooded male in obvious confrontation with the officer. Nevertheless, the image points to the concept of gender/class/age/race all being relevant factors in that the image is of a male, who is young and white. The particular interplay between the stratifications of class and race are such that this youth (a white youth) in discussion with the officer, is less stereotypically troublesome and therefore represents a less threatening scenario, than if he had been a black youth.

© Peter Macdiarmid/Gettty Images

Thus in this chapter, we also begin to expose more nuanced gendered representations and cultural constructions of crime and victimisation in society. These themes are further developed throughout the remainder of this book where you will also notice the reoccurrence of the themes concerning the over-locking nature of social divisions.

News coverage of young people and crime cyclically focuses on a slightly more unusual aspect of unruliness, that of young women and girls. Once every ten years or so there is a media furore about girls' involvement in youthful violence. Girl gangs were newsworthy once again after the actress Elizabeth Hurley was robbed at knifepoint in Chelsea and threatened with a broken bottle allegedly by a gang of four teenage girls in 1994 (Knowsley, 1994). Almost a decade later there was another surge of interest in young women's alcohol consumption leading to the female equivalent of men behaving badly, the 'Ladette' (Walklate, 2001). This has since been reproduced and has occurred more frequently, recently taking the following forms: 'Menace of the violent girls' (*Daily Mail* 31.07.08), 'The ladette louts' (*Daily Mail* 21.07.08), 'The Feral Sex: The terrifying rise of violent girl gangs' (Bracchi, 2008), and in May and June of 2009 Tom Whitehead writing in the *Daily Telegraph* drew our attention to teenage girls and the growth of the 'ladette' culture in a series of articles – 'Rise of "ladette" culture as 241 women arrested each day for vio-lence' (Whitehead 01.05.09), 'Number of "ladette women" fined for drunk and disorderly behaviour rises by a third' (Whitehead 14.06.09). These and similar articles describe these very young girls' physique as threatening and unbecoming, of them becoming menacing gang or 'crew' members who speak and act violently and sadistically.

Such headlines are made sense of by reference to a unique combination of news values where the gender bias is played upon to make girls' activities more interesting and spectacular, unpredictable, odd and quirky. These young people are those whom we don't expect to be uncivilised, threatening and undisci-plined. In a similar vein, gendered headlines in relation to sex crimes, paedo-phile and murderous women have always been highly newsworthy (for a more developed discussion see the sections on 'crime news' and 'murderous women' and Figure 3.1).

Let us reflect on some of the themes explored above. The dominant, highly visible and popular commonsensical representations of crime, offending and perpetrators that have been illustrated leave in their shadow a number of important and significant criminological and victimological wisdoms and knowledges. These struggle to become known to mass mediated audiences. Nuanced gendered knowledges are masked by representations that tend towards unitary, generic and exclusive definitions of the crime, offending and perpetrator problems. These problems are oversimplified and become generalised to one of offending young men. Less visible, indeed well hidden, are the finer and more nuanced exceptions to the general gender pattern rule. These anomalies and individual exceptions can remain buried, unreported by victims and unrecorded by police and other measuring devices. If these anomalies do come to light and are reported by victims for example, or are discovered by whistle-blowers or by investigative journalists and they can attract sufficient **newsworthiness** and a toxic combination of news values, they become sensational crime news. Let us now examine how this might occasionally happen.

Crime news: socially constructed and gendered in nature

At all geographical levels, from the global and international through to national, regional and local areas crime tends to feature high on news agendas. Crime news tends to top the league as compared with almost any other area of social life that contemporary news programmes and news reports comment upon. Where sports news tends to fill the back pages of newspapers and money matters are scattered throughout, crime news will frequently find its way onto the front pages and will make headline news. It is now commonplace for crime and the media sections in criminology textbooks to note that, not all crime is newsworthy. Some crime news stories are so powerfully loaded with a toxic combination of **news values**, the informal professional imperatives adopted by editors and followed by journalists (Jewkes, 2005a, following Galtung and Chibnall, 1977 and Ruge, 1965) that govern and impact upon whether or not a potential crime story gets into print or is otherwise made visible to mediated audiences, that they generate much column space in news-papers and air-time on news programmes. According to Reiner's longitudinal study of crime news reports, their content has increasingly focussed on victim related matters (Reiner, 2002).

Whilst crime is generally newsworthy, it is a range and combination of vari-ous 'news values' that help push a potential crime story into an actual crime story. To briefly illustrate this it is useful to refer to Jewkes' articulation of 12 news values for the twenty-first century. These are headlined and briefly explained in Table 3.2.

Gender, together with a focus on crime and /or victimisation cuts across several of these news values and links them to produce toxic combinations producing highly newsworthy material. There is some debate amongst media theorists on which are the most powerful 'news values'. Jewkes argues vio-lence is the news value most common to all media. Greer (2003) has argued that the notion of proximity – the spacial and cultural relevance of the news item – is the over-arching news value. It seems that violence lends itself to

Table 3.2 News values for a new millennium

1. Threshold	Relates to the level of perceived importance or drama. For example, vandalism and robberies (petty crimes) are likely to feature in the local press but it takes offences of a greater magnitude to meet the threshold of national or international media. Supplementary and new thresholds are often added after the main feature to give a longer life to a news story.
2. Predictability	This value fits in with existing knowledge and expectations. So, for example, we might come to expect news reports of hooliganism, rioting or protest and policies.
3. Simplification, or 'unambiguous'	This refers to a clear and definite process of reporting that tends to have no shades of grey, with a tendency to over-simplification. Stories are reduced to sound bites, manageable, bite-sized chunks.
4. Individualism	Individual cause, individual focus or pathology is pre-eminent. Individual definitions, descriptions, micro-solutions and immediate reactions, to crime, criminality and victimisation are emphasised. Thus there is often a focus on inter-personal crimes of sex and violence, on victims and offenders, celebrities or notable people.
5. Risk	Crime stories tend to be increasingly victim-oriented and play upon and capitalise upon people's fears and anxieties. Stories that can stress palpable risk and the immediacy of risk as well as the likelihood of lasting danger, are newsworthy.
6. Sex	Stories that have a potential or major sex angle to them are 'a good story'. Jewkes argues this is one of the most salient of the 12 news values. Research has shown that newspapers over-report news of a sexual nature and the links between sex and violence are often played out to emphasise value number 5 – risk. There are exceptions to this toxic mix of newsworthiness.
7. Celebrity or high status persons or notable individuals	Galtung and Ruge (1965) call this 'elite-centricity – powerful or famous nations or people. Chibnall (1977) refers to this obsession with notable individuals or celebrities as 'personalisation'. Alternatively this category can include high status officials e.g. church/clergy, politicians, business elites, pop personalites, footballers. Futhermore, some individual criminals have achieved celebrity status in the media.
8. Proximity	Greer (2003), has argued that the notion of proximity is the over-arching news value. This refers to the spacial and cultural relevance of the news item and how meaningful it is in terms of its 'nearness to home'. This refers not only to geographical nearness but the story's personal relevance, how it directly connects to you as well as how it connects to the current 'climate of opinion' on issues. Is it topical?
9. Violence	Jewkes sees violence as the news value most common to all media. Violence lends itself to many of the other features of newsworthiness. Yet not all violent crimes meet the threshold for becoming a top media item.
10. Spectacle or graphic imagery	TV news is especially capable of providing a strong visual impact to crime and victimisation. Emotive language often accompanies the visuals whether they are still mugshots or video-nasties. Under this heading Jewkes also notes how there has been a blurring of the boundaries between the 'real' and 'fake', fact and fiction. Osborne (2002) has coined the phrase 'infotainment' to describe such reporting.

(Continued)

Table 3.2 (Continued)

11. Children	Children are a prime example of the focus on individuals. Whether as victims or offenders, children tend to make a news feature more newsworthy.
12. Conservative ideology and political diversion, or deterrence, detraction and repression – from wider problems	This signifies a conservative 'status quo' agenda, where appeals to morality are often used to create deviants or issues are dressed up so that indignation is instilled in us, often against marginal groups who are used as scapegoats to divert attention to more deep rooted social divisions and problems.

many of the other features of newsworthiness, sex combined with violence, together with a focus on children – either as victims or offenders or both – tend to make a feature more newsworthy and together with the news value 'novelty' will almost guarantee a reported or visible crime will make the news agenda. Crime stories that can stress palpable risk, the immediacy of risk as well as the likelihood of lasting danger, are newsworthy. The case of 4-year-old Madeleine McCann, who went missing from an apartment in Praia da Luz, Portugal, on 3 May 2007, is a good illustration. Risk was and remains a lasting danger and a key factor in terms of newsworthiness. Madeleine has never been found and no one has yet been held accountable. This helped put this incident on the worldwide crime news agenda and has in part helped it remain there, on and off ever since. In part because this has been assisted by her parents and Kate McCann in particular whom the media has variously represented as 'anguished parent, to grieving mother, to suspect' (Herbert, 2007) and back again to anguished parent.

Risk in combination with sex has greater potency. Stories that have a potential or major sex angle to them are 'a good story'. Indeed Jewkes argues that this is one of the most salient of the 12 news values. Research has shown that newspapers over-report news of a sexual nature and the links between sex and violence are often played out to emphasise risk. There are important and significantly gendered exceptions to this toxic mix of newsworthiness e.g. domestic violence, child abuse in the home. Risk in combination with sex and (some types of) violent crime is an even more potent mix. Interpersonal crimes, for example sex and violence, can more easily be portrayed as dramatic and titillating than non-violent crimes, especially if children can be added to this increasingly toxic mix of news values. Children, whether as victims or offenders tend to make a potential news feature even more newsworthy. Additionally, Greer (2007) has drawn attention to how the visual has become an increasingly important news value. Thus, for example, crime news stories that combine the key ingredients of risk, sex, violence and children with dramatic visual images can be guaranteed media exposure.

In Soham, Cambridgeshire in 2002, the murder of Jessica Chapman and Holly Wells hit worldwide headlines. These reports were accompanied by pictures of the immensely photogenic girls. Ian Huntley and Maxine Carr were arrested days after the girls' disappearance and pictures of the accused were also well publicised. Although there are speculative expectations about sex in relation to the Madeleine McCann case, it was overt in the Soham case. The story was newsworthy all round the globe with the key ingredients all being present – risk, sex, violence and children with dramatic visual images of both victims and offenders – the latter simply represented as good and vulnerable versus the accused as twisted and bad.

Media misogyny

Whilst sex, violence, risk and children can often combine to produce a good crime story, as indicated above, there are exceptions which a gendered perspective makes clear. We shall now explore some of these anomalies starting with media misogyny. Several poignant questions serve as a short cut to illustrating 'media misogyny' and a 'virulent form of vilification that is directed at female offenders' (Jewkes, 2005a: 108). The following questions are adapted from the discussion of standard narratives used by the media to construct women who commit very serious crimes as discussed in a chapter entitled 'Media misogyny: monstrous women' by Yvonne Jewkes (2005), which readers are encouraged to read at this point.

- When women commit serious crimes:
    - Why are their crimes polarised and women constructed as either sexually promiscuous or sexually inexperienced/frigid?
    - Why are they subjected to intense scrutiny regarding their physical appearance and attractiveness?
    - Why are they the epitome of the 'bad wife'?
    - Why are they ascribed a 'bad mother' motif?
    - Why are they frequently depicted as vampires or mythical monsters?
    - Why are they psychiatrised and abnormalised and variously labelled as psychotic or psychopathic 'mad cows'?
    - With men, why is it that *she* is the instrumental 'evil manipulator' and the burden of guilt is on *her* shoulders?
    - Why does the media turn us into 'non-agents'?

Thus returning to the examples noted above, in the Soham case Maxine Carr was and remains portrayed by the media as an enigma, a woman who cannot be understood, in a similar vein to Myra Hindley and Rosemary West (see below and Figure 3.1). A more recent example of a woman everyone can easily be persuaded to despise is the 39-year-old mother of two, Vanessa George. George worked at Little Ted's Day Care Unit in Plymouth. Along with her co-worker Angela Allen and Facebook partner Colin Blanchard, George was proactive in a range of paedophile activities. In December 2009 she was given a minimum of seven years in prison having admitted seven sexual assaults on children and six counts of making and distributing indecent pictures of children. All of these cases were highly newsworthy, they also introduce have misogynist overtones.

Murderous women

A number of monstrous women have been identified by press reporting of murderous women over the centuries including one-off as well as serial killers dating back to the eighteenth and nineteenth centuries. Illustrative cases can be pinpointed from across the world, including Australia, America, Mexico and the United Kingdom. In America these include names such as Lizzie Borden and Aileen Wuornos and in Britain some people may remember Ruth Ellis, the so-called 'Finchley baby farmers', Annie Walters and Amelia Sach and Myra Hindley and more recently Emma Humphreys and Sara Thornton or perhaps Beverley Allitt. Whilst all were murderous women, as we shall explore here, they are remembered for different reasons linked to the 'fascinating' facts as reported.

A chronology of murderous women is shown in Figure 3.1. Some of the key details about these murderous women, including significant offender-victim relationships, are provided in the brief notes included in the figure. Standing alone Figure 3.1 is simply a voyeuristic and sensational reproduction of media misogyny and the endless fascination with murderous women. It is not intended to be read in this way and should be used a platform for critique and for practising critical analysis. Use this chronology as a springboard from which to engage in a critical expose of media reporting of crime news and extremely violent crimes committed by women. Ask yourself a number of questions about this chronology:

- Are there any deaths perpetrated exclusively by women, or with women involved, that are omitted from this chronology? Give dates, examples and brief notes.
- From this list can you establish any:
  - types of murders?
  - patterns to any types of murders?
  - common themes, relationships between offenders and victims?
  - commonalities of motivation for the murders or any particular types of murders?

1960: **Sharon Kinne**, a 19-year-old mother, briefly succeeded in blaming her husband James Kinne's murder on their 2-year-old daughter. She was later also indicted for the murder of Mrs Patricia Jones and then also for the shooting of a middle-aged Mexican man Francisco Pardes Ordóñez. Sentenced to 13 years in prison the newspapers in Mexico called her 'La pistolera'.

1963: **Magdalena Solis and her brother, together with 12 other cult members**, were each sentenced to 30 years in jail. Magdalena was described as a Monterey prostitute and the priestess of a murderous sex cult. Dissenters and unbelievers were killed, victims sacrificed, beaten and hacked to death.

1963: **Delfina and María de Jesús**, Mexican sisters who, after a discovery in 1963, were found responsible for the deaths of more than 80 girls. Their vice ring and murder of migrant workers was supported by corrupt networks that enabled horrific and shocking activities including ill-treatment, torture and murder to be carried out by the sisters. They were sentenced to 40 years in prison.

1964: **Mary French along with 23-year-old Charles Schmid and friend John Saunders** were convicted of the murder of three teenage girls in Tucson. In 1964 they lured a young woman for a drive, then raped her, killed her with a rock and buried her. A year later the trio were involved in strangling sisters Gretchen and Wendy Fritz. Schmid was sentenced to two terms of life imprisonment; Mary French received five years and Saunders life.

1966: **Myra Hindley and Ian Brady** became known as 'the Moors murderers'. They were jointly found guilty of killing two children, Edward Evans, and Lesley Ann Downey. Brady was also found guilty of murdering John Kilbride and Hindley was his accessory. They assaulted and killed children and both received life sentences that year. Several other missing children in the Greater Manchester area have since been linked to Hindley and Brady.

1968: **Mary Flora Bell** At a trial commencing in December 1968 Mary Bell, aged 11 years-old, was found guilty of manslaughter of a 3-year-old boy and a 4-year-old boy in Newcastle-upon-Tyne. Strangulation and violence were used.

1980: **Blanche Wright**, referred to as America's first hit woman, described herself and her partner as contract killers for drug dealers. Wright operated in New York. Aged 21 on her arrest she was sentenced to 18 years for shooting drug dealer Marshall Howell and 15 years to life for her part in the murderous shooting of Martha Navas and her neighbour Luis Martin.

1980: **Alice Lynne Chamberlain** was the 32-year-old mother and central figure in the so-called 'Dingo Baby' murder case. At the setting of Ayers Rock, Lindy Chamberlain claimed she saw a dingo rush out of the tent where baby Azaria lay sleeping on the second day of the Chamberlains' holiday, seconds before she discovered the baby was missing. Alice Chamberlain received a life sentence with hard labour.

1981: **Susan Barber** In May 1981 she poisoned her husband by putting weed-killer (Gramoxone) in his steak-and-kidney pie. After being arrested in 1982 she was jailed for life for murder.

1985: **Emma Humphreys** a 17-year-old, stabbed Trevor Armitage with whom she lived with a knife. At her trial she pleaded provocation but was convicted of murder and sentenced to life in prison. She spent ten years in prison before being freed by the Court of Appeal in London.

1986: **Ulrike Meinhof and Gudrun Ensslin**, two of the ruling triumvirate of the Baader-Meinhof gang, a left-wing terrorist group whose revolutionary activities included extortion and murder commencing in Frankfurt in 1968, with the planting of incendiary bombs.

(Continued)

(Continued)

1987: **Valmae Beck** assisted her partner in the abduction, rape and murder of a 12-year-old girl in Queensland, Australia.

1989: **Tracey Wigginton** killed a man by stabbing him 27 times, almost decapitating him and reportedly drinking his blood in Brisbane, Australia. She was sentenced to life imprisonment by the Supreme Court in 1991.

1989: **Kirnjit Ahluwalia** was convicted of the murder of her violent husband and sentenced to life in prison. She had poured petrol over her husband's feet whilst he was sleeping and set them alight. He died five days later. Her conviction was quashed in 1992 at a retrial. The court accepted new evidence and she plead guilty to manslaughter on the grounds of diminished responsibility whilst suffering depression. She was released from prison.

1990: **Sara Thornton** received a life sentence having been convicted of murdering her husband after stabbing him in 1989. In 1996 she was freed after a retrial ordered by the Court of Appeal in London. At this trial she was found not guilty of murder but was convicted of manslaughter. She had served five and a half years in prison.

1992: **Aileen Wuornos** received two death sentences having preyed upon older lorry drivers and having been found guilty of killing seven men while working as a prostitute in Florida. She spent 12 years on death row for multiple murders before being executed in Florida in 2002.

1993: **Beverley Allitt** was jailed for the murder of four babies and injured nine others between 1991 and 1993 (BBC News, 1999) in Lincolnshire. Dubbed the 'Angel of Death', and diagnosed as suffering from Munchausen's syndrome by proxy, she was given 13 life sentences in 1993 with a recommendation that she serve a minimum of 30 years in jail.

1995: **Rosemary West** was convicted of serial murder. Over a period of 16 years she was found guilty of murdering ten young women in Gloucester. Rosemary West and her husband Fred were co-accused and Fred committed suicide in prison before the trial.

1996: **Tracie Andrews** reported the murder of her fiancé Lee Harvey, after a 'road rage' incident in Worcester, England and later made an emotional appeal for his murderer. She was later arrested and charged in connection with the murder which she denied. She was found guilty and sentenced to life imprisonment in 1997.

2007: **April Bright**, following a carnival in Bristol, 18-year-old April stabbed 35-year-old Mohamoud Hassan in the neck at a pub. Although admitting to manslaughter she was convicted of murder in 2008 and given a life sentence.

2008: **Jennifer Shelton** was accused of killing her mother, 84-year-old Bertha Martin who suffered a severe head injury and died of a brain haemorrhage. Facing a charge of manslaughter, Jennifer was found guilty having smashed her mother on the head with an ornamental horse in Sunderland. She was jailed for four years.

2008: **Maxine Williams** 22-year-old Maxine from Wales, was found guilty of murdering Bernard Evans her mother's partner with a a knife that cut through a main artery in his arm. She was given a life sentence.

Figure 3.1 A chronology of murderous women 1960–2008

(adapted from Wilson, C. And Seaman, D. (1983) *Encyclopaedia of Modern Murder.* London: Book Club Associates and various web-based searches)

As Figure 3.1 demonstrates, women murderously victimise by a wide range of means including shooting, bludgeoning, bombing, cannibal killings, child murders, cult murders and dismembering murders. Their murdering has made use of drugs, gangs, hatchetings, kidnapping, large scale murder, poisoning, sex, shooting, stabbing, strangulation, suffocation and terrorism. There are on average 750 murders every year in the UK and some receive more media attention than others. Gender, combined with sex is often key to heightened publicity. As noted in Figure 3.1, women murder alone, with accomplices and as part of a mixed couple in 'team killings' and in sadistic sexual homicides. They kill strangers, people in their care and engage in consecutive filicide (Scott, 1996).

You were encouraged to read this list with a particular eye on offender–victim relationships which might have led you to a consideration of 'domestic' murders. Furthermore, whilst you might have unearthed a range of gender related issues in your critique, particularly relating to stranger and non-stranger violence, your critique might also have raised issues concerning women's motivations for committing murder. The list may well have conjured up a range of relevant questions suitable for examination. For example:

- Is murder by women an economic crime?
- Is it financial in nature?
- Is murder by women a result of impoverishment and oppression?
- Is murder by women motivated by power or greed?
- Is murder by women sexual in nature?
- Is murder by women for mercy or revenge?
- Is it self, and/or family, protection or defence?
- Are women pulled towards or pushed into committing murder?

Such questions, arising from a more detailed critique and questioning of the chronology of murderers outlined in Figure 3.1 has lead us away from simply being superficially fascinated by women who kill, to a much more serious set of queries. This set of criminological and victimological queries suggests several levels of analysis and poses serious questions about murderous women and their crimes, relationships, desires and motivations.

Some of these relationships, desires and motivations have been more fully exposed in media representations of murderous women than others. Criminological inquiry has not been much more rigorous in its examination of such issues which we will pursue further in Chapter 5. Sporadic news reports of murderous women have made links to a number of medical conditions and legal defences. The nurse Beverley Allitt, referred to above, brought Munchausen's syndrome by proxy (MSBP) into the public spotlight. A Cardiff mother brought MSBP back to the Crown Courts where she admitted to two charges of child cruelty after subjecting her child to unnecessary surgical procedures causing risk and discomfort (BBC News, 2003). Another syndrome, Sudden Infant Death (SIDS) has also featured in topical news stories during the last two decades. Infanticide, the murder of a new born infant is a highly gendered term that has achieved legal status by being written into defence arguments alongside the notions of diminished responsibility and post-natal depression or psychosis. As such, it is a defence in England appropriate for women only (Jewkes, 2005a). This type of murderer therefore is always assumed to be a woman.

The subject of 'women who kill' is of course of recurring interest in mediated representations of crime news. Myra Hindley and Rosemary West have withstood the test of time in terms of standing out as child killers in partnership with their male partners. Less prominent as time passes are husband/partner deaths of the type committed by Emma Humphreys and Sara Thornton whose cases focussed on the use of the 'plea of provocation'. This, together with the notion of 'psychological self-defence' (Walklate, 2001) tend more recently to go hand in hand when reporting on cases when women kill their male partners. Jewkes confirms this. Spousal homicide – 'the unlawful killing of an individual by their spouse or partner' (Jewkes, 2005a: 231) by women would appear to be increasingly newsworthy in the latter years of the twentieth century and into the new millennium. One such report made front page headline news in the *Daily Mail* which put its particular slant on such cases: 'Women who kill abusive partners could escape a murder charge. 'GO SOFT ON THE WIVES WHO KILL IN COLD BLOOD' (Slack, 2008). In Australia one report claims there is a history of domestic violence in more than 70 per cent of such cases (Bagshaw and Chung, 2000). Whilst there are pockets of criminological interest, this has done little to challenge or impact upon the stereotypical representations of women who kill that continue to dominate popular media. Less well remembered incidents where women have been involved in others' deaths include those where the death is connected to child abuse cases and inquiries.

The very first question you were asked to consider in relation to Figure 3.1 was: 'Are there any deaths perpetrated exclusively by women, or with women involved, that are omitted from this chronology? Female child abusers featured on that list only in so far as criminal investigations were mounted and therefore a crime (and criminological) interest is assumed. The question suggests that some women are doing harmful deeds – perhaps equivalent to murder – that do not register in this chronology. This headline – 'Mothers who kill: not as rare as we think' (*Independent*, 1999) – is one of an array of media reports that tend to report under the banner of child abuse and neglect. A social service rather than criminal representation of the incident tends to dominate, even when a criminal investigation might be parallel to the social service investigation and part of the multi-agency inquiry. Whilst we have referred to occasional media references to infanticide, the reporting of women who are abusive and neglectful to children tends to have a rather different agenda from crime news reports. In some ways this agenda has a similar gender agenda to it but it differs in others.

Some of these complex issues are returned to below and also in Chapter 5 but for the moment you are encouraged to do the following tasks:

1 Develop your own chronology of child abusers/cases as derived from news headlines over a similar time period to that done for murderous women in Figure 3.1, 1960–2008.
2 When you have done this ask yourself a series of questions about the gender agendas that are represented in this chronology and make a list of them.

And the men?

Similarly to women, men are involved in a full range of murder methods. Whilst several poignant questions serve as a short cut to illustrating 'media misogyny' and a 'virulent form of vilification that is directed at female offenders' (Jewkes, 2005a:108), as shown above, the interesting gender questions are rather different for men who commit serious crimes. For men the questions we might pose in respect of mediated reporting are also complex and sometimes ambiguous. In some instances of serious violence, media reporting is almost cavalier and accepting of the orthodoxy of murderous and seriously violent and abusive men. In other instances the climate of opinion is whipped into a type of misanthrope similar to that hatred directed at murderous women. Thus, when men commit serious crimes:

- Why are they treated in a gender-neutral way?
- Why is masculinity not problematised?
- Why aren't they the epitome of a 'bad father'?
- Why aren't they ascribed a 'bad father' label?
- Why are media and public responses less exaggerated than they are for women?
- With women, why is it that *he* disappears, often as the 'unfortunate bearer of a tormented psyche'?
- Why is the media less reticent to confront them as rapists and murderers?
- In sum, why are they simply 'just boys doing business' (Newburn and Stanko, 1994)?

Although the chronology of murderous women provided earlier is far from comprehensive, a relatively small number of monstrous women have been identified by press reporting of murderous women over the last 50 years or so. Compared with men, women murder infrequently. Mediated reporting is quantitatively and qualitatively different in respect of murderous women's male counterparts, accomplices and lone male killers. In stark contrast to those crime news stories where women feature as murderers of their partners and husbands there appear to be many fewer published instances where men are spousal murderers. Few of the men who kill the on average two women per week in this way, make big crime news and neither do their victims.

Signal crimes, sex crimes and child abuse

Following Innes (2003, 2004) Greer claims that '**signal crimes**' – can have a lasting influence on crime reporting (Greer, 2007:2 8). He argues that in the wake of one such signal crime,

> (T)he sexually-motivated abduction and murder of 8-year-old Sarah Payne in the summer of 2000 by a convicted paedophile crystallized fears around the image of the predatory child sex offender and fuelled debate on 'risk and dangerousness', 'surveillance and control', …

Predatory sexual violence was rendered more newsworthy, and its newsworthiness intensified through the lens of sex.

So, returning to some of the questions posed earlier including what counts as offensive and anti-social behaviour; what crimes are considered the most heinous, damaging, harmful and serious; who gets labelled, classified and treated as a victim; who gets labelled as a criminal, classified as a perpetrator and treated as an offender, and following scholarly and gendered understandings of mediated representations, we find violent and sex crimes are drastically over-reported out of all proportion to their apparent incidence at least according to official counts .The 'law of opposites' (Surette, 1998) applies, where the pattern of crimes reported in news stories is almost the obverse of official statistics. Table 3.3 draws attention to some of the oversimplifications which give rise to mythological beliefs about who is responsible for certain types of sex crimes and abuses. The populations of whom we are encouraged to feel fearful and concerned about are also noted.

Table 3.3 Sex crimes, folk devils and criminaloids

Sex crimes	Folk devils		Criminogenic population	
	Are	Are not	Are	Are not
Rape and sexual abuse	Predatory strangers Bogeymen	Female Siblings: brothers, sisters Parents: mothers, fathers	Single, lone predatory men	Women, family members Friends Relatives
Paedophilia	Predatory strangers Bogeymen Monsters, beasts	As above	Male perverts, sex beasts	Female
Child abuse	Fathers, wicked step dads	As above, including aunts, uncles, babysitters	Strange bogeymen	Female Family
Domestic violence	Male partners	Of the same sex as the abused	Angry men	Female
Prostitution	Street walkers	Men and boys	Women	Male Children

Cross referencing the above with the most toxic combinations of the news values referred to earlier in this chapter is useful for understanding why and how some crime news is big news and why and how some crime news is even bigger crime news. It is also instructive to do this through a gendered lens. In this way we have begun to discover some interesting criminological and victimological oddities.

The confusion and combination for example of gender and sex in less orthodox ways with violence, children, proximity, and risk will likely guarantee excessive hypervisibilty. Specific examples include paedophile women, child abusing and murderous women, men battered and killed by their male or female partners, none of which currently feature in the ideal typical paradigm (see Table 3.1) of gendered sex crimes. Where a crime news story includes a folk devil that is not usually female or the story can include a criminogenic population that is not the norm, the story will score high in news values and newsworthiness can be demonstrated as excessive. In the examples provided above, the women are represented as 'not real women' and the men as 'not real men'. Where women are suspected of heinous sexual and murderous crimes they tend to be seen as exceptions to the rule (Carrabine et al., 2004) and this is precisely what makes such stories highly newsworthy. This is where victimological wisdoms and knowledges are instructive in helping to understand better how and why gender matters in understanding mediated representations of victimisation.

Child abuse

If the concept of a 'signal crime' has a lasting influence on crime news reporting, then several child abuse cases fall into this 'beacon' category. **Child abuse** is one form of the maltreatment of a child or young person under 18 years of age. Four major categories of child abuse can be identified. First is physical abuse and amongst the forms this can take, are hitting, shaking, throwing, poisoning, burning or scalding, drowning, suffocating. Second, sexual abuse involves forcing or enticing a child to take part in sexual activities. Persistent ill treatment of a child can also be by way of emotional abuse whereas a more passive form of child maltreatment is neglect. The former causes severe adverse effects on the child's emotional development whereas the latter represents a failure to meet a child's basic physical and/or psychological needs and can result in serious impairment of a child's health or development.

The risks to the very young of being seriously and repeatedly and variously victimised are staggeringly high and a more detailed overview is offered in Chapter 5. This chapter is concerned with popular representations of child abuse and as such uses it as a case study. Mediated representations, are often taken as approximate barometers of common sense opinions about current social problems and those directly or indirectly related to legal, crime and victimisation policy are especially newsworthy material. Such stories throw up a number of gendered themes, anomalies and complexities. If we were to compare and contrast depictions and representations of sex crime with child abuse this would be well illustrated. As less populist knowledges recognise, child sexual abuse occurs in the familial context more frequently than it does in public spaces and by predatory paedophile strangers. This knowledge is at odds with representations of the crime and victimisation problem that would be apparent in popular media and political discourse as we saw in the earlier part of this chapter.

Child abuse is a subject that, on the face of it, fits all of the major criteria for being newsworthy. It includes children as victims and sex, three toxic news value ingredients. Unsurprisingly therefore, there is a substantial media archive on the subject of child abuse. Strong verbal headlines together with powerful visual images abound. In the first nine years of this century there has been a variety of different headlines in relation to child abuse. Even the most perfunctory analysis of mediated texts and messages suggest that there are different concerns and gender agendas being articulated and there are significant criminological and victimological issues that merit consideration. There appears to be a broad divide in reports about serious harm to children and serious case reviews and inquiries. First, let us note the commonalities. Most adhere strongly to the criteria for newsworthiness and both tend to report upon the most 'sensational' or extreme 'miscarriage' cases. All focus upon an adult, often a parent, family member or carer as the perpetrator and all take very seriously the need to protect children from all forms of serious harm and abuse, to minimise the risk to children, to prevent child abuse tragedies and offending, to properly detect abuse, to bring offenders to the attention of the relevant authorities and to do justice for vulnerable young victims. However, this is where the similarities in reporting end. What distinguishes one set of reports from the other is the major argument that forms the focal point to the report.

BOX 3.3

BABY P CASE STUDY

A horrific but highly appropriate case study for dissecting the nature of news reporting on serious child abuse is that of Baby P. Born 1 March 2006, he died on 1 August 2007 following abusive neglect and a range of physical injuries (see 'Baby P: a Timeline – the damning dossier', as prepared by prosecution lawyers via Telegraph.co.uk).

One set of headlines and reports focuses in the main upon the child's experience of harm as the tragedy. Criminologically this is a focus upon the 'innocence of the child'. According to such journalism this is where the audience's sympathy's should lie. These reports emphasise the neglect, the abuse, the harm and suffering of the child, and draw out the failings of various social service provisions and lack of response to signs of danger, risk and abuse. In terms of responding to the victimisation, this reporting highlights the inadequacies and failures of communities to intervene, the work social services and social workers in particular, health service and medical professionals and belated police and criminal justice interventions. The reports focus on paradigms of bad practice (Melia, 2004) and portray how state interventions into families and parenting practices have been unobtrusive, how social workers and other care professionals have been overly soft, permissive, naïve and sentimental during investigations and inquiries. Favourable interpretations on the behaviour of parents similar to those reported upon in the Jasmine Beckford Inquiry that showed the social worker approach followed a 'rule of optimism' (Parton, 1997) are echoed. Reporting of this nature emphasises the 'pro-family social worker' who is insufficiently assertive and child protectionist and fails to identify children at risk (Corby, 2000: 49). Headlines which echo these sorts of sympathies have recently been aired in relation to Jaycee Lee Dugard who lived in California in captivity for 18 years raising two daughters she had to her kidnapper Phillip Garido, a convicted sex offender who abducted her when she was 11 and also in relation to the Austrian, Josef Fritzl, who kept his daughter imprisoned in the basement of their home for 24 years having fathered seven children by her. Victimologically, although these reports are child focussed, and do focus on a key individual as perpetrator, they also tend to diffuse the responsibility for the victimisation and find others partially culpable.

BOX 3.4

MEDIA RESEARCH AND CHILD ABUSE

Further relevant cases studies can be examined to dissect the nature of news reporting in addition to those of Baby P. These are likely to include some that are related to those headlines you will have uncovered as part of the research you were directed to conduct earlier in this chapter suggesting you chronicle child abusers/cases. Indeed, over the last 30 or so years there have been over 40 major inquiries, with an estimated 90 SCRs per year (Redner and Duncan, 2004). Major inquiries and reviews were conducted following the deaths of: Maria Colwell, 1973, Jasmine Beckford, 1984, Kimberley Carlile, 1986, and this century, Victoria Climbie, 2000. See: Laming, Lord (2003) *The Victoria Climbie Inquiry. Report of an Inquiry by Lord Laming.* London: Health and Home Department. In addition you are likely to come across the Cleveland Affair, 1987. All of these were well reported upon, still remembered and are useful case studies.

Another set of headlines and reports prioritise a rather different message. They focus on the perpetrator, the responsible adult(s), often the parents, the mother, the father or other carers. Rather than our sympathies focussing exclusively upon the vulnerable young child's experience of harm, the audience's sympathies in these reports are encouraged to lie also with those who are accused of inflicting the harm. Such reports emphasise the harm and suffering of those assumed to be responsible and on occasion those falsely accused, blamed and held responsible. See, for example, 'Two-year nightmare of the family torn apart by "abuse" case blunders' (Savill, 2006), 'Complaints cause doctors to shun child protection' (Batty, 2005), 'Consultant accused mother of killing child' (Davies, 2006), ' A system that abuses the whole family' (Jardine, 2006). These implicate the net-widened intrusion by the state into family life (Parton, 2006) and state surveillance of families (Broadhurst et al., 2007). Acting prematurely, doing too much too soon, defensive professional practice (Munro, 2004), institutional self-preservation, over-zealousness and insensitivity (Corby, 2000) are key themes and attention is drawn to the unjust and unfair consequences for those accused, assumed guilty, deemed responsible and blamed.

In a broad and popular context, then, there is a general fascination with and abhorrence of, serious forms of harm experienced by children. Such subject-matter inevitably stirs very strong emotional responses. If you engage in a case study approach to analysing some of these news reports a number of confusing and complex gender issues in relation to public and private, popular and populist as compared with more rounded knowledges about child abuse and sex crimes present themselves. With particular reference to this chapter you should note who is 'innocentised' and who is 'demonised', who is fore-grounded and who is rendered 'invisible'. Think further about news reports and 'ideal type' victims/offenders. Are men visible as victims and women as 'normal' offenders?

Public/private locations: gender, crime and victimisation

Where does victimisation happen? As outlined earlier, mediated representations of the crime and victimisation problem lay strong emphasis on certain types of visible criminal victimisations that occur in public places; accessible places and spaces which are not too difficult to find. Examples of popular and well worn sites for disorder and criminal victimisation are on the streets of our cities, towns and local centres particularly at night time (Winlow and

Hall, 2007). They include areas surrounding key institutions and amenity areas such as football stadiums, shopping precincts, outside pubs and clubs, in car parks and places where young people tend to gather. These can all be classified as public arenas, places that are outside rather than inside, open rather than closed and private areas. They are sites where crime and victimisation 'appear' to be.

Public/private sites for harm

Radical, feminist and critical perspectives in criminology following pioneering work in the 1980s have all exposed the domestic sphere as a key site for the violence and sexual abuse experienced by women and children (see, for example, Dobash and Dobash, 1979, 1998; Hanmer and Maynard, 1987; Hanmer and Saunders, 1984; Kelly and Radford, 1987; Stanko, 1985, 1988, 1990a). These knowledges, 'get behind the mere appearance of things' (Mawby and Walklate, 1994:19) and at the events that 'go on behind closed doors' (Walklate, 2005) that we do not 'see' (Walklate, 2007b: 49). As such, they provide a strong challenge to popular constructions and dominant mediated representations of the crime and victimisation problem and where it resides.

Such knowledges challenge and problematise the focus on ideal typical locations for victimisation. They also problematise gender stereotypical strategies that focus on risks to fragile, vulnerable and passive, elderly and young and youthful females who frequent public places at night time. These challenges to the ideal victim in the public domain at night time reveal the partiality of mediated representations of who offenders are, who is at risk to criminal victimisation and where and when harms can be experienced. The private domain of the home, as one indoor site for criminal victimisation remains relatively hidden in crime news stories as do the risks of serious violence and abuse, particularly to those women and children who spend much of their time at home with those they know and often trust the most. Thus despite the feminist exposé of serious forms of victimisation behind closed doors, crime news stories tend not to expose these gendered risks. Risky places tend not to be defined as those where women are for much of their time and where they experience being most frequently harmed. (For a continuation of this discussion of researching crimes and victimisations in private and hidden places see Chapter 4). This points towards a conclusion that suggests that safety in our commuter zones, by-ways, off-road areas and indoor locations tend to remain marginalised and the gendered risks to harms that are experienced in these locations are obscured (Davies, 2008).

Summary conclusion

Crime news reporting and media images have an overall tendency to reproduce myths and stereotypes of crime, criminals and victims. We are provided with an exaggerated picture of violence in society and sex crimes. Crime is depicted as a basic confrontation between good and bad, which fits in with the 'oversimplification' news value. All of this can have very real consequences and impact upon individuals and groups. Where some sex, violence and abuse is over represented, others are under-represented – those behind closed doors – either in the home (domestic and sexual violence and abuse) or in the boardroom (the corporate and white collared workplace) and in private or closed institutions (state offices, nursing and care homes, prisons).

Media images tend to reproduce myths and stereotypes not only of the crime problem, but also of who criminals are. They are depicted as youthful, poor, often black and male. All of this can have serious consequences in terms of those who are selected as perpetrators and who are labelled and ostracised as part of a problem 'demon' category. Where these sorts of criminals are over represented, others are under-represented, those who have the power to evade traditional policing strategies and who are shielded and protected from becoming dealt with by the formal criminal justice system. Male perpetrators of domestic and sexual violence and abuse in the home have some such power as have corporate and white collar criminals.

Media images tend also to reproduce myths and stereotypes of not only the crime problem and of whom criminals are, but also of who are and can be victims. Victims tend to be depicted in ideal stereotypical ways and women are expected to match this stereotype. The media seems fascinated by the figure represented by 'little-red-riding-hood-female', young and vulnerable, brought into sharp relief in contrast to the 'big-bad-black-wolf-man'. Criminologically we can adopt the notion of 'otherness' to make sense of the gendered nature of media representations of criminals and victims, the concept of the 'criminal other', for women criminals, and the 'victimological other' for men as victims. Crime news stories rarely depart from the traditional gender stereotypes appropriate for crime victims and for criminals, except where the quirkiness of the story is guaranteed to sell copy. Where young men who break the law might be seen as just lads doing the business and celebrating their masculinity, criminal women have stepped outside the bounds of femininity, motherhood and cultural expectations related to all of these and so they are already mad and bad and by breaking the law too they are doubly deviant. Where the former is standard fare and not especially newsworthy, the latter in contrast, is not (standard fare) and is (newsworthy).

Gender as a key identity

This chapter concludes that by using gender as a key identity we can begin to make criminological and victimological sense of popular media representations of crime, criminals and victims. This chapter has revealed the partiality of mediated information on the crime and victimisation problem in society. Conclusions are offered in connection with three key areas. First, we have noted there are very specific and stylised representations and cultural constructions of crimes, criminals, offending and offenders as well as victims. Media mythologising contains an exaggerated picture of gender stereotypes. This is seen particularly in representations of violence and sex crimes. Second, deconstructing crime news we find simple and complex gendered discourses. In these, men are likely to be criminals, offenders and victimisers, reinforcing and confirming the dominance of maleness and their criminogenecy. It reproduces beliefs that victims of sexual violence are always female (and all the perpetrators male), that men are not victims, that men are never, vulnerable, fearful or at great risk to victimisation and this leaves men relatively invisible as victims. Third, the nexus between structural and locational bias is evident.

In the next chapter we turn the spotlight upon feminist research methodologies and ideologies. In particular we will focus on the principles that have underpinned the critical approach used in the deconstruction of media representations of crime and victimisation as adopted and encouraged in Chapter 3.

STUDY QUESTIONS/ACTIVITIES

Throughout this chapter a variety of mini-case studies have been used to illustrate how, as criminologists and victimologists, you might adopt a critical approach to the reading and use of mediated sources of information on crime and victimisation. In addition, you have been encouraged to adopt such an approach for yourself having been pointed towards a number of case study materials. Ensure you engage in these activities and consider the questions that have been posed throughout the chapter too. In addition:

- Revisit the glossary terms foregrounded for this chapter: Cultural constructions, Folk devils, Ideal type, Gender-blind, Gender bias, Stereotype, Newsworthiness, News values, Signal crimes. Write your own definitions of each and provide a brief example to illustrate your understanding.
- Revisit Table 3.2. Make a list of examples that illustrate each one of the 12 news values described in Table 3.2.
- Select a major crime news story and critically compare the coverage of this in a range of different newspapers. How are/is the crime/s, criminal/s, victim/s represented?

SUGGESTIONS FOR FURTHER READING

In her book *Media and Crime,* and in Chapter 5 entitled 'Media misogyny: monstrous women', Yvonne Jewkes gives a useful overview of psychosocial and feminist approaches to understanding mediated accounts of seriously violent female offenders. She usefully offers eight standard narratives used by the media to construct women who commit very serious crimes. These are given the following labels: sexuality and sexual deviance, (absence of) physical attractiveness, bad wives, bad mothers, mythical monsters, mad cows, evil manipulators and finally, non-agents.

Two chapters in *Doing Criminological Research,* second edition, (forthcoming), P. Davies and P. Francis (eds) are useful and instructive with lots of examples and illustrations. See Chapter 11 'Using the media to understand crime and criminal justice', by Rob. C. Mawby and Chapter 10 'The media and criminological research' by Yvonne Jewkes.

4

FEMINISM, IDEOLOGIES AND RESEARCH

GLOSSARY TERMS

Feminism

Positivism

Victim perspectives

Critical victimology

Feminism

Victim – prone/precipitation/blaming/culpability

Ideal victim

Survivor

CHAPTER AIMS

- Demonstrate the positivist underpinnings to criminological and victimological knowledges
- Outline feminisms as they relate to the sub-discipline of victimology
- Provide examples of feminist knowledges and show how these can be used to critique other (mediated) knowledges and public policy
- Further develop feminist inspired research methodologies and gendered theoretical knowledge
- Exemplify and illustrate gender and other salient 'power' issues connected to doing criminological and victimological research

Introduction

This chapter has two substantive sections. Both consider the contributions of feminist ideologies to doing research in criminology and in studying victims in society. The first substantive section will refer to the inherent 'legacy of positivism' as part of the broader and problematic context of doing criminological and victimological research. It also focuses on feminist ideologies and their points of similarity as well as different feminist perspectives and feminisms and their points of divergence in the criminological and victimological research, theory and policy contexts. Since feminist critiques (see also Chapter 5) contributed towards the search for alternative ways of measuring and documenting criminal victimisation and feminist ideologies have greatly influenced the way in which we approach the study of criminology and victimology in the twenty-first century it is important to give significant space to these developments. One particular illustration is provided on 'rape knowledges'. Through focussing on this case study illustration some simple to complex beliefs, understandings and contested knowledges about the crime of rape are outlined.

The second substantive section of this chapter moves from the more general level where positivist underpinnings to criminological and victimological knowledges are outlined and feminist principles and ideologies are discussed to the more specific level of doing and operationalisation. This part of the chapter draws heavily on the main case study illustration 'women and crime for economic gain', in order to consider some of the key hallmarks of valid and reflexively ethical (feminist) research practice. Thus some of the significant feminist features to doing research that can lead to feminist informed theorising and policy-making are explored. This is achieved by focussing upon a piece of research that involved doing interviews with female offenders in both the community and the prison setting. Here I draw on my experience of doing original fieldwork with female offenders. In the context of examining 'women and crime for economic gain' this case study illustration serves to highlight a number of important gender and other salient 'power' issues connected to doing criminological research.

Key questions for Chapter 4

- Can radical, critical and/or feminist ideologies supplant positivist understandings of crime and victimisation in society?
- What are the main characteristics of a feminist methodology?
- Why should criminological and victimological researchers ask the 'gender question'?
- How can criminological and victimological researchers conduct gender sensitive research?

- Are women still held to blame for rape?
- How might interviews with female offenders raise wider gender issues for the researcher, the researched and for offenders and victims more generally?

The legacy of positivism

Some enduring legacies persist in both the criminological and victimological enterprises. Several of these have a strong impact upon how a gendered approach has taken shape in these disciplines and upon how research is approached and conducted. Using perspectives dominant in the study of crime victims, we will now explore the enduring and problematic legacy **positivism** continues to hold over research, theory, policy and practice in the discipline of criminology and the sub-discipline of victimology.

Three main **victimological perspectives** have been articulated during the past half century (Mawby and Walklate, 1994). The three perspectives are:

- positivist victimology;
- radical victimology;
- critical victimology.

Positivist victimology

Positivist victimology, sometimes referred to as administrative or conservative victimology can be dated back to the emergence during the mid-twentieth century of the discipline of victimology itself, and specifically the work of Mendelsohn (1940), von Hentig (1948) and Hindelang et al. (1978) (Davies et al., 2003). Indeed, von Hentig and Mendelsohn are portrayed in much of the literature as the founders of the discipline of victimology and the author of its 'domain assumptions' (Walklate, 2007). A number of general points can be made about this victimological perspective. First, much of this early work was purely speculative rather than empirically grounded. Second, that which was empirically grounded relied upon the officially recorded criminal statistics provided by central and local government departments, at least until the introduction of the victimisation survey of the late 1960s (Walklate, 1989: xiii). As a result, these early victimologists were unaware of the 'true levels' of crime or victimisation. Third, scholars working within this perspective focussed attention towards what they variously term **victim proneness, victim precipitation** and victim lifestyle. They were interested in the extent to which victims of crime contributed to crime and to their own victimisation. Thus von Hentig (1948) considered victims' lifestyles and their proneness to victimisation. In

doing so he identified 13 psychological and sociological classes of victim, ranging at one end of a continuum where young people, females and the elderly
feature at the opposite ends of the spectrum of proneness where the 'fighting
tormentor victim' featured (Walklate, 2007a). Mendelsohn (1949) focussed
upon the responsibility of the victim for a criminal event occurring. As Walklate
highlights, '[t]his notion of making victims responsible, to whatever extent, for
their own victimisation, "blaming the victim", has been a considerably problematic one for victimology' (1989: 2–3). The contribution of individuals to their
own victimisation, including the concepts of **victim blaming** and **victim culpability** can be seen further in the work of Wolfgang (1957) who introduced the
term 'victim precipitation' whilst Hindelang et al. (1978) introduced the
notion of victim lifestyle which equated an individual's risk of personal victimisation to his or her own particular routine daily activities. More significantly for victims of rape, since Amir's work in 1979 this violent sex crime has
been associated with the controversial phrase 'victim precipitation' the legacy
of which continues in connection with some women's experiences of seeking
justice. The fourth point is that within much positivist victimological thought
there is a clear focus upon visible victims – that is victims of conventional crimes
such as interpersonal crimes of violence and street crime. This has produced a
focus on public spaces – as opposed to private ones such as the home – as locations
for criminal victimisation.

The legacy of the positivist victimological perspective is as follows. First, it
has ensured the development and refinement of quantitative measures of victimisation. Second, it has clearly influenced the way the state, various criminal
justice agencies, voluntary institutions and organisations respond to victims of
crime and victimisation. This can be seen in particular in the self help philosophy so often promoted alongside a call for retributive justice. Positivist victimology has, however, also attracted criticism. Largely as a result of its focus
upon conventional crimes, the 'private sphere' has remained until recently a
neglected site for victimological research and intervention, as have the victims
of the state and its agencies as well as corporate excesses. Moreover, reliance
upon unsophisticated data and method has meant that much positivistic
research has attempted to play down the risk of victimisation and often presented a random picture of victimisation (Hough and Mayhew, 1983).
Particular types of victimisation including most gendered forms of victimisation
continue to remain unsophisticated. Finally, its denial of any political and/or
structural analyses has meant a complacent view of the victim and more generally, an intellectual and conceptual naiveté.

The work of these and a handful of authors writing in a similar vein produced a domineering positivist framework for the consideration of victimisation which persists in the twenty-first century and impacts upon our
understanding of how victimisation is researched, how it occurs, what form it

takes, how often it happens, why it happens, when and where it takes place and who it happens to. Thus thinking about Von Hentig's 13 categories critically, it is possible to see that he thought the normal person against whom the victim – typically women, children, the elderly, the mentally subnormal etc. – was to be measured was the white, heterosexual male (Walklate, 2007a). Whilst the positivist legacy has been strongly challenged, it has not been extinguished. Some of those that impact upon a gendered victimology are summarised later in this chapter.

Radical victimology

Radical victimology developed in response to the partiality of the positivist perspective and as a result of the ongoing politicisation of victimology during the 1970s and 1980s. The emergence of radical victimology is partly associated with the feminist movement, new left ideals and the protest and counter cultures (Davies et al., 2003). In response to the positivist agenda, radical victimology has been concerned with combining analysis of the state and its actions with the lived experiences of victims of crime (Young, 1986). As Young (1986: 23) argues, 'a radical victimology notes two key elements of criminal victimisation. First, that crime is focussed both geographically and socially on the most vulnerable sections of the community. Second, that the impact of victimisation is a product of risk rates and vulnerability'.

Consequently, radical criminologists have engaged in locally orientated political struggles, drawn attention to state excesses, acknowledged the experiences of victims of crime in many socially deprived neighbourhoods and worked alongside the voluntary, feminist and left wing movements as much as they have the state (Davies et al., 2003). This particular spread of work contextualised victimisation within a broader socio-economic and political framework. The violences and abuses suffered by women and children in the home was exposed and 'grass root' supportive provisions in the form of refuge provision and rape crisis were born in this era.

Critical victimology

Critical victimology is a perspective which endeavours to incorporate the interests of radical victimology and also those of **feminism**. For Walklate (Davies et al., 2003) critical victimology takes seriously the need for a development of an empirically based, rational and objective science, but in direct criticism of radical victimology, one which gets 'beyond the "mere appearance" of things towards understanding these mechanisms which underpin and generate their appearance'.

Victim perspectives

The unfolding of these ways of thinking about both victims and offending produced new ideologies and ways of doing research. Many lessons about women and their experiences of violence and victimisation and about men and their misuse of power are inextricably linked to the feminist critique of criminology which Carol Smart initiated in the 1970s (Smart, 1976; see also Chapter 5). Pioneering scholarly work followed throughout the 1980s that had major implications in terms of understanding women as victims of violent and sexual abuse from men as we also saw in Chapter 3 (see, for example, Dobash and Dobash, 1979; Hanmer and Maynard, 1987; Hanmer and Saunders, 1984; Kelly and Radford, 1987; Stanko, 1985, 1988, 1990a). This era of work from the late twentieth century also shaped our understanding of criminal women so that their criminality has been for the most part explained in terms of social and economic marginalisation and dependency. This has tended to have the effect of reframing criminal women as suffering at the expense of unjust, sexist, biased and patriarchal systems and institutions (see, for example, Carlen, 1985, 1988, 1998; Eaton, 1986; Gelsthorpe, 1989; Carlen and Worrall, 1987). Views of women as vulnerable and socially and culturally victimised proliferated and all of this has had an impact upon how a gendered perspective has been incorporated in the victimological enterprise, upon how victim research has been conducted and upon the choice of subject matter under investigation (Davies, 2007). Some of the consequences of this are summarised also below.

In terms of the history of gendered victim policies, the second wave of feminism and the political climate in the United States and later in the United Kingdom fuelled radical and left unrest and activism. Radical and left realist scholarship was simultaneously published throughout the 1970s, and 1980s reflecting criminologically this changing political mood. This body of work challenged and critiqued conventional and traditional definitions of the crime problem and positivistic victimology. It also offered an alternative focus for the crime problem focussing upon the role of the state and also upon women's roles and experiences in public and private and in some cases a strong policy agenda for placing previously marginalised victims more firmly centre stage. This critique and the aims to incorporate lessons of feminism, together with political activities and initiatives, many of which were specifically aimed at providing a response to women's unmet needs, resulted in the formation of Women's Aid and Refuge provisions for female victims only of domestic abuse, rape crisis interventions and later rape suites (provisions which are considered in more detail in Chapter 8), all of which helped put gender onto the victimological agenda (Davies, 2007). In addition to a whole variety of different social harms and injustices being highlighted, for a select few scholars (see, for example, Pearce and Snider, 1995; Perry and Dawson, 1985; Szyockyi and Fox, 1996) their victims became worthy of study and are sometimes included within the parameters of victimological study.

These historical developments within the academy and from political-social and economic pressures forced a proliferation of feminist ideas connected to both the criminological and victimological enterprises. These ideologies are now considered.

Feminist ideologies

Various strands of feminism have impacted differently on both victimology and criminology (Walklate, 2004b: 94). In many respects, feminism challenges the very heart of the conventional victimological agenda (Walklate, 2000) which has been outlined above. **Feminist** research practice has been explored by various writers (Gelsthorpe and Morris, 1994; Maynard and Purvis, 1994; Naffine, 1997; Stanley and Wise, 1993) and many others have brought their own feminist perspective to bear on their fieldwork and analysis of different areas of sociology (Carlen, 1985, 1988; Heidensohn, 1996, 2003, 2006; Maher, 1997; Walklate, 2004). This work demonstrates that there is no single feminist viewpoint or perspective. Nevertheless as Naffine has argued:

> Many feminists are of the view that the angle from which the dominant class views the world, is one which provides a poor field of vision. Subjugation, and reflection upon that status, makes for a better appreciation of the world. (Naffine, 1997: 51)

A variety of feminist positions and feminisms are now evident including liberal feminism, radical feminism, socialist feminism, cultural feminism, 'women-of colour' feminism/womanism and post-modern feminisms (Kahn, 2009). There are some common features across feminist positions regarding the female victim of crime as well as female offenders. They all tend to have the so-called 'woman question' in common (see, for example, Cain, 1990; Carlen, 1998, 2002; Harding, 1987; Hudson, 2000; Walklate, 2000, 2001, 2003b, 2004). In terms of doing feminist research, this means doing research for example, *for* rather than *on* women (Smith and Wincup, 2000). The key characteristics of liberal, radical, socialist and post-modern feminisms as they relate to the study of victimology (and criminology) are compared and contrasted here according to six criteria. The criteria for comparison include the following:

- What each perspective argues against in the study of victimology?
- What each perspective argues for in the study of victimology?
- The theoretical approach each perspective chooses to focus upon?
- The policy issues that are promoted?
- The preferred methodological approach to the study of crime and victimisation?
- The political strategy adopted by each perspective?

Whilst each of the feminist perspectives identifiable within victimology and the broader criminological enterprise has significant differences according to each of these six criteria, they have two things in common. First each challenges a conventional agenda. Second, each has a common focus in asking the 'woman question' and thus in being oriented *for* rather than *on* women (Smith and Wincup, 2000). The key characteristics of liberal, radical, socialist and post-modern feminisms are illustrated in Table 4.1.

Thus we can see that several feminist approaches to the study of crime and victims rather than a unified 'sisterhood' can now be identified. For liberal feminists the woman question might include the investigation of sexism; to radical feminists it includes analysis of men's power over women; to socialist feminists the compounding of social class and patriarchy are crucial to understanding social justice and victimisation, whilst post-modern feminists problematise the notion of 'the other' and celebrate difference (Walklate, 2003, 2004) acknowledging that different women have different needs.

The influence of radical feminism has perhaps been the most enduring and influential in the study of victims of crime. Radical feminism, through its critique and reaction to the failures, omissions and partiality (Davies et al., 2004) of the early positivists fuelled debates about the notion of the gendered victim and the salience of gender to the study of victims more generally. It contested positivism and brought gender issues, men's and women's victimisation to the fore in understanding broader questions of social justice.

Radical feminism however, can be seen as a pro-women rather than a fully gendered way of thinking. Different feminist ideologies offer different preferences in terms of political and policy strategies. Thus we find that it is generally the case that in the context of policy issues gender-neutrality is wedded to the equality based feminist positions whilst gender-specific policy advocates are wedded to difference based perspectives (Daly, 1994). Philosophically feminists have warned that gender-neutrality simply equates to the male standard where masculinity and maleness are the yardsticks against which judgements of others are made (MacKinnon, 1987). Daly pointed out over a decade ago: 'The equality-difference debate has haunted women activists for more than a century' (Daly, 1994: 9) and when it comes to gender-wise policy, as Chapter 5 will consider, transcending such dichotomies remains problematic.

Table 4.1 Feminism and victimology

Key hallmarks	Liberal feminism	Radical feminism	Socialist feminism	Post-modern feminism
Argues against	Inequality and discrimination	Men's oppression and controlling power over women, the neglect of structural analyses	The neglect of structural analyses	The uncritical and the universal, phallocentrism and assumptions of unity
Argues for	'Fair play' and equal opportunities between the sexes	Women's knowledge, women suffering violent and sexual abuse	Women's knowledge, the interplay between patriarchy and capitalism, intersectionalities of class-race-sex/gender-age	Woman as 'the other' and celebrates difference
Victim context	Challenges masculinist assumptions – a white, male middle class, heterosexual views in relation to victimisation, prioritises women as a disadvantaged group	Challenges men's sexual power over women and raises questions about men, masculinity and sexuality	Focuses on the social system and socio-structural conditions as an explanation for victimisation, draws on 'transgressive' debates outside criminological and victimological domains	Focuses on difference, plurality and gives voice to diversity, challenges mainstream thinking and concerns about victims and victimisation
Policy	Challenges sexism in theory, policy, practice and research and promotes equality	Focuses on sexual violence and harassment, rape, domestic violence, child abuse, intimate and domestic relations	Campaigns for social justice	No policy agenda, challenges conventional links between science, rationality and policy making
Methodology	Focuses on empirical methods of data gathering and 'adds women in' as victims	Includes women and strives to allow women speak for themselves as victims	'Standpoint knowledge' admits to 'whose side we are on' and elevates women as victims research done 'by women, with women, for women'	Challenges and critiques feminist science and feminist victimology, deconstructs ideas, language and structures
Political strategy	Focuses on the discriminatory practices of the legal and criminal justice system on equal legal rights, the implementation of 'correct' (PC), unbiased procedures	At one extreme they challenge positivist notions of victim precipitation at the other they ask whether all men are potential rapists?

To reconstitute sexuality promotes women as survivors | To explore social justice and expose how there is a compounding effect of, for example, racism, sexism and classism which impacts upon women's experiences of victimisation | Gives voice to the silenced: emphasises diversity in women victims' experiences: white, black, lesbian |

Sources: Carlen, 2002; Walklate, 2000, 2001, 2004a, 2004b

The purpose of the above was not to provide a thorough chronological history of the development of victim perspectives, nor to provide any detailed critique of women and crime or the activities of the women's movement and how each of these relate to crime, criminology and victimology. These have been well documented elsewhere (see Marsh et al., 2004; Mawby and Walklate, 1994). Rather, the purpose of this selective potted history of feminist ideologies simply serves to provide a flavour of the context within which criminology and victimology have developed and how these subject areas have been shaped by questions tangentially related to gender issues. A second purpose, is that it takes us a stage further in terms of exploring some of the stereotypes, caricatures and conundrums that have come to be associated with gender, crime and victimisation.

What then are some of the key features of the positivist legacy? How has a gendered perspective been incorporated into the victimological and criminological enterprises? What are the consequences? Within the study of victimology women were originally characterised as victim-prone; indeed women were generally ascribed **ideal victim** status (Christie, 1986). Some women however, for example, those with risky lifestyles such as prostitutes and drug users continue to be viewed in legal and paralegal decision making as culpable and held responsible as precipitous victims. Women and particularly female children have tended to be visible and classically fragile and vulnerable as well as often passive victims (but only in public spaces and places). There has also been a presumption that all the victims of sexual violence are female and all perpetrators of it male and that all women are always fearful. However, whilst these are problematic historical legacies, the impact of feminism has been significant in that it has become clearer for example that the private domain of the home as a potential site for criminal victimisation has been obscured as have the risks of serious violence and abuse, particularly to those women and children who spend much of their time at home with those they know and often trust the most.

In contrast to this characterisation of women, are men. However, women are not simply the opposite of men, but are hierarchically subordinated to men. In particular white, heterosexual men, according to 'domain assumptions' and positivist legacies, are the norm or gold standard against whom the (irrational, fearful, victim prone female) victim are compared. Men have been (and are) largely exempt from victim status and have been (and are) rendered invisible as victims. Men and males are fearless criminals and there has been (and is) a presumption that all the perpetrators of sexual violence are male and all its victims female (see also Chapter 3). These caricatures, myths and stereotypes, have persisted despite clear and consistent evidence from survey based research such as the British Crime Survey dating back to the early 1980s, that men are most at risk from almost all forms of criminal victimisation but especially those serious forms of inter-personal violence that occur on the streets and in public spaces (see Chapter 2). However whilst risky places have been defined as those where men are, men refuse to be fearful. And despite the feminist exposé of serious forms of victimisation behind closed doors, risky places tend not to be defined as those where women are frequently harmed. This has impacted upon the pace, standard, quality and availability of support for victims and upon appropriately gendered provisions in particular. Clearly this is not a neat and tidy picture where lessons for the gendering of victimology are concerned. Our criminological and victimological knowledges are fraught with stubborn and persistent legacies, unequal equations and paradoxes and contradictory sets of discourses (Davies, 2007).

Rape knowledges

In exploring feminist approaches to the study of victims and victimology the example of rape can be used as a form of case study to exemplify and illustrate some key themes and issues. In one newspaper article earlier this century (*The Times*, 2005) the headline read as follows: 'Women still held to blame for rape'. The clear message from this headline is that general opinion or common sense beliefs subscribe to the view that women who are raped by men have only themselves to blame. The headline implies that such opinions are longstanding ones yet they ought perhaps to have changed. This is clearly a highly gendered headline implying several confusing and contradictory conventional wisdoms in particular about women as victims but also about men as offenders. The article beneath the headline goes on to explain the research which uncovered these opinions. The article also offers a variety of critical comments about the research and its findings derived from different bodies. Supplementary data is offered on the 'facts' relating to rape, on convictions for rape and on issues concerning the reporting of rape. Extracts related to some of these aspects of the report are reproduced in Box 4.1.

BOX 4.1

FINDINGS FROM AMNESTY INTERNATIONAL UK

- More than a third of people believe that a woman is totally or partially responsible for being raped if she has behaved in a flirtatious manner.
- 26 per cent of adults believed that a woman was partially or totally responsible for being raped if she was wearing sexy or revealing clothing.
- 22 per cent held the same view if a woman had had many sexual partners.
- 30 per cent said that a woman was partially or totally responsible for being raped if she was drunk.

Vera Bird, MP, Fawcett Society, Commission on Women and the Criminal Justice System:

> We tend to blame the low conviction rate on failures in the police and judicial systems. But if juries are thinking like this then improving the procedures is not going to make much difference.

Jenny Watson, Equal Opportunities Commission:

> There still seems to be an assumption that women are sexually available, so if a woman has gone out to have a good time, then she must want to have sex.

Sheila Coates, Director of South Essex Rape and Incest Crisis Centre:

> victims – who often blame themselves – are reflecting the blame they can face from society.

The above illustrations fall firmly within a twenty-first-century analysis of the state of knowledge on rape. The article that gave stimulus to this case study was written in 2005. It is therefore hugely disappointing to have read much more recently still, 'Half men arrested for rape not prosecuted' (*Daily Telegraph*, 2009). The furore for some continues surrounding the attrition rate for rape cases, reflecting the ongoing struggle to bring more sex attackers to justice and do justice for their victims. Even more disconcertingly, in February 2010 BBC news reported 'Women say some rape victims should take blame'. The news item refers to results from a survey of more than 1,000 people in London. Findings show that people are still quick to blame the victim for rape if she had dressed provocatively or gone back to the attacker's house for a drink. The women were less forgiving than men. The article referred to above in the *Daily Telegraph*, published only in December of 2009, draws from an annual Violence Against Women Crime Report in which the Crown Prosecution Service (CPS) provides figures as shown in Box 4.2. The CPS have very recently felt the need to publish a raft of guidance aimed at standardising methods of policing and prosecution and dispelling persistent myths about the crime of rape.

BOX 4.2

CROWN PROSECUTION SERVICE: RAPE KNOWLEDGE

- CPS solicitors considered the cases of 6,597 people, the vast majority of whom were men, arrested for rape in 2008–9.
- 3,511 (53 per cent) did not face prosecution.

- 3,495 were tried.
- 2,018 were convicted (this includes those found guilty of lesser offences).
- 42 per cent of the charges were unsuccessful.
- The most common reason for an unsuccessful conviction is the difficulty in proving that the victim did not give consent to sex, particularly when alcohol is involved.

These illustrations of rape knowledges demonstrates how contemporarily, conventional, common sense wisdoms continue to trickle through, permeate, confuse and cloud understanding of how rape might, according to more sophisticated and scholarly knowledges, be most effectively researched. How rape occurs, what form it takes, how often it happens, why it happens, when and where it takes place, who perpetrates it and who experiences it are all influenced by positivist legacies, domain assumptions and mediated knowledges as discussed in Chapter 3.

Section summary

Sticking with the example of the study of crime victims, feminist challenges to the conventional victimological agenda that have insisted on pursuing the 'woman question' have highlighted three significant features relating to gender and victimology. First, they have succeeded in establishing that women suffer almost exclusively from some forms of victimisation and disproportionately from others. Second, they have demonstrated a gender patterning to risk and fear of victimisation. Third, they have pointed towards a gendered approach in responding to victimisation and supporting victims. In terms of major feminist achievements, feminism has put more emphasis on hidden processes; it has shown how the gender of the perpetrator has often been hidden (Morley and Mullender, 1994) and as Goodey has stated 'feminist research has done much to recast women outside the stereotype of passive victims of male aggression' (Goodey, 2005: 83). Perhaps most significantly, by employing the concept of **survivor** rather than 'victim' (London Rape Crisis Centre, 1984) feminists have made several points about the gendered nature of victimisation and its impact and about gender issues in the recovery from victimisation. The concept of 'survivor' challenges the ideologies and scientific basis of positivist victimologies and in particular public perceptions of the female victim as passive, helpless, powerless, blameworthy or victim-prone. Moreover, the concept carries with it positive connotations and is forward looking. It signifies all of the negotiating and coping strategies women employ to live their daily lives (for further discussion on the notion of survivorship see Chapter 8).

Thus we can identify some interesting and potentially fruitful avenues for further research *for* women (and *for* men) that might inform our gendered knowledge. Moreover, the omnipresence of the woman question should properly include all identities of women including for example, immigrant women's experiences of victimisation and the suffering and harm experienced by the whole matrix of combined female identities. Thus young black/white women's experiences might be compared and contrasted with older white and ethnic minority women's experiences. Walklate has raised some interesting prospective areas for a gendered research agenda in criminology and victimology. For example, the white, heterosexual male as the victimological other: 'that which cannot be spoken' and that also of women as the criminological other. These questions are explored further in Chapters 3 and 6.

Interviewing female offenders

This part of the chapter focuses on a piece of research that involved doing research through interviewing female offenders. In particular it draws on experience of conducting interviews with female offenders in the north east of England and how this research was operationalised. This exemplar is used to highlight a number of important gender and other salient 'power' issues connected with doing criminological research. These reflective dynamics are often evident in feminist inspired work on women and crime in both America (Daly, 1994; Maher, 1997) and Britain (Carlen, 1988; Carlen et al., 1985; Hudson, 1994). These accounts 'tell it like it is' and expose the place of subjectivity in fieldwork-based research. The following discussion relates to a part of the research that investigated women who commit crime for economic gain (see Davies, 1999) as referred to in Chapter 1. Whilst the fieldwork encompassed various different strategies and stages of gathering data, the major part of it has involved one-to-one interviews with women who have committed 'economic crimes'.

Interviews were conducted with 29 women in total. Twenty-one took place in prison and five in the community with women who were either on probation or were no longer under the jurisdiction of the courts. In terms of their biographies, all the women interviewed were white and can be loosely described as working class. The majority were in their twenties although their ages ranged from 17 years to 46 years. Sixteen of the women had a total of 33 children between them with two of these same women pregnant again in prison. Thirteen had a partner whilst 13 described themselves as single.

All but one of the women was serving a sentence of the court or a court order and all had been convicted of at least one, and in the majority of cases several, criminal offences. Dispositions ranged from being remanded in custody and awaiting trial, prison sentences ranging from three months to two years and probation supervision with and without various conditions. The crimes the women were most frequently engaged in, and discussed in interviews, were thefts, in particular shoplifting, fraud and deception but also employee and car theft. Burglary, drugs and prostitution related offences also figured significantly in their offending profiles whilst a variety of other offences were also included in the range of crimes they had committed. Summarising the female offenders interviewed, these women would generally be characterised as 'hustlers' (Campbell, 1991; Maher, 1997). The women are economically marginal and are committing petty offences (Steffensmeier and Allen, 1996). Crime appeared to constitute a major source of income for these women.

Marrying interviews and feminist ideology

Gender issues already to a large extent governed the decision to adopt the use of interviews and gender issues remained at the heart of other dilemmas that were confronted during fieldwork. My decision to employ the use of personal interviews and a semi-structured interview format was largely based upon the nature of the research (feminist inspired) questions being explored. These questions included exploring the types of crimes the (female) interviewees engaged in and details on the ways in which they conducted them. Pilot discussions had shown similarities between the women in respect of the types of crimes committed. There were also commonalties between the ways in which the crimes were executed and these factors could have suggested a structured interview format. However I already had a preference for keeping the research grounded and for maintaining respect for the narratives of the individual women as far as that is possible. Grounded research might involve several of the following principles; first, collecting data at first hand from informants; and second, collecting it in their own terms and in the light of what they think is significant (not what pre-existing theory thinks is significant) and third, developing theory grounded in the actor's words and/or actions (Glaser and Strauss, 1967). In this way my research would hopefully elicit common data but also differences and variations whilst remaining faithful to the sources from which the information came (Davies, 2000). These latter points also raise issues pertinent to doing feminist and ethically imbued research.

Decisions about doing qualitative interviews with female offenders – the example drawn upon here – were influenced by the attempt to follow good reflective research practice – which some call feminist research – but other issues add to its feminist orientation. These issues include conscious choices made at the outset by a female researcher; the fact that all the informants were female; and that the subject matter explores a research question that has a specific gender bias to it. The use of the semi-structured in-depth interview method is generally seen as consistent with feminist research because such interviews seek not to be exploitative but to be appreciative of the position of women.

Other decisions that have gender issues at the heart include decisions about how to introduce the research and how best to describe what it is all about to the various levels and sexes of gatekeepers as well as the female interviewees. Decisions about where interviews might take place and how interviews will be conducted all have safety implications which are particularly significant for a lone and relatively inexperienced female interviewer.

Feminisms' empathies with ethical research

Ethical dilemmas are endemic to social research. This is especially so with respect to research on sensitive topics such as those connected to crime and victimisation, criminal and social justice, and research carried out with or amongst vulnerable and relatively powerless populations. Informed consent, anonymity, confidentiality and respect for the researched are all issues that connect with high ethical standards and can marry well with feminist approaches to conducting research.

Informed consent is an ethical principle implying a responsibility on the part of the social researcher to strive to ensure that those involved as participants in research not only agree or consent to participating in the research of their own free choice, without being pressurised or influenced, but that they are fully informed about what it is they are consenting to (Davies, 2006). Research must not harm or put the researched at risk in any way and the researcher has a responsibility to conduct themselves with honesty and integrity and with consideration and respect for the research subjects whose rights should be respected. This particular responsibility that researchers have towards research participants implies that researchers should base research so far as possible, on the freely given informed consent of those studied. Research participants should be made aware of their right to say no, decline or refuse permission and to participate. They should be able to exercise this right whenever and for whatever reason they wish. Moreover, whilst the researched may agree to participate generally they should nevertheless also feel free and be free to exercise their powers of veto during the research process and reject the use of specific data-gathering devices such as tape recorders and video cameras.

Therefore, for consent to be fully informed it is incumbent upon the researcher to explain as fully as possible, and in terms meaningful to participants, the questions of what, who, why and how. That is, what the research is about, who is undertaking and financing it, why it is being undertaken, how it is to be promoted and how any research findings are to be disseminated. None of these aspects of the research design are clear cut or straightforward. *Who* for example are the participants in the research? It is one of the responsibilities of the researcher to determine who informed consent must be obtained from. If access to research is gained through a 'gatekeeper' for instance, informed consent should be sought directly from the research participants to whom access is required. This may mean adhering to the principle of informed consent at several different levels of access (this is illustrated on page 80). Special care in this respect must also be taken where research participants are vulnerable by virtue of factors such as age, social status, or powerlessness, or are ill or infirm or where proxies may need to be used in order to gather data. Doing interviews in the prison setting brings forth several ethical considerations about informed consent and decision making and the Prison Service has its own ethics committee which examines all research proposals that might give rise to ethical concerns. As Martin has observed, 'one distinct advantage of carrying out research among such a literally captive audience is that the refusal rate is usually low' (Martin, 2000: 228). Ethically though, this could be a worrisome issue.

There is also a strong onus on the researcher to decide what is meant by anonymity and confidentiality and the researcher and the researched should be clear and in agreement about what each of these mean. Research participants should be informed about and understand how far they will be afforded anonymity and/or confidentiality. My own respondents provided me with a name which may or may not have been their given name. I changed all names and gave respondents pseudonyms, which goes only some way towards providing anonymity but no guarantee. The researchers' responsibility extends to a careful consideration about making promises or unrealistic guarantees that might later be difficult, impossible or tempting not to keep.

Whilst informed consent ought to be integral to any robust and effective research design this can prove difficult to adhere to in practice during the conduct of social and criminological research and research done in prison in particular. Informed consent might be seen as an ideal-typical principle to which all social research should aspire towards. In reality it may be impossible to achieve consent that is fully informed and in practice informed consent is never likely to be fully attained (some of these issues are also illustrated below).

The lone female researcher and access, safety, case selection and politics

Prior to entering the field, although some degree of access will already have been successfully negotiated, further matters concerning individual case selection present themselves. Politics may complicate matters as well as practical difficulties such as finding suitable interview locations. Although fieldwork is often a part of the research process to look forward to, doing interviews with known criminals who have apparently done something serious enough to warrant their loss of liberty can be a daunting prospect nevertheless.

In respect of minimising fears for safety it is possible to exercise some measure of control over who to interview through case selection procedures. In respect of the type of offence allegedly committed by the offender, the offence categories which were of interest to me the researcher and interviewer were made explicit. I emphasised that economic crimes; that is fraud and forgery, thefts and shoplifting-type offences (hence I thought this would exclude violent women and violent offences including murder) were to be investigated. Such parameters can be built into the research design for genuine reasons related to the research question but also they help to assuage concerns about safety at the pre-interview point. Another concern when conducting prison based research is of being taken hostage, particularly if there are ongoing grievances in particular establishments or if there are current political issues in respect of the treatment of prisoners. Some of these safety issues are discussed further below.

The offering of inducements to interviewees can usefully cut across issues concerning case selection. But, should payment be offered to the women for the interviews? Others conducting research with vulnerable, impoverished and relatively powerless women had done so and there are valid arguments both for and against this practice. For many this option is fairly swiftly dismissed, as funding is often not available even if it was preferred but other 'inducements' might be considered. In carrying out my own research small quantities of cigarettes were taken to all interview venues together with a lighter (with permission from wing staff in the prison). This practice could be seen as part of the 'research bargain' and proved particularly useful in the prison setting.

Snowball sampling is a way of selecting a sample (which is akin to a 'chain letter'). In this experience of fieldwork initial contact with one or two willing interviewees was achieved in both the prison and community settings and these women put me in touch with other women also willing to be interviewed. In this way snowball sampling is a self-selecting sample. It is also an acceptable and ethical method of sampling, although there are problems associated with this method in respect of typicality, representativeness and bias.

Having identified several female (ex) offenders in the community willing to be interviewed, further thought and planning was required prior to and during the interview process. For example, if probation-building space was not available or appropriate, alternative venues would be required in which to conduct the interviews. At this stage practical, ethical and safety concerns (re)present themselves. The majority of the interviews took place in prison. Several took place on probation premises, some in a café and one woman was interviewed several times at length in her own home. Each interview location brought with it its own particular idiosyncrasies. Some safety concerns can be assuaged by being assiduous about informing home and work, of your whereabouts and likely time of return. Interviews in prison dominated my early experiences of interviewing female offenders. Several prison staff members were always aware of my presence on a wing and a member of staff was always either within earshot or a panic button available nearby.

In terms of the prison sample, having described to the officers on the wing the type of offences (and therefore I hoped the type of offender) I was researching, the selection of inmates to approach was initially at their discretion. In the event the vast majority of the women had at some time committed offences relevant to the research. This was mostly established early on in the interview as the purpose of the discussion was described, and it was soon discovered what each of the women were currently being detained for. On the first afternoon of interviewing however, I was introduced to a diminutive woman who I later discovered was on remand for alleged murder. We continued our discussion talking about her circumstances and her life in general before the meeting ended whereupon she politely thanked me for spending time talking with her. The member of staff as usual after each interview was curious to know once again how it had progressed. *He* was clearly amused and was testing out my reactions and how I would cope. It was all done in good humour and although the interview had proved an interesting experience it was not useful for the purposes of gathering hard data. After this occasion greater control was exercised over the selection of interviewees in prison. This was achieved by asking women who were particularly helpful and forthcoming about their committing of 'economic crimes' to suggest other inmate's names to me for interviewing purposes. This snowball sampling method signified a more grounded form of research practice but also a degree of collusion and connection with the inmates was achieved that allowed them to become self-selecting. Several inducements – cigarettes – were also clearly contributing to this pattern of recruitment.

In the prison setting, inducements come in many forms, especially for those women sentenced rather than on remand. The prison grapevine works quickly and efficiently. Not only was there a 'Miss' (later I became Pam) who wanted to talk to them – which held out the prospect of getting them out of cleaning the floor, or their cell, or simply doing nothing – but she had cigarettes with her. This spread of rumour, interest and curiosity all combined to the advantage of the interviewer who was becoming known in the prison. Self-selecting interviewees were presenting themselves whilst checks and balances within the interview schedule were ensuring that the stories were their own and individual accounts were emerging.

Subjective reflection

Reflecting on the experiences of interviewing is natural and ongoing and it is useful to adapt the use of a reflective research diary to record these 'extra' ideas and thoughts, concerns and feelings. This may appear to end the process of doing interviews; however this process is an emotionally and physically draining form of interaction and upon returning home from interviews the researcher may feel not only exhausted but also there may be a feeling of anti-climax. To immediately commence the time consuming task of writing up is not realistic. After a period of being alone subsequent to interviewing the need to get the interviews down on paper or talked about is important. Talking about the interviews without disclosing confidences or compromising anonymity is a useful practice and serves several functions, including diffusing feelings of stress and euphoria after the intensity of the interview situation as well as preparing for their analysis and discussing fieldwork with other colleagues and supervisors.

Discussions inevitably involve some distressing stories about problematic and abusive childhood relationships, backgrounds and circumstances, some of which might be expected but nevertheless might be distressing to both disclose and to hear about. On occasions such experiences of interviewing may have effects on the interviewer as researcher in the longer term. Secrets and confidences divulged by the interviewee can have a traumatic affect on researchers who are unprepared for them or who have built up a relationship and rapport with a female interviewee.

Highly reflexive research can significantly enrich the (ethical) validity of any research. Some of these considerations are explored by Piacentini who argues 'for a process of acquiring penal knowledge based on criminology of emotional attentiveness' (Piacentini, 2007: 153). In my own research the vast majority of those interviewed within the prison suffered from an addiction to drugs – in the main speed, amphetamines, heroin and cocaine – but also to alcohol. At the time of conducting the prison based interviews, I was both surprised and shocked to discover the high proportion of female inmates who had a drug problem. Since these interviews were conducted, increased numbers of women received into prison have been sentenced for drugs related offences. In 2004 the Home Office reported that 66 per cent of the sentenced women in prison were either dependent on drugs or drinking heavily before they came to prison (Medlicott, 2007). Although drugs offences were not generally the reason for their most recent sentence, many of the women I interviewed were close to, or involved with, drug use. This complicated their patterns of offending; exacerbating the extent of it particularly their crimes for economic gain, and it also affected the way in which some of the interviews were conducted. The provision of cigarettes to smoke during the interview, to some small extent, helped calm and compose the women who often found concentration and conversation difficult to maintain.

Continuing to expose my own subjective reflections and personal statements about feelings that were evoked for me during the fieldwork and interviews, it is not unknown for some commentators to denigrate research conclusions based on interviews with known criminals (see, for example, Jupp, 1989) and drug users. The research described here also relies on self-report data provided by offenders. In self-reports there is always a risk of underreporting or of over exaggeration. The fact that some of the women discussing their experiences of committing crime were drug users invites criticism of the research. Some women interviewed in prison did exhibit signs of restlessness and an inability to concentrate but the majority were keen to talk and be listened to. The discussions primarily focussed upon the manner in which they carried out their activities, the locations in which they took place and details on the methods and networks they were a part of. Little of the information could be exaggerated or specific crimes referred to made up. Most respondents were highly comfortable narrating their criminal activities and expertise. The greatest problem experienced was in finding the detail. Stealing and 'grafting' had become such a way of life and routine activity for many of the women that they took it for granted that the methods and techniques employed to carry out their crimes were commonly known and understood. Although the women interviewed had in the main been labelled dishonest by the police and courts, there is no reason to suggest that their stories and narrative accounts in interviews were fabricated.

Summary conclusion

This chapter has operated on two levels relating to both ideology and practice. It has, through exemplification and illustration wedded the two together in order to fulfil the chapters aim's which were to demonstrate the positivist underpinnings to criminological and victimological knowledges, outline feminisms as they relate to the sub-discipline of victimology, provide examples of feminist knowledges and show how these can be used to critique other (mediated) knowledges and public policy, further develop feminist inspired research methodologies and gendered theoretical knowledge, exemplify and illustrate gender and other salient 'power' issues connected to doing criminological and victimological research.

STUDY QUESTIONS/ACTIVITIES

Revisit Table 4.1: Feminism and victimology. Look at the key methodological hallmarks belonging to each of the four feminisms: liberal, radical, socialist, post-modern. Think about how, from each of these feminist perspectives, you would go about explaining why women do the following activities: shoplifting, prostitution, violence.

SUGGESTIONS FOR FURTHER READING

Davies, P. (forthcoming) 'Doing interviews with women in prison', in P. Davies and P. Francis (eds) *Doing Criminological Research,* second edition. London: Sage.

Maher, L. (1997) *Sexed Work. Gender, Race and Resistance in a Brooklyn Drug Market.* Oxford: Clarendon Press.

Taylor, A. (1993) *Women Drug Users: An Ethnography of a Female Injecting Community.* Oxford: Clarendon Press.

5

FEMINIST AND GENDERED PERSPECTIVES: EXPLAINING AND THEORISING OFFENDING AND VICTIMISATION

CONTENTS

GLOSSARY TERMS

Discrimination	Classicism
Feminisation of poverty	'Doing-gender'
Gender difference	Hegemonic masculinity
Agency	Masculinity

CHAPTER AIMS

- Contextualise feminist theorising on offending and victimisation
- Query whether or not criminology has explained gendered patterns of offending in an adequate manner

- Provoke further feminist inspired knowledges and theorising on crime and victimisation in society
- Encourage feminist and critical scholarship to confront some key challenges around gendered offending and victimisation
- Promote a more sophisticated and nuanced set of knowledges about the relevance of gender-class intersections
- Offer a tripartite challenge to scholarship on crime, offending and victimisation in society

Introduction

Chapters 5 and 6 are both devoted to exploring feminist and other gendered perspectives in historical and contemporary understandings of the crime problem and of criminal victimisation. The first of these two chapters mainly examines the way in which women's criminality has been explored criminologically. It outlines the origins and development of feminist influences in criminology and albeit to a lesser extent, in victimology too. This chapter considers the backdrop to the feminist critique of criminology, the critique itself and its impact in terms of pioneering work and feminist influences in understanding crime and victimisation. In doing so, Chapter 5 focuses upon a range of key social and criminological concepts including those of patriarchy, marginalisation, oppression, social control, male domination and sexism.

Leading on from the evidence and illustrations provided in Chapter 2, where the predominant gender patterns to crime and victimisation were examined, the early part of Chapter 5 inevitably addresses criminological theorising on menboys and more men and not so much on women's criminality, but their conformity within the law. Whilst this has not protected women from being enmeshed within the apparatus of social control systems and processes it has apparently in part justified criminological attention on crime as the business and work of men and as a game for the boys. Simultaneously it has concentrated the social scientists' and the victimologists' gaze in particular, upon women and girls as victims, both of crime and of an unjust society more generally. The complex interplay of these knowledges has had real impacts and consequences upon appreciations and understandings of criminal women and crime as a pursuit of women and girls. This is explored further as the chapter goes on to critique a selection of gendered explanations through suggesting there is an 'explanatory gap' in feminist theorising. Building upon the example promised in Chapter 1, where I introduced the research on women and crime for economic gain, and in Chapter 4 where I elaborated a little on some feminist ideologies to doing research through focussing on my interviews with female offenders, this part of the book resumes the use of this example and considers not only how this 'gap' in the literature and series of explanatory theories and postulations can be revealed but also how emergent theorising can result.

Key questions for Chapter 5

- How has a feminist inspired criminology challenged positivistic knowledges of the crime and victimisation problem in society?
- How has a feminist inspired criminology steered explanations and theories about who is victimised and where?
- Do criminologists tend not to take female offending seriously?
- What is the relationship between femininity and violence?
- Do criminologists tend to ignore the extent to which women incur financial victimisations?
- Can a feminist inspired criminology continue to be insightful for explaining and theorising offending and victimisation in the twenty-first century?
- What are the dilemmas and challenges faced by feminist and gendered perspectives in explaining and theorising offending and victimisation in the twenty-first century?

Contextualising feminist perspectives

As we are reminded above and in Chapter 2 where much greater detail is shown on this, when scrutinising women's overall participation in crime over time, it is clear that women have always been more law-abiding than men. Though the data is rarely drawn together, this appears to be the case across all regions of the world in English-speaking countries (Evans and Jamieson, 2008), and where the data is more readily available and accessible, in England and Wales. Men commit the majority of crimes. In Sweden, men and women accounted for 83 and 17 per cent respectively of those found guilty of offences in 2005. The proportion of women has increased from 13 to 17 per cent since 1975 (Wittrock, 2005), thus as in England and Wales dating from the latter years of the twentieth and the first decade of the twenty-first century, there are some increasing concerns with ideas of convergence of male and female rates (Heidensohn and Gelsthorpe, 2007). In terms of crime and victim classifications there are also distinct patterns. Men commit more frequent and serious crime than do women and girls. In England and Wales various data sources continue to confirm there are more male than female victims of violence with domestic violence being the only category of violence for which the risks to women are higher than for men (Levi et al., 2007). Similarly in the Federal Republic of Germany clear sex-related and age-related differences among victims can be identified (PCS, 2006).

Having established that as suspects, defendants and offenders, females are in the minority (Fawcett Society, 2007) in England and Wales and also on a more global level, the context within which budding criminologists and victimologists began to explain the amount of crime in society and how they began to explain it is clearly important. Part of our consideration of this historical context must also address the wider social and economic realities of any given time and in any given jurisdiction. Criminologically this requires due consideration be given not only to founding figures but also the socio-economic era in which they were a part. Thus, consideration should not only be given for example to Lombroso's theories of criminal behaviour, but also to the nineteenth-century Lombrosian era more broadly, where there were newly reformed institutions such as prisons and the nascent discipline of psychology was making its presence felt. Victimologically this requires due consideration be given not only to key figures such as Mendelsohn and Von Hentig, but also to the United States and the late 1940s where they found themselves working as two émigré lawyers as a consequence of World War II and 'the holocaust connection' (Walklate, 2005, 2007). It was in this broader context that their concerns to better understand the relationship between victims and offenders led to their devising of victim typologies. All of these broader socio-economic and historical concerns are highly relevant and pertinent to gaining an understanding and appreciation of the forming and shaping of what we now refer to as positivist criminological and victimological theorising. In terms of a backdrop or context to the feminist critique of criminology, clearly crime and victimisation patterns are significant as is the broader historical, social and economic environment. The situated nature of crime and victimisation in society accounts for particular as well as differential understandings of the crime problem and of criminal victimisation in particular, as well as in differential ways of explaining and theorising offending and victimisation.

Lombroso-ism, Von Hentig/Mendelsohn-ism and positivism

In the twentieth-century criminology was largely the domain of doctors, psychologists and psychiatrists. Scientific study was complemented by psychological studies which purported that many criminals were of low intelligence and feeble-minded and that criminality reflected a heritable degeneracy. Characteristics were identified that apparently predisposed individuals to crime and those innate or 'born with' differences between law abiding and non-law abiding, 'normal', personalities could be identified and held as key to abnormality. The typical criminaloid could be spotted as having prominent cheek bones, close knit and dark eyebrows, hair on the back of the hands. Stereotypes of criminals based upon these misconceptions and myths are still very much in evidence today. There is still a common sense belief that outward appearance reveals inner characteristics. See also media representations of women as offenders and victims as explored in Chapter 3. The legacy of Lombroso is that of individual positivism. From a gendered perspective however there are several layerings belonging to the Lombrosian/positivist legacy.

What did all of this mean for women criminals? Clearly women criminals have always existed albeit in small numbers and there have been many seriously violent women throughout history. These women are the victims of the majority of women's conformity. They stand out, being highly visible and newsworthy (see Chapter 3) and these are the women everyone is quick to and loves to hate. The standard narratives used by the media (Jewkes, 2005) for serious women offenders are strikingly similar to the Lombrosian hallmarks of the female offender. Thus the few but obvious and abhorrent women criminals are:

- sexually deviant, virile, lascivious;
- primitive, savage, physically unattractive and often man-like;
- bad wives, mothers, monsters, mad cows, evil manipulators and irrational non-agent spectacles;
- Criminologically they are: mad, bad, manipulative whores whereas victimologically they are: innocent, preyed upon, vulnerable and passive Little Red Riding Hood figures.

What is 'the feminist critique'?

The feminist critique refers to a critique of criminology and the sociology of deviance that pre-dates the 1970s. Part of this critique, which originates from a group of female scholars, claims that knowledges, readings, representations, interpretations, appreciations and understandings of the amount of crime in society and how to explain it had been dominated by men, studying men from a male perspective. Male scholars and practising criminologists had studied a predominantly male populous and had done so from a man's standpoint.

In the late 1960s Frances Heidensohn was researching the subject of delinquent girls and in 1968 she drew attention to this ignorance of women as deviants and lack of interest in women's criminal connections (1968). However, it is generally accepted that it was with the publication of Carol Smart's *Women, Crime and Criminology* (1977) that concerns about gender and its relationship to crime and social control were sharpened. Smart's critique in 1977 and her later work (1989) pointed out that criminological attention had been preoccupied with men, boys and more men. The study of crime and deviance, the courts, judicial and criminal justice systems and processes were male dominated and legal centric. Criminology in effect was exhibiting the power of men and maleness. It had a male gaze typical in an already patriarchally dominated society.

Thus viewing early criminological theory and research and more latterly victimological studies through a gendered lens has shown how women have been either neglected or explained by reference to their biology and physiology. Individual biological and pathological determinism have become virtually institutionalised within criminology. Yet, this is flawed fundamentally. Individual positivist theories have framed women criminals of the past and present in very specific ways. Smart refers to how the ideology of these early theories contains 'myths about the "inherent" evil in women or their lack of intelligence and ability and their natural passivity' (2008: 6). Referring to the work of Lombroso (1895), Pollack, (1950) and Cowie et al. (1968) Smart points out those women who commit offences are judged to be either criminal or pathological. They are certainly represented as 'odd women'.

The feminist critique had a tremendous impact upon criminology and empirical inquiry. It brought to the fore a range of sociological concepts including those of patriarchy, marginalisation, oppression, social control and male domination. Feminist inspired theoretical work flourished too. It generated a spate of sociological and criminological empirical studies exploring issues of bias and **discrimination**, sexism and questions about legal and judicial harshness and leniency. Various studies in the 1980s examined aspects of victimisation, the stereotypes of female offenders, and the treatment of women by the various criminal justice agencies and the way in which law and order policies impacted upon women. Feminist criminologies have raised issues about formal and informal modes of control, forms of socialisation, the role of punishment and the notion of justice. Thus a whole range of sociologically and criminologically pertinent and interesting questions emerged prompting research that sought answers to questions including the following:

Are women treated fairly/unfairly by the:

- police?
- probation service?
- courts, magistracy and judiciary?
- Are women treated fairly/unfairly by professionals and volunteers in the criminal justice system?
- Are girls and women treated fairly/unfairly in
- young offender institutions?
- prisons?
- Are women treated more leniently/harshly than men by the criminal justice system as a whole and by its constituent agencies and professionals within them?

- Are any gender differences justifiable?
- Do women suffer double doses of punishment?
- Is there a just measure of pain for men and women?

Women and girls have now been systematically examined in several criminal justice contexts, including as offenders, albeit by a small group of feminist criminologists. Indeed, throughout the 1980s a plethora of criminological research emerged and it seemed that criminology and the sociology of deviance had become more than the study of men and crime (Smart, 1976: 185). Smart's 1977 publication is now generally viewed as a seminal work on women and the crime problem and recently has been described as 'significant in instigating and legitimating the study of 'women and crime' (Evans and Jamieson, 2008).

The legacy of difference

The impact that feminism has had on explaining and theorising offending is often explored in a roughly chronological order. Whilst some have been preoccupied with women's absence in the literature and thus engaged in the project of 'putting women back in' to the theories of anomie, labelling, differential association, delinquent sub-cultures and critical criminology' (Heidensohn, 1996: 153), others variously explored sex differences, sex roles, divisions and stereotypes. The concept of social control has been extensively used to explain how and why women and girls are in control and controlled as has patriarchal society and culture. One or two flirted with the notion of emancipation and women's liberation being responsible for their offending.

Since the 1980s there is evidence of empirically informed theorising. Substantial effort has gone into examining the economic marginalisation of women and the feminisation of poverty thesis is part of this vein of theorising. There is a good range of authors whose work should be read in the original on each of these and several texts summarise these feminist inspired developments in respect of explaining and theorising offending (see further reading at the end of this chapter). Especially notable is the work of Pat Carlen in the UK (1985, to date), and together with Worrall (1987, 2004), as well as Eaton (1986, 1993), Gelsthorpe (1989), Gelsthorpe and Morris (1994), Hedderman and Gelsthorpe (1997), Heidensohn (1985, 1989, 1996, 1997, 2002, 2006), Worrall (1990, 2002). A further new wave of feminist criminologists including Daly (1994), Maher (1997) and Miller (1998, 2001) has persisted in the task of making the subject of offending behaviour empirically grounded and understood in gendered terms. Here, rather than following a chronological order a different approach is adopted whereby I use my own effort to expose an explanatory gap in the literature to reveal progressive as well as deficient theorising in respect of understanding the criminality of some women, namely those who commit crime for economic gain.

Feminist criminology and new theorising

The most convincing and durable of feminist inspired explanations for women's involvement in crime have tended to dwell for the most part on issues concerned with marginalisation and impoverishment, economic powerlessness and similar such forms of need and want. This has been to the nearly complete exclusion of greedy needs and desires, excitement and other explanations that feature more often in mainstream criminological theorising. Ungendered, 'malestream' explanations for crime in general and for property or 'economic crime' in particular have dwelt on the latter. Hedonistic excitement and a grabbing form of greed for possessions and money – economic gain – unobtainable by legitimate means are explanations for crimes that we tend to recognise in connection with troublesome youths (read boys) and calculating (read male) burglars. Conversely and dichotomously, explanations for female offending tend to dwell on need and want and women are often characterised unwittingly but largely, as passive, acted upon by social, economic and environmental forces, which have shaped their actions. Thus economic marginalisation, poverty, inequalities and economic dependency are drivers that push marginal and vulnerable women – particularly as young mothers – into crime. Some approaches verge upon a form of sociological determinism to the extent that criminology has seemed unable or wanting in terms of producing full explanations for, and solutions to, such offending.

I therefore argue there is another avenue to explore further here before abandoning the feminist inspired criminological ambition to better explain and theorise offending and victimisation. By explaining away women's crimes (such as their committing of property or 'economic crimes'), their crimes become lost and forgotten, and the focus having been repositioned away from criminal women, to impoverished women. Criminal women are all re-fashioned as survivors, or more often, as victims. Whilst not denying the validity and significance of such insightful explanations, the strength and breadth of the refocussing of feminist scholarship has been almost comprehensive. This broad brush approach to understanding women's lack of power, in particular their lack of economic independence and their gendered shackles, has obscured some avenues to the class-gender side of the coin. My own research began to focus on questions concerned with understanding women's motives for committing economic crime and this opened up some interesting avenues for further exploration. In revisiting some of the key literature it seemed that female offenders' lives and activities might not always be fully accounted for via explanations which appeared to push women into illegal solutions to their economic marginalisation and that such accounts of female offender's lives and activities may not always be consistent with women's motives for committing crime. When women's motivations rather than others' post-hoc justifications are foregrounded and when criminal women's voices and their complex and often ambiguous accounts are heard and listened to, there is evidence in feminist empirical work that supports different theoretical conclusions. Some feminist criminologists have explored economic motivations and in particular the consequences of the 'criminalisation of poverty' for criminal women – the **feminisation of poverty**. As noted above, the work of Pat Carlen is exemplary in this respect. Nevertheless, most of those economic explanations that have been thoroughly examined tend to be restricted to versions that view the offending behaviour of women as less than purposeful.

Criminal women's responses to their marginalised socio-economic positions, feminists agree, is often the result of a complex of forces and responses related to their immediate and structural circumstances – the classic **agency**-structure dilemma. For the most part it would seem that structure has dominated in feminist inspired criminological theorising. Whilst this does not entirely preclude such women from choosing another lifestyle or 'solution' it is almost always presented as an inevitable outcome. Women as offenders are seen as being propelled into action of an illegitimate nature, to make ends meet, that is, to survive economically. Some women's criminality, as Carlen has briefly acknowledged, appears more rational and genuinely pursuant of pecuniary reward (Carlen et al., 1985; Carlen, 1988; Carlen and Worrall, 1987) or more wilfully economic in nature (Davies, 1999; Hudson, 2002) than the feminisation of poverty thesis implies. Persuasive and powerfully evidenced, argued and theorised work from within feminist criminology often also serves to obscure the exceptions to the rule, the minor threads that are evident and that occasionally suggests that some crime committed by some women, some of the time might be understood under a rather different range of motives.

Is economic crime a man's game?

For me it seems that whilst feminist scholarship is increasingly sophisticated it still only partially explains why women engage in 'economic crimes'. 'Economic crimes' might not be such backward looking solutions to women's problems. Rather, 'economic crimes' might be solutions to women's ambitions to achieve. Women might therefore, be more actively resisting male subordination and economic marginalisation than current well respected feminist inspired theorising implies. If the majority of the criminal activities that women commit are property crimes, they might be crimes that are financially motivated and committed as a rational response to a lack of money or ability to obtain sufficient money from traditional and legitimate sources. This is of course highly contentious as are the following questions and speculations. Why, for example, are we so reluctant to believe that some women can mean to commit crime and intend or elect to commit crimes for economic gain? Is it possible that these women might be using crime as a resource for moving from exploitation to independence? These criminal women might be economically rational, like 'economic men', and they might be rational and purposeful in their actions. These women might be showing consistency with economic rationalism. Thus some crimes might be primarily committed, at least by some women, for different economic reasons than much feminist theorising implies.

Some types of criminal activity that women and girls take part in might be strictly financially motivated. Prostitution, shoplifting, theft, fraud and forgery and drugs related offences are all ways of achieving economic reward. If we can think of such crimes as economic crimes can we claim that criminological theorising adequately accounts for their motives for committing them? Is it possible that economic greed is in evidence? Some scholars have begun to investigate through imaginative theorising on the gendered nature of crime, both gender-difference and gender similarity in crime. Gender can now be viewed as a situated accomplishment; girls and boys 'do' masculinity and femininity. Crime is used as a resource for **doing-gender**: in other words male youth crime is a resource used for accomplishing masculinity (Messerschmidt, 1994, 1995). These more recent theoretical constructs might be useful in respect of more closely examining women's motivations to commit violent types of crime as well as economic crimes: girls might achieve femininity through committing shoplifting, for example. At the very least, provided feminist scholars are willing to contemplate these possibilities no matter how uncomfortable and class-gender problematic, these interesting questions suggest there are identifiable gaps in the criminological literature and that there may be problems of theoretical connectedness that warrant further attention. What emerged from all of this for me was a set of research questions focussed around women's motivations to commit economic crime in the context of both need and greed, and in the context of women's rationalism.

Whilst space prevents a thorough exposition here of all the literature reviewed, a very brief summary of the findings from the literature reviews I conducted can be given. I found that much of the substantive subject literature, for example that related to economic and financial crime, business and white-collar crime and the informal/criminal economies, could be described as gender, free/neutral/blind. Using the concepts introduced in the introductory chapter, the man/woman question was absent. The vast majority of the literature assumed men as the subject and 'yardstick'. There were few exceptions and few instances where masculine bias was not explicit.

Campbell's unique study of communities in Oxford, Cardiff and Tyneside in the 1980s and 1990s brings a feminist analysis to bear on the 'riots' of 1991. In graphic detail Campbell draws attention to the *'desperate local economies'* (Campbell 1993: xi) in which men and women across Britain abide. This work stands alone in terms of its inclusion of women's roles in the maintenance of local informal and criminal markets and women's modes of survival in harsh economic locales. Although women's relationship to the informal economy has been examined in relation to work patterns and the gendered experience of work and men's relationship to criminal economies has been partially examined, women's contributions have not attracted much attention. The classic studies rarely focus upon women, whether as primary or supporting actors in criminal economies.

Few authors devote any attention to the gendered nature of allegiances to illegal work. With no claims to being a criminologist, Madeleine Leonard's work (1994) regarding the informal economic activity in Belfast is a singular example of women's ways of making a living income. Criminologically, McLeod's (1982) study is a rare but now dated example of prostitution as women's work and Maher's (1997) study of sexwork in a Brooklyn drug market is a more recent but equally rare exception. As she points out, women's position in the informal economy is such that even secondary sector employment is becoming difficult to locate and that little is known about the participation of women or the impact of sex/gender in structuring participation in informal sector work especially in the criminal or drug economy.

Indeed I found that the whole notion of a criminal economy would appear to be dominated by an assumption of rationality (Davies, 2005). This is evident in the work of those who have explored the parallels between normal or legitimate work routines and illegal or illegitimate trades and activities (see McIntosh, 1975; Maguire, 1982; Walsh, 1986; Bennett and Wright, 1984). It was evident that rationality is an underpinning assumption within this literature generally and that a particular form of *economic* rationalism emerges as a dominant theme. Ultimately, women's agency in the committing of crime and very specifically women's self-assessed motivations seemed under-explored. The tendency to dichotomise women's motivations is made explicitly clear in the way that women tend to be portrayed, particularly in literature from the US, as either 'passive victims' or 'gangsta bitches' (Maher, 1997). For me, the extent to which women might be motivated to commit different types of crimes more for greed than need (Croall, 2001; Davies, 2003; Davies and Jupp, 1999) seemed under explored.

Instrumental/economic rationality, the dominant way of accounting for property crime generally, is the one explanation seldom offered when women's offending is being considered. It seemed that some forms of offending by women might be more purposefully rational than has hitherto been thought. Economic gain, the attraction of money and economic reward, as a pull factor could be a further 'pathway' into crime for some women. Additional and/or alternative economic explanations may help deepen our understanding of some of the crimes women most frequently commit. Traditional explanations rarely included instrumental economic rationality as a motivating factor for women. Criminality is 'assumed to be a masculine attribute and women criminals are therefore perceived to be either 'not women' or 'not criminals' (Worrall, 1990: 31). Women as criminals thus tend to emerge in theoretical accounts as passive actors rather than strategising resisters. The possibility that women offend rationally and purposefully for need or greed, tends to be obscured.

Emerging from all of this it seemed there is space for another avenue if not an entire pathway into crime for women, one that is more of their own selection and choosing. Women following this route enter crime as knowing criminals, as active decision-makers, more in charge of their own destiny and more rational and calculating in their choice of criminal activities than present feminist inspired theorising allows for. For some women, crime might be an attractive economic proposition a compelling, alluring attraction that holds out the prospect of a less thrifty and meagre lifestyle, a lifestyle that looks more lucrative and successful. In this view, crime is a prospective solution and ambition, a promising pathway and alternative way of achieving a different lifestyle. This represents a different starting point for understanding female offenders and for appreciating the types of crimes they regularly and routinely commit as well as their motives for committing them. This alternative or additional perspective on women who commit crime for economic gain where women are assigned offender status rather than excused from it demanded a full examination and critique of the rational choice perspective in criminology.

Rational man

My investigation inevitably led me to consider whether or not the rational choice perspective might be inclusive of women and girls and to ask questions about whether or not this perspective was generalisable. Would rational choice and instrumental/economic rationality be suitable as an explanation of women's experiences and motivations to commit economic crime as they would appear to be for men? Can we generalise this mainstream explanation, rational choice theory, to explain some of the main criminal activities that women engage in?

In short, I found that the rational choice perspective that had become significant within criminology during the 1980s and had growing resonance in the

1990s could be readily dismissed as a potentially useful hypothesis or testing ground from which to develop my investigations of women's motives for committing crime for economic gain. The way in which criminology had popularly embraced 'the economic' was via the rational choice perspective and the orthodox economic 'choice theoretic'. This method of incorporating the economic within criminology demonstrates clearly the 'pervasiveness of **hegemonic masculinity**' (Scraton, 1990) within the discipline (Walklate, 1995: 29). I found this to be a selective and unitary model, that excludes whole areas of legitimate economic activity that are important for women in particular (e.g. homeworking, domestic labour, child care, unpaid work, etc.) and lead to only partial understanding of what social (economic) life is really about for women. Thus, at best, rational choice appeared to me to represent a concept and form of rationality that might be peculiar to **masculinity**, where rationality is an entrenched male attribute. The utility of the rational choice perspective for better appreciating and understanding women's experiences and motivations for committing crime for economic gain seemed negligible. The perspective follows traditionally masculinist vocabularies of motives for criminality and remain fundamentally tied to the economic as-business-as-money-as profit. I concluded that they are gender-specific, neglect women, femininity and motherhood and the significance of familial relations and women's conceptualisations of social life.

Where feminist criminologists have addressed purposeful rationality they have done so only partially. Adler (1975a, 1975b) and Simon (1975) touched tangentially upon women's rationality. They envisaged women's criminality would increase rapidly and that women criminals would become either more violent, like men, or become involved in a wider variety of criminality through assuming traditional male social roles. In this way, like men, women would begin to assert themselves; in typically male ways they would become 'aggressive, pushy, hard-headed' (Simon and Landis, 1991: 2). This is a classic female liberation causes crime argument. In these views, this was the logical and rational end product of the increased emancipation of women. Adler and Simon's theses has been severely criticised and were virtually dismissed in the late 1970s–1980s. However, this perspective has some empirical support in the light of women's apparently increased rates of participation in violent and drug-related crimes. Other feminist scholars continue to dismiss the thesis on the grounds that it is too simplistic and smacks of liberal feminism, leaving unchallenged what the yardsticks of our understanding might be (Gelsthorpe, 1989; Walklate, 2001).

In the early 1980s Steffensmeier broached the question of rationality, unusually, through a gendered lens. He looked at an organisation's criminal enterprise in the context of 'sex-segregation in the underworld' and suggested, 'rationality refers to the link of means to ends or the extent to which expeditious means are used to achieve goals' (Steffensmeier, 1983: 1025). Such approaches are rare and could be more developed. Gender sensitive approaches could combine with gender specific appreciations to bring about greater understanding of the gender patterning of crime and criminality. For example, two authors writing about women sex workers have advocated a 'presumption of wilful rationality' (Scrambler and Scrambler, 1997: xv) to capture the idea that the background of prostitutes cannot be denied as important when considering recruitment into the sex industry but the idea of free and informed choice might be important too. Such an approach recognises 'committing crime' is one's own free will and choice (wilful). However, at the same time it can be regarded as exercising one's reason (rationality). The notion of 'wilful rationality' might be appropriate for considering other forms of crime for gain that women 'do'.

The brief summary of my findings arising out of multiple literature reviews convinced me that there were theoretical spaces ripe for further investigation related to women's motivations for committing economic crimes.

Feminist theorising: the offending-victimisation dilemma

This chapter has focussed on both women's conformity and more latterly women's victimisation/criminality. It has briefly contextualised the feminist critique and noted some of the impetus this critique has created for theoretical and empirical work around women and crime. Some of the insights that this feminist inspired work has had have been explored here and others are expanded upon in the remaining chapters. Before this chapter closes there are three caveats and a number of highly complex dilemmas that warrant criminological and victimological confrontation and debate if a fully gendered understanding of the crime problem and of victimisation in contemporary society is to be achieved. First the caveats and then the complex dilemmas or 'knotty problems' for feminist, gendered and criminological theorising are flagged up around one major challenge for the reader to reflect on and for the criminological academy to confront and debate.

Three caveats to Chapter 5

[i] The latter part of the chapter focussed on 'economic crime'. This categorisation has not been fully explained, exemplified or illustrated. Its definition here remains unresolved and contestable. For a fuller exploration of this generic categorisation and connected definitions of terms see Croall, 2007; Davies, 2005.

[ii] This chapter omits or skirts over a number of incremental and formative empirical and theoretical landmarks which most texts on women, crime and criminology incorporate as standard practice. There are key authors that might be expected to appear in literature that purports to discuss feminist criminology. Relevant contributions by some of these authors, from the key historical period pre-dating Lombroso right through to the twenty-first century is not covered comprehensively within the pages devoted to this short chapter (although some are scattered throughout the remainder of the text). For the reader who wants a more traditional and roughly chronological timeline overview of such authors' work and theoretical perspectives I direct you elsewhere as this has been admirably more comprehensively done by several other writers. In particular I would suggest the following:

- Heidensohn, F. (1996) *Women and Crime*. second edition. London: Macmillan.
- Gelsthorpe, L. (2002) 'Feminism and criminology', in M. Maguire, R. Morgan and R. Reiner (2002) (eds), *The Oxford Handbook of Criminology*. third edition. Oxford: Oxford University Press. There is also a succinct summary section entitled 'The Early feminist critique of criminology', in Chapter 13 'Gender and crime', by Frances Heidensohn and Lorraine Gelsthorpe in M. Maguire, R. Morgan and R. Reiner (2007) (eds) *The Oxford Handbook of Criminology*. fourth edition. Oxford: Oxford University Press.
- Chapter 15 'Feminist criminology' in T. Newburn (2007) *Criminology* gives a clear overview of early criminology and the female offender, the development of modern feminist criminology and an assessment of contemporary feminist criminology.
- See also suggested further reading in Chapter 3 by Jewkes, 2005.

A major reason for choosing a different format for this chapter was to:

- push forward feminist inspired and gendered criminological and victimological thinking;
- provoke, stimulate and encourage readers to grapple with some current and emerging difficult feminist headaches;
- take up the immense challenges that lie ahead for feminist inspired criminological and victimological scholarship;
- contemplate the wider gender issues.

Three starting points are provided at the end of this chapter.

[iii] Feminist and gendered perspectives – this chapter has been pre-occupied with feminist explanations and understandings. It has focussed almost exclusively upon women and this, given the histories of gendered theorising is inevitable and justifiable. In this way the chapter has prepared the ground for furthering debates and encourages these to become more complex, nuanced and sophisticated along feminist but also gendered lines. This chapter therefore lays the foundations for the chapters that follow which deal with how the feminist agenda has ignited theorising about masculinities, crime and victimisation is increasingly explored.

Summary conclusion – the challenge:

Reconciling women offenders as victim with women as real offenders

This key challenge can be sub-divided into three parts consistent with the themes of this chapter and the book as a whole.

[1] There is a difficulty in reconciling thorough and respected feminist and socialist inspired criminological wisdoms concerning criminal women as more 'sinned against than sinning' with evidence that women commit serious economic crimes and other violent victimisations that warrant more sustained and rigorous criminological inquiry. Several provoking questions sum up the quandary here.

- Is it justified that all women's crimes be explained away by recourse to economic and patriarchal pressures?
- Do dominant feminist criminologies tend to cast women as victims rather than as survivors?
- Does feminist inspired theorising contribute to beliefs that women's crime is not 'real' crime and that 'real women' do not offend?

Not to deny or undermine the huge importance of this work, it is perhaps now timely and hugely important too, to face up to mounting concerns about increased punitiveness towards and panic-like media attacks upon, women and girls who offend. This chapter makes a case criminologically, for re-assessing and re-positioning feminist inspired theorising about women who commit economic crime, for example. Not all female offenders are victims and perhaps not all female offenders are best served by criminological denial of the wider range of women's vocabularies of motives for committing 'economic' and perhaps other crimes too.

[2] As the reader has been reminded several times, this chapter has mainly focussed on women's conformity and women's criminality. However, the chapter to a lesser extent, and the book to a much greater extent, has also focussed on victimisation. This part of the challenge requires the reader to foreground also, the significant and further complex feminist and gender inspired findings, patterns and theorising emerging from the sub-discipline victimology.

Thus in taking up this challenge, the conundrums and ambiguities signalled from within a growing body of victimological work need equal and parallel foregrounding. The details of these knowledges are scattered throughout the pages of the remainder of this book. In short our knowledges of both men and women as real victims is growing and other gendered knowledges are emerging which are relevant too. Some provoking questions have already been posed in relation to these themes in earlier chapters. Here is a reminder of the sorts of questions that warrant confrontation in this challenge.

Can men and boys be victims?

Or

Do dominant and/or feminist victimologies always cast men as offenders and women as victims?

Can men be hurt by other men and women?

Are men survivors and 'winners' in patriarchal society?

How can we build on our knowledge of the gender patterning to victimisation?

[3] The third part of the triangulation that forms the challenge demands that we take women seriously as real offenders. This controversially includes facing up to murderous and child abusing women (if only to put sensationalist tabloidism to bed, see Chapter 3). This is perhaps the trickiest and most delicate part of the challenge, yet a part that cannot be avoided for very much longer if we are to seek gendered justice. By raising this as a serious criminological question for feminists there is a danger of alienating scholars and practitioner audiences alike and more importantly of providing ammunition to the neo-liberal project, populist punitive ideals and the carceral clawback counter-culture. Nevertheless, there are enlarged pockets of scholarly activity and factors related to the current socio-economic and political climate that mean it is timely to suggest a confrontation despite the risk of a feminist stand-off. A feminist backlash undercurrent is being felt already and inspirational theorising must be a strong and forceful backbone in the search for gendered social justice.

Ultimately however, if each part of this triangulated challenge is taken up it may well be as Wykes and Welsh (2009) have suggested:

> Once it becomes clear through feminist work within criminology that women's place in crime is largely due to their lack of economic power and their place in sexual and familial relations, and often both in conjunction, then criminology becomes largely a redundant source of explanation. (Wykes and Welsh, 2009: 65)

Thus neither criminology nor feminism can address the problems of crime by men and/or women. It might prove beyond the ability of criminology to marry up the knowledges we have amassed so far here (and including those in future chapters too) about gender patterns to crime and experiences of victimisation. How do we continue to highlight women's suffering at the hands of violent men at the same time as foregrounding women's violences to other women, men and children, at the same time as appreciating the historical-socio-economic position of women with multiple identities?

STUDY QUESTIONS/ACTIVITIES

This chapter has included more than enough questions for you to ponder on and contemplate. The most important of these are those under the section entitled 'Summary conclusion – the challenge' directly above. Additionally, several reading materials have been suggested. More are to be found below.

███████████████ SUGGESTIONS FOR FURTHER READING ████████████████

Fawcett Society (2007) *Women and Justice. Third Annual Review of the Commission on Women and the Criminal Justice System*. London: Fawcett Society.

Heidensohn, F. (1968) 'The deviance of women: a critique and an enquiry', *British Journal of Sociology*, 19 (2).

Smith, C. and Wincup, E. (2009) 'Gender and crime', in K. Hale, A. Hayward, E. Wahidin, and E. Wincup (eds), *Criminology*. second edition. Oxford: Oxford University Press.

In addition, there are various chapters in all editions of *The Oxford Handbook of Criminology* edited by M. Maguire, R. Morgan and R. Reiner. Some have already been referred to earlier in this chapter. An other is:

Levi, M., Maguire, M. and Brookman, F. (2007) 'Violent crime', in *The Oxford Handbook of Criminology*, fourth edition. Oxford: Oxford University Press.

6

FEMINIST AND GENDERED PERSPECTIVES: ON FEAR, RISK AND VULNERABILITY TO VICTIMISATION

GLOSSARY TERMS

Fear of crime

Quantitative research

Qualitative research

Victimological other

Repeat victimisation

> **CHAPTER AIMS**
>
> - Outline key predictors and gendered findings from the researching fear project
> - Engage in a feminist inspired and critical critique of survey derived knowledges on fear, risk and vulnerability
> - Provide examples and illustrations of hidden/invisible victimisations and the gender patterning to them
> - Consider gender sensitive risk-taking
> - Bring a masculinities sensitive perspective to victim studies
> - Provoke further gender based knowledges and theorising on victimisation in society

Introduction

Chapters 5 and 6 are both devoted to exploring feminist and other gendered perspectives in historical and contemporary understandings of the crime problem and of criminal victimisation. The previous chapter focussed on the historical origins and development of feminist influences in criminology and to a lesser extent in victimology and how these have shaped and might yet further influence criminological debates and provoke new theorising. Whilst there was a detailed focus on identifying feminist imprints on theorising it also identified gaps and avenues ripe for further feminist inspired explanations and perspectives. It opened up dilemmas and indeed it concluded by throwing down a gendered gauntlet to those engaged in criminological and victimological scholarship. There are then specific challenges in respect of the 'woman question' as well as the 'man question' and this chapter focuses in some respects upon some rather narrower yet highly significant (mainly) victimological concerns – fear, risk and vulnerability – that arise in part out of some of these recent developments in theorising around gender, crime and offending.

Although there is some disagreement as to the exact definition of fear of criminal victimisation, over the past 40 years, attempts have been made to identify the specific individual characteristics strongly associated with such fears. The **fear of crime** is generally taken to mean the personal worry about becoming a crime victim, although it is sometimes seen more vaguely as the feeling of being unsafe, particularly when out alone at night. (Ditton, 2008).

The first section of this chapter provides an overview of such characteristics or predictors of fear of crime and victimisation. It critically reviews where criminological and victimological empirical knowledges come from focussing on fear of crime research. The principal methodological tools and form of questioning is central to this gendered critique. The chapter outlines and critiques knowledges around the fear of crime project as a precursor to exploring men's apparent lack of fearfulness and women's heightened fears of criminal victimisation. The remainder of this chapter explores developments around our understanding of women's fear of criminal victimisation as a result, at least in part, of serious forms of violence between intimate partners in the home but also due to other peripheral and hidden 'quasi-crimes'. Featuring towards the end of this chapter is an analysis of how 'the man question' emerged and how masculinities are relevant to an understanding of crime and victimisation in society. Some recent turns in masculinities theorising concerning hegemonic and other masculinities, are outlined and considered via the concept of the **'victimological other'**. Gender-related barriers to understanding more fully fear of crime, risk and vulnerability to victimisation are noted before an additional development to the complex gender dimensions to fear, risk and vulnerability to victimisation is introduced highlighting gendered practices on risk-taking. This final section also reminds us of the gender salience question and re-visits how gender and risk are interlinked and often mutually constitutive (Hannah-Moffat and O'Malley, 2007).

Key questions for Chapter 6

- Who has what fears of crime?
- How does fear of victimisation connect with vulnerability and risk?
- Do women distort and exaggerate their risks to victimisation?
- Do men underestimate their risks of being violently attacked?
- What and whose fears are warranted, rational and well-founded?
- What and whose fears are extraneous, excessive, undue, fanciful and irrational?
- Does women's fear differ from men's?
- What are rational and irrational fears of crime?
- Are risk avoidance and risk taking gendered?
- Is a gendered victimology forging the way ahead?

Predictors of fear of criminal victimisation

Earlier in this book and elsewhere with colleagues I have been concerned to elucidate the nature of victimisation in relation to the major intersecting and overlapping social divisions of class, race, age and gender in England and Wales. Following the theme of social divisions, we have explored social class and social exclusion, the winners and losers (Croall, 2007: 54) – in society. Neighbourhood characteristics, such as perceived neighbourhood problems are also predictors of fear of victimisation. Thus social class appears to combine with community and residential postcode location. Race, ethnic minorities and criminal victimisation patterns, the fixation with viewing young people as criminals, as opposed to victims (Francis, 2007), has been a feature of our work whilst the elderly as a socially constructed and problematic category together with simplistic assumptions about 'the elderly' having 'irrational' fears of crime has been examined by Wahidin (2004) and Wahidin and Powell (2007). Others confirm that older age is related to differential fears of victimisation. Moore and Shepherd (2007) suggest that age is differentially related to fear of victimisation in that younger individuals tended to fear violent crime while older individuals tended to have a greater fear of property crime. Certainly relationships between old age and fear of crime are far from straightforward.

The gendered nature of victimisation has also been previously addressed as part of the effort to explore the socially and structurally divided nature of victimisation in society. Previously myself and co-editors Francis and Greer (2007) have split the issue between male victims (Walklate, 2007a) and females (Davies, 2007b). This particular social division, gender, has been prioritised for exploration in this book where I have already noted the gender bias to the patterning and nature of risk, people's experiences of criminal victimisation, and, as I have yet to explore, the gender bias to social and criminal justice responses to victimisation (see Chapter 8). Whilst continuing to fully acknowledge that there are complex findings emerging, all confirm the significance of social divisions and multiple inequalities and where the intersectionalities of class/race/age/gender variously combine as intersecting, interlocking and contingent (Daly, 1993 and see also Chapter 3). One factor that has the potential to be related to fear of criminal victimisation is the degree to which individuals take avoidance or precautionary measures, such as participating in self-defence courses, carrying a weapon, avoiding being alone or frequenting certain places, planning to move away, or other preventive measures (e.g. installing alarm systems, extra locks, obtaining guard dogs). The motivation for such behaviours could certainly be to protect oneself or those around them, but questions remain as to whether such behaviours are associated with lower levels of fear of criminal victimisation. For example, although (Anon 326 article) found that older age is predictive of less fear of victimisation, while being male is predictive of greater reported amounts of fear, there was a significant interaction between gender and age for fear of criminal victimisation, as well as preventive efforts. Thus, interpreting these main effects may be misleading. Instead, it appears that reported fear of criminal victimisation increased with older age for males, but decreased with older age for females. Further, preventive behaviours increased with older age for both males and females, but to a significantly greater degree with older males. Although these findings support previous investigations in that both age and gender were significantly related to fear of criminal victimisation (Akers et al., 1987; Warr and Stafford, 1983), the significant interactions found indicate that these relationships may be more complicated than previously thought. We recognise how African American ethnicity, being female, or having a low socio-economic status has also been associated with fear of criminal victimisation (McCrea et al., 2005; Warr, 1984; Warr and Stafford, 1983). Such characteristics are hypothesised to be related to fear of victimisation as first, individuals possess a self-perceived vulnerability to crime and second, consequences of actual victimisation could be especially difficult for such individuals. These issues connect well with debates about rational and irrational fears of crime and victimisation and by prioritising gender these complex relationships are more easily demonstrated.

Gendered findings from surveys

So where has the information on the above such associations, correlations and relationships come from? In the main the information has been derived from questionnaire based survey work including crime surveys and victim surveys where in both instances, there is a direct questioning of the victim of crime. Fear of crime research took off in the 1980s when questions on fear were included in the first British Crime Survey. Survey work has since built upon this bank of data which has proved crucial to the victimological enterprise. Since then fear of crime has been measured by a number of proxies most popularly under the generic banner 'worry', but 'concern' and 'anxiety' about crime are part of the fear project. Within this, relationships between fear and the likelihood or probability of experiencing victimisation have been explored. Findings suggest some evidence that perceptions are to an extent associated with actual level of risk (Kershaw et al., 2001). Effects on people's quality of life have been measured too through questions around safety and well being. What emerges is a complex picture often related to particular variables such as age and gender, and residence, themes that have already been identified earlier in the introduction to this chapter. The first British Crime Survey (Hough and Mayhew, 1983) and virtually all fear of crime surveys since have reported women as more fearful of crime and victimisation than men (Pain, 2001). This holds true in the home, in the workplace (Upson, 2004) and the city. There are strong relationships between sex and race and worry about crime and feelings of safety and well being in particular; women are more worried than other groups are about burglary and they are also far more concerned about violent crime. The latter finding is linked to issues around women's personal safety, particularly safety from various forms of violent personal criminal behaviour including assault and rape.

All of the findings reported on above have had the effect of transmuting what has previously been a social concern about crime and the generalised other (Walklate, 1998) into a personal problem of individual vulnerability (Ditton, 2008). Walklate's critical appraisal usefully identified what she has called four conceptual shifts in the fear of crime debate (2007b) where fear has been:

1 rational/irrational;
2 safety;
3 anxiety;
4 trust.

All of these transmutations have interesting gender angles to them which will be explored below. However before doing so, this overview of gendered findings, derived in the main from questionnaire based survey work including crime surveys and victim surveys and direct questioning of the victim of crime, attracts a gendered critique all of its own. This has feminist inspired as well as masculinities concerns stamped across it.

Researching fear: a positivist project?

The ideas behind researching the fear of crime were partly linked to a belief that by generating and publishing more accurate and valid information, the record would be put straight and people's fears in early 1980s Britain would be put in perspective. As two of the key authors of *The British Crime Survey* later explained:

> It was thought within the Home Office that distorted and exaggerated ideas of crime levels, trends and risks were widespread among the public; information on crime risks would demonstrate the comparatively low risks of serious crime and puncture inaccurate stereotypes of crime victims. In other words, the survey was envisaged in part at least as a way of achieving what might be called the 'normalisation' of crime – to help create a less alarmist and more balanced climate of opinion about law and order .
>
> (Hough and Mayhew, 1988: 157)

The survey approach however, is strongly associated with a particular type of social scientific research methodology. In short questionnaire based survey work is wedded to an approach that is essentially **quantitative** in nature.

Despite the findings from such survey work having become increasingly sophisticated and nuanced in terms of throwing up patterns and associations between fear, worry, concern, anxiety, safety, risk and so on, more **qualitative** approaches to research that are sympathetic to victim populations show there are inherent difficulties that prevent the adequate cataloguing and documenting of experiences of crime and victimisation in society in this way alone.

Pockets of qualitative and case study research, as referred to later in this chapter, suggest that positivist research tools are blunt instruments and poor tools of the trade for discovering the gendered nuances to the fears, risks and vulnerability to victimisation. Obsessions with social scientific methods that mimic the pure and natural sciences approach to doing research facilitate the continued thriving of positivist, conventional and conservative victimological legacies. Together with the reproduction of problematic images, and rhetoric (as seen in Chapter 3) all of this adds up to what might be called a positivist project in the researching of fear, risk and vulnerability to victimisation. This stranglehold is troublesome at a number of levels which have already been alluded to and prohibits theoretical, policy and practical developments around understanding the gendered terrain of victimisation. It is complicit in compounding the features of invisibility around knowledge, statistics, research, theory, control, politics, panic (Davies, et al., 1999: 3–26, Chapter 2 in this volume). The legacy of positivism is propped up by an over-riding message that quantitative measures of victimisation count most, and that victimisations measured as voluminous in this respect are most serious and harmful. This has policy implications that influence whether or how the state responds to victimisation and what types of victims of crime attract supportive provisions. It also means that there are neglected sites for victim research and intervention including the 'private sphere' which remains private along with a neglect of victims of the state and its agencies together with a lack of attention on corporate excesses, killings and maimings and other social harms caused by multinational corporations and companies across the globe. Thus some of the risks of victimisation are played down, whereas others are exaggerated. In sum, positivist victimological approaches dominate the research project and remain inadequate. They offer only a partial and thus limited understanding of the victim of crime, trends, and rates and in particular gendered experiences of victimisation are distorted and improperly captured.

Women's fears as connected to risk and vulnerability

Stanko suggests all women are 'universally vulnerable' (2008). In order to understand how and why she arrives at this statement we need to understand the social world from a woman's position with all of the historical and social-cultural baggage that this encompasses. In order to more fully understand fear, risk and vulnerability to crime and victimisation we need to have a more comprehensive landscape of victimisation in our criminological and victimological visions. One way to facilitate a less strait-jacketed approach to the terrain of victimisation that currently dominates the community safety landscape is to encourage thinking about hidden or invisible victimisations and where these sites for criminal and other types of social harm occur – the neglected geographical locations at global and local levels (see below).

Hidden/invisible crimes and violences

The reader is reminded of the concept of hidden or 'invisible' crimes. Invisible crimes were defined in Chapter 2 and in general terms these refer to:

- specific acts of crime which are not recorded in official crime statistics;
- categories of crime which are either not represented in official statistics or which are significantly under-recorded.

Furthermore a template was offered as a heuristic device for helping understand why some crimes (and their victimisations) are less visible than others. This was called the 'seven features of invisibility'. The way in which each of these individual features compound means that there are real knowledge gaps and terrains of victimisation that remain deeply buried and hidden from victimological (and criminological) visionary landscapes.

The gender agenda to hidden and invisible crimes and victimisations

Tapping into the more qualitative and case study knowledges that remain relatively hidden/invisible/peripheral, it is already evident that there is a gender map to such experiences despite the gendered nature of victimisation across workplaces having been little researched (Davies and Jupp, 1999). For example, there is some evidence to suggest that traditional male workplaces are risky environments and the mining industry, unsafe building sites and the construction industry generally are classic examples where men are at risk to victimisation at work (Croall, 2001), Furthermore, using data from the 1992–6 National Crime Victimisation Survey, Fisher and Gunnison have recently found that specific types of jobs place females more at risk of experiencing a violent incident (robbery and assault) than males in the same types of jobs (Fisher and Gunnison, 2001). As Croall has stated, it cannot be argued that women or men are more at risk to victimisation in the workplace; risks are affected by the gendered division of labour (Croall, 2001).

As Marsh has recently noted, 'it is still the case that a neglected area of victims of corporate crime is that of women as victims' (Marsh et al., 2004: 126).

This statement, made more than a decade after Gerber and Weeks (1992) pointed out that the corporate victimisation of women is particularly in need of feminist theorising. It suggests the continued androcentricity of victimological work generally and the corporate victimisation of women more specifically as well as the absence of gynocentric approaches that see the world from a female perspective. There has been only one significant publication on this very subject in 1996 (Szockyi and Fox, 1996). Victimisation can embrace a wide range of anti-social experiences and many alternative labels that might justifiably constitute victimisation include abuse, atrocity, disaster, accident, scandal and exploitation all of which can be employed to deny official harm and victim status as well as obscure the gendered terrain of victimisation.

Social change and glocal gendered victims

With respect to the victimisation of women workers, the edited volume referred to above notes how Imperial Foods has been implicated in the killing of black women workers (Szockyi and Fox, 1996). More recently, and linked to economic globalisation, there has been an apparent reappearance of sweatshops where 90 per cent of all workers are young – and in the West, immigrant – women, working in the garment industry and where 'operators are notorious for avoiding giving maternity leave by firing pregnant women and forcing women workers to take birth control or to abort their pregnancies' (Feminist Majority Foundation, 2001). There are also indications from other case studies of corporate crime that the pharmaceutical, cosmetics, health and medical industry has harmed women as consumers on a mass basis (Finlay, 1996; Mintz, 1985; Peppin, 1995; see also Croall, 1995, 2001, 2007a 2007b; Perry and Dawson, 1985; Slapper and Tombs, 1999; Swasy, 1996).

Other evidence supports the understated nature and extent of victimisation of women. For the last ten years or so Tombs and colleagues have concerned themselves with exposing the subject of corporate victimisation and with raising the profile of toxic crimes and harms in particular. They have estimated that as many as 20 million women's jobs entail toxic risks (Pearce and Tombs, 1997, 1998; Slapper and Tombs, 1999). Certainly there is evidence of hundreds of polluting companies in England and Wales involving emissions of cancer-causing chemicals (Brown, 1999: 5). Dramatic but rare exposures of such hazards have spawned pockets of empirical research into the effects of toxic chemicals including pesticides, dioxin, and hazardous waste on the public. Lynch and Stretesky's (2001) review notes a Norwegian study that evidences birth defects linked to exposure to environmental toxins. There have also been some high profile and recurrent attempts to expose scandals affecting women and their babies. Switzerland's largest industrial company Nestlé, the world's largest artificial baby milk producer, has been targeted for its unethical marketing and its part in causing malnutrition amongst infants in the global south and an estimated 1.5 million infants to die each year (Corporate Watch, 2004a). The same industrial giant has also been the focal point for pollution incidents and the target of feminist opposition groups in relation to its sponsoring of beauty contests and thereby perpetuating sexism (Corporate Watch, 2004a). Monsanto has similarly been the focus of Corporate Watch. This body claims Monsanto has an impressive history of committing corporate crimes, several of which have a direct bearing on the health of women, including their marketing of a genetically engineered hormone BST where evidence suggests BST milk may cause breast cancer (Corporate Watch, 2004b).

Watts and Zimmerman (2002) have pointed out an increasing amount of research is showing violence against women in a global context. This includes intimate partner violence, sexual abuse by non-intimate partners, trafficking, forced prostitution, exploitation of labour and debt bondage of women and girls, physical and sexual abuse against prostitutes, sex selective abortion, female infanticide, the deliberate neglect of girls and rape in war. A variety of recently reported incidents are beginning to impact upon the global victimological land-scape. Other research has recently uncovered how women do not always classify their experiences as rape (Kahn et al., 2003) and cultural issues appear to mili-tate against those women from diverse social and ethnic groups publicly admitting their victimisation or seeking out help (Chigwada-Bailey, 2003).

Evidence is emerging in relation to women's suffering following conse-quences of economic globalisation and during and in the wake of military vio-lence. These derive initially from journalistic reports and are followed by academic interest. Newspaper journalism has commented upon war crimes against women, 'Bosnian Serbs jailed for rape and sexual slavery' (Bishop, 2001). Since the break-up of the former Soviet Union and in the wake of relaxed border controls, there are increased opportunities for freedom of move-ment which haveе resulted in a proliferation of research focussing upon traf-ficking of women and girls often for the purpose of sexual exploitation in the form of prostitution, pornography, escort agency work (CWASU, 2002; Goodey, 2004; Hughes and Denisova, 2002; US Department of State, 2003). Smuggled migrants suffer in similar ways to those subjected to trafficking and violence against immigrant workers has also been apparent (Raj and Silverman, 2002). Europol, the European police agency has recently confirmed that cul-turally sensitive 'honour killings', in which young women who are often fleeing forced marriages, have been murdered, remain well hidden but appear to be increasing in Europe (Bennetto and Judd, 2004).

Whilst there has been a limited research agenda devoted to the gendered nature of victimisation, key case studies suggest the victimisation of women warrants further research. With respect to war crimes against women, whilst this is not a new phenomenon (Askin, 1997) there has been recent interest on the part of some criminologists (Cohen, 2002; Ruggiero, et al., 1998) to bring the crimes and victimisations of war within the remit of that discipline. Jamieson (1998) has acknowledged the ways in which feminists for example have focussed upon rape as expressions of the gender order and how although gender features in our understanding of war crimes there are limits to and gaps in our knowledge. Those that pertain to women include 'the need to identify the processes which produce the intensification of the sexual victimisation of women in wartime' (Jamieson, 1998: 496). There are others who have similarly argued that gender matters in understanding militarism and violence and that sexual violence against women and girls as a weapon of war is a serious human rights issue (Caiazza, 2001). Askin (1997) argues that whilst women are subject to the same atrocities as men, they are also victims of additional crimes – rapes and enforced pregnancies, forced maternity – because of their gender. This is supported by Ristanovic's investigations of wartime victimisation of refugees in the Balkans (Ristanovic, 1999, 2004).

Women as multiply victimised

The impact of victimisations on women includes women as wives, as mothers, as single parents, as workers and employees, as consumers, as citizens, as investors, as passengers, as residents and tenants, as female youths, children and babies (Croall, 1998; Davies, 2007a, 2007b; Sheley, 1995). Spaces, places and venues for women's victimisation include public and private places, the street, the home and care home the institution, the workplace, the battlefield and the war zone, the shopping mall and public transport. As women, and as indirect victims, we feel the pains, harms and victimisations of those close to us (Davies, 2008). This suggests a bias in the gendered nature of victimisation where women appear to bear the brunt of harm and suffering and victimisation. One of the commonly shared characteristics of victimisation is the notion of being harmed (Miers, 1989). Harm, can be physical, emotional and/or psychological and financial. Harms can involve very many forms of suffering including exploitation, mental abuse, violence, disease, deformity and deprivation. Harms can be multiple and serious as well as long lasting and debilitating. The British Crime Survey has shown that those victimisations that remain relatively invisible are not always or necessarily the least serious forms. Vast amounts of financial hardship remain un-criminalised and whilst men and women suffer, there are indications that there is a gendered impact here too. Smith (2001) has pointed out how the privatisation of retirement income affects men and women differently. Due to women's employment patterns during their life course their low wages are replicated in low retirement incomes resulting in many women living in poverty in retirement. As the many examples provided here demonstrate, serious forms of financial, physical, sexual, abuse and assault, corporate victimisations at home, at work, in peace and in wartime are experienced in very specific ways by women.

Feminist scholars and philosophers have persuasively argued that women are differently connected to the social world to men that women's needs and experiences differ greatly from men's. Women's social existence is connected, dependent and interdependent ways (Nelson, 1996) and more orientated towards an ethic of care and responsibility towards others in relationships (Gilligan, 1982). For women the family, the home, emotions, nurturing and caring are central to social life and these are generally considered feminine characteristics. Women's suffering, as wives, partners, (single) mothers, carers, sisters, and daughters is intricately connected to these. Even when ostensibly victimising others – committing property and acquisitive crimes particularly shoplifting and prostitution – we do so ostensibly and in the main for others' benefits, for families, partners, neighbours and friends (Davies, 2003a, 2003b). Following feminist criminological theorising (Carlen, 1988; Worrall, 1990) on criminal women this leads to a victimological dilemma for women who find themselves doubly victimised and doubly suffering, as opposed to doubly deviant and doubly suffering (Carlen, 1988).

Whilst those who more closely approximate characteristics typically associated with femininity are likely to feel others' suffering more readily and easily than those who don't, it does not follow that *women* necessarily bear the brunt of harm and suffering. Nor does it imply that *women* have a monopoly on suffering and hardship. A fully gendered approach to the understanding and appreciation of victimisation in society should not allow for *women* to hijack harm and suffering for themselves. Whilst harm, suffering and victimisation occur on a gendered terrain, men can exhibit so-called feminine characteristics and women can similarly exhibit those characteristics most commonly and routinely associated with men and traditional notions of masculinity. Women can do female or male gender; men can do female or male gender (Davies, 2007a).

What the positivist researching fear project insufficiently emphasises is the extent to which women in particular suffer from several or multiple forms of victimisation. Women are direct as well as indirect victims of criminal acts and omissions but they also suffer secondary, repeat, multiple and serial forms of criminal and non-criminal victimisations. Their direct victimisation can take visible and less visible forms and those most likely to be officially recognised are those that can be read off in the Criminal Injuries Compensation Scheme (2001) booklet (see also Chapter 8). In sum, multiple, secondary and repeat victimisations point towards how women's victimisation is complex and multi-layered, and how ungendered research designs and projects can render many of our experiences invisible. Whilst examples here have pointed out the lack of comprehension around women's experiences of victimisation, there is even more scant knowledge about men's 'real' experiences.

Dichotomising fears: rational/irrational, public/private

As already noted above, there is a number of interesting gender angles through the various transmutations rational/irrational; safety; anxiety; trust to be explored. The first of these has been raised on a number of occasions in earlier chapters and now warrants further discussion.

The findings from surveys deemed women (and the elderly) amongst the most fearful of crime. Such fearfulness has recently been deemed at best paradoxical (Ditton, 2008) and when such findings were first released, and at worst, exaggerated and irrational because the same populations were the least likely to be victimised. Radical, critical and feminist inspired criminological inquiries have since made more sense of these apparent paradoxes and conundrums. For instance:

> 'Realist' social surveys suggest that a proper account of women's subjection to domestic, work-related and other peripherally visible forms of victimisation, their experience of other harassments and marginally criminal incivilities, their unsatisfactory experience of police protection and the multiplication of each of these problems by factors of race, class and age, entirely dispels the apparent disparity between risk and fear. (Jones et al., 1986; Crawford et al., 1990: 40; Sparks, 1992: 9)

Furthermore in relation to exaggerated fears, women's fear of crime is often regarded as exaggerated; yet it is linked to routine experiences of sexual harassment and related 'quasi-crimes' that shape their interpretations of risky situations, though usually they fall beneath the gaze of the law (Campbell, 2005; Holgate, 1989; Hannah-Moffat and O'Malley, 2007: 5–6).

The quotations above make references to several types of criminal victimisation including domestic violence. Domestic violence is a highly gendered crime type and a classic example of **repeat victimisation**. They also refer to other peripherally visible forms of victimisation. Examples of the latter will include serious forms of interpersonal violence against women that take place in the domestic and/or workplace and which remain un- or under-reported and under-recorded and therefore are peripheral or invisible. Alternative data collection methods and techniques aimed at discovering the size of the 'dark figure' have found that women are subject to staggeringly high levels of violent victimisation in different settings.

- A man has physically or sexually abused 1 in 5 women at some time in women's lives (Venis and Horton).
- The BCS estimates 13 per cent of women have been subject to DV [domestic violence], sexual victimisation or stalking in the last 12 months (Home Office, 2004) and states that *'women are the overwhelming majority of the most heavily abused group'* (Home Office, 2004).
- Women's Aid claims that every week two women are killed in DV situations (Women's Aid, 2004).

This once again raises the question of public/private, visible/invisible locations for victimisation and sites for criminal and other forms of victimisation (see also Chapter 5). Real risky places for women are not well understood and the messages from radical, critical, feminist and gendered perspectives are still to be brought (literally) home. Furthermore they suggest there is a routineness, normalcy or taken-for-grantedness about some of the harassments and activities that women put up with and the affronts that they bear. This connects with the notion of lack of knowledge or interest (media, politics, moral) that the crime has been committed and victimisation is routinely occurring as referred to above (awareness, normalisation, ideology, collusion). There is a normalisation of the 'little evils'.

This latter point is taken up below in relation to women's ways of coping. The first quotation also refers to women's unsatisfactory experience of protection from the police which also colours women's perceptions about their own personal safety. Their dissatisfactions with protection might also be extended to encompass criminal and social justice matters where women have been treated less than satisfactorily by various institutions of the criminal justice system as well as other state and compensatory bodies (see below and Chapter 8).

Let us reconsider for a moment some of our knowledges about gendered crime patterns and gendered crimes and victimisations: first, the data connected to that presented in Chapter 4 on 'rape knowledges'; second, that connected to women's experiences of domestic violence and domestic violence as a repeated crime type.

Rape knowledges re-visited

Data:

- 80 per cent of rapes are committed by someone known to the victim.
- The number of rapes reported to the police has gone up in recent years.
- The number of convictions for rape has remained constant in recent years
- A drop in the conviction rate from 33 per cent in 1977 to just over 5 per cent today.

(*The Times*, 2005).

Elsewhere I have explored knowledge about how gender issues connect to crime and victimisation (Davies, 2007a, 2007b). In summary there is an unacceptably high number of women raped every year in the UK, and risks to non-stranger rape. These 'facts' about rape are indeed understandably worrisome. And, since risks are highly gendered, women's worries are indeed well founded As scholars of victimisation and victimology, what exactly do we know about gender and rape? We know that:

- Rape is an exception to the more general pattern of victimisation, which is usually higher for males than females.
- Rape is a highly gendered crime and type of victimisation.
- Rape primarily affects women.
- The majority of women's assailants with respect to interpersonal violence are men and men who are known to the raped woman.
- Age combined with sex renders some women more at risk to sexual violence.
- Gender and age structure women's fear of sexual violence with women being particularly fearful of violence from men.
- Women fear, perceive and deal with risk and experiences via different day-to-day coping strategies and support networks.

We know therefore that women suffer almost exclusively from some forms of victimisation and disproportionately from others. We know there is a gender patterning to risk and fear of victimisation. And in terms of major feminist achievements, we know to put more emphasis on hidden processes. We also know the gender of the perpetrator has often been hidden (Morley and Mullender, 1994). Feminist commentators generally agree that we fail to adequately capture women's real experiences or approximate the real extent of their suffering and that an unquantifiable number of such victimisations often remain or are rendered invisible. Some have argued the term 'domestic violence' renders women's experiences invisible by hiding the gender of the perpetrator (Morley and Mullender, 1994) and the gendered nature of the offence and victimisation generally.

Gendered rationality

Reminding ourselves of the dualistic theme of rationality/irrationality commented upon in Chapter 5, a debate was ignited in 1983 that called into question the rationality of women's fears of crime. Crime survey data appeared to prove that women's fears were irrational. Shortly after Stanko (1988a, 1988b, 1993) began to deconstruct women's irrational and rational fears of crime and victimisation and since then others have offered counter responses to the claims that women's fear of victimisation from men is irrational. More sensitive research tools used in the local measurement of crime and victimisation since 1982 (see Crawford et al., 1990; Hall, 1985; Hanmer and Saunders, 1984; Jones et al., 1986) have produced results that help to support these arguments. Feminist research in the area of domestic violence has explained the reasons why women stay in violent relationships revealing women's rationalism rather than their irrationality and irresponsibility (see Mooney, 2000; Walklate, 1998). As part of the counter argument, these writers have pointed out that if women are fearful they have just cause to be so and they remind us of the huge 'dark figure' of sexual crimes and domestic violence against women as noted earlier.

Other aspects of the counter argument coalesce around the issue of women's rational response to victimisation. The ways in which women do rationality are as mediated by gender as any area of social activity. Walklate has argued that what a man may consider rational may not be considered so by a woman (Walklate, 1995: 63). In the context of exploring and explaining the gendered nature of sexual violence, Lees has commented that 'It appears that there are different conceptions of rationality, which may be determined partly by the social and gendered background and experiences of individuals as well as the really different possibilities which exist between men and women. (Lees, 1997: 139). Philosophically it has been acknowledged that women's fears are not always unreasonable. Women's negotiation of risk points to their understanding of risk as gendered (Chan and Rigakos, 2002) and further suggests that women know the risks they face and adapt their behaviour and lifestyles to minimise, negotiate and cope with these day-to-day living conditions. So in terms of supporting victims through experiences of victimisation, at one level women 'do it for themselves' by negotiating their own safety and minimising risks, they actively and routinely engage with and negotiate their own safety in their daily social life (Stanko, 1990b). In other words, women rationally negotiate their own safety and rationally work through their experiences of victimisation and abuse. This can mean that women often stay in violent relationships (Mooney, 2000). However this does not imply that risk is universalised in sex/gender terms. Recent research has reported fearful men and fearless women (Gilchrist et al., 1998; and see section 'Men, masculinities and victimisation', page 121).

Negotiating unsafety

Thus we have seen how women might be deemed 'universally vulnerable' and know that they are living always in 'climates of unsafety' where:

In effect, women's feelings of fear may relate to their tacit understanding of the likelihood of experiencing male violence and the lack of protection they receive from those around them, and in particular, from those in positions of authority to protect them from abusive situations. (Stanko, 2008: 72)

However, rather than this being a passive and fatalistic form of submission to violence this is a rational and active resistance to the threat from it. Women engage in precautionary strategies to protect their physical safety. And, even after physical assault, survivorship rather than victimhood is a preferable place to be.

Not everyone who suffers victimisation likes to think of themselves or to be called, a victim. Feminists including those involved with Rape Crisis centres prefer to speak of survivors, for a number of reasons. First, using the term 'survivor' makes clear the seriousness of rape as, often, a life-threatening attack. Second, public perceptions are shaped by terminology and the word 'victim' has connotations of passivity, even of helplessness. In the context of a movement which aims to empower people who have been victimised, this is clearly inappropriate: 'using the word "victim" to describe women takes away our power and contributes to the idea that it is right and natural for men to "prey" on us'. (London Rape Crisis Centre, 1984, iv)

The notion of survivorship is significant for women. Miers (1989) has pointed out that being a victim is an accorded status, which carries with it a set of expectations. A female victim might have expectations that the criminal justice system – from the police though to the CPS, the courts, the judiciary and the prison system – treat her with respect, dignity and due process. There may also be expectations that others will have of her. Family, friends, colleagues and criminal justice personnel might expect female victims to be dependent, passive, inert, fatalistic and tolerant. When women have appeared in court as defendants and have not conformed to the expectations others have of them as a victim, they have been described as not subscribing to the 'gender-deal' (Carlen, 1988). When women have appeared in court as victims and witnesses and have failed to do the gender-deal and strike a gender-specific bargain, they have been treated less than sympathetically and have experienced 'secondary victimisation' often through 'victim blaming'. Through being gender-deviant and failing to enter into the gender-contract (Worrall, 1990), women have found themselves treated more punitively than if they had conformed to a more respectful and respectworthy stereotype of the dutiful wife/partner, caring mother as victim.

As well as women doing survivorship for themselves, they do so on behalf of others too. The ways in which women help other women are evident in the voluntary and mutual support work carried out under the auspices of

Women's Aid. Other ways in which women are instrumental and pro-active in encouraging and promoting survival from victimisation and disaster are often less self-evident. Indeed, women's valuable contributions often remain invisible and incalculable. One example is in the area of youth violence and community safety. Pearce and Stanko (2000) note the complexity of women's relationship to fear creation and alleviation. Contrary to finding young women as always in need of protection from young men, they find young women often take an active role in either disrupting or stabilising the feeling of safety and order within communities. Several writers have challenged the notion that all women are always worried, afraid and fearful of crime (Gilchrist et al., 2008; Pearce and Stanko, 2000; Walklate, 2001) with Gilchrist and colleagues finding fearful men and fearless women (Gilchrist et al., 1998, 2008). Furthermore, as the edited collection by Enarson and Hearn Marrow (1998) shows, women are in fact present in every disaster response 'as mitigators, preparers, rescuers, caregivers, sustainers and rebuilders' (1998: 6) and women's survival assets stand them in good stead as resource managers with specialised knowledge of coping and survival strategies during and after disasters. Women not only feel and experience victimisation on behalf of others but they help in reconstructing lives and communities shattered by disaster and rioting (Campbell, 1993).

Section summary

The above illustrates how gendered inroads have been made in the victimological enterprise. However these developments also reveal gaps and omissions, and indicate where we might yet search in order to devise more gender-sensitive theories, polices practices and research. We might for example, impose a gendered insight and locate our research efforts into different locations and spaces for example in the home as well as on the street, at the workplace and at war, at school and in the playground as well as in institutions such as the care home, the hospital and the prison. Additionally, we have a scant level of understanding of the direct and indirect impacts of different types of victimisation on women in different settings. Thus we can identify some interesting and potentially fruitful avenues for further research *for* women (and *for* men) that might inform our gendered knowledge. Moreover, the omnipresence of the woman question should properly include all identities of women including for example, immigrant women's experiences of victimisation and the suffering and harm experienced by the whole matrix of combined female identities. Thus young black/white women's experiences might be compared and contrasted with older white and ethnic minority women's experiences.

Men, masculinities and victimisation

In early victim studies we are often presented with a homogenous portrayal of the crime victim. Where gender distinctions were evident however, there was often a homogenous portrayal of who women are and an equally homogenised portrayal of whom men are. These homogeneities are persistent and remain key obstacles to a more fully gendered understanding of victimisation. The same obstacles limit an improved understanding of masculinities, gender and victimology. Where women have been characterised as ideal victims, indeed as victim-prone and blameworthy, men have quite simply been characterised as victimisers. Whilst this has not necessarily ensured that all female victims of all types of victimisations have been visible and whilst this has not always corresponded with support provisions available to female victims, it has contributed to the continued and unchanging assumptions and presumptions about men as victimisers. It has also bolstered presumptions that all the victims of sexual violence are female (and all perpetrators male) and that men are never vulnerable, fearful or at great risk to victimisation. On the contrary, white, heterosexual, rational, men have been the norm or yardstick against whom not only females but also all other victims could be compared. Men have not been ascribed legitimate or real victim status and have been largely invisible as victims.

Even with the advent of more sophisticated measurements of victimisation following the first British Crime Survey in 1982, and with the data we have accumulated since on risky places and venues, the ways of thinking about men and women that are illustrated above remain difficult for victimologists of the twenty-first century to dispense with. Men, in self-report surveys continue to confirm lower levels of fear (Sutton and Farrall, 2005). So, although risky places ought to have been redefined as those where men go and where women live, more innovative and imaginative research narratives indicate there are still private experiences of victimisations in different locations and settings, between individuals and groups that victimology has yet to properly contend with. There are several barriers that contribute to the difficulties in exposing and explaining these gendered experiences, risks and fears. Just a few suggestions as to what these barriers might be can be gleaned from a handful of research studies connected to a small selection of victimisations. Some of the general barriers and some of the more specific barriers to exposing and explaining men's experiences and therefore gendered experiences include the following:

- obsessions with scientific and often empiricist quantitative research methodologies and techniques and the need to discover clear patterns and rates (this tends to obscure nuances and irregularities);
- absence of research methods that provide an adequate representation of women's violence to men in a context of no violence from the man (Babcock et al., 2003; Bacon, 2004; Dobash and Dobash, 2008: 95);

- prejudices and constraints of time and resources militate against institutions and war crime investigators researching, investigating and documenting male sexual assault during war preventing detection and punishment;
- failures to address the question of 'maleness';
- macho concealment of fear and socially desirable responses in surveys: it might be shameful and embarrassing for men to express fear and thus they may be unwilling to report it (Sutton et al., 2010);
- power relations among men based on a hierarchy of masculinities – hegemonic and subordinated masculinities (Messerschmidt, 1998, 2009);
- hegemonic masculinities that suggest: men aren't real victims; men and big boys don't cry (Goodey, 1997);
- the stigma of male rape, men's fears that they will be considered to be homosexual and myths regarding the promiscuity of gay men all conspire to prevent both heterosexual and gay men from reporting their experiences to the police (Gregory and Lees, 1999);
- 'men's hesitation to disclose vulnerability' (Stanko and Hobdell, 1993: 400);
- the problem of intimate partner violence is primarily one of men's violence to women partners and not the obverse (Dobash and Dobash, 2008: 95);
- women who do not want to be portrayed as victims and who do not want always to feel vulnerable and in need of protection.

Victimology has therefore thought about men mostly as victimisers and has generally not contemplated men as victims. In discussing feminism, gender and victimology the historical developments have been very much associated with both the domain assumptions derived from the founders of victimology in the 1940s and 1950s as well as the feminist critique within criminology, which originated in the 1970s. This time frame has produced many lessons for the study of victims and victimology in terms of understanding the nature and extent of women's experience of victimisation and how this might be accommodated in relation to criminal justice policy. The time frame relating to the exploration of the nature and extent of understanding men's experience of victimisation is much shorter still and in terms of the likely impact of this understanding and in particular how this might be accommodated in relation to criminal justice policy the lessons are perhaps still to come. Research on gender, masculinities and crime can be traced back only 20 or so years to the 1980s when new studies focussed on criminal masculinities (Carrabine et al., 2004; Walklate, 2004). These developments were inspired by feminist scholarship and initially, the notion of masculinity was employed to help explain men's oppressive power over women and in particular men's violence against women. In this view violent men can be seen to be acting out, demonstrating and asserting their machismo. Thus this early application of the notion of masculinity emerged as a concern to explain and understand men as victimisers and women as victims and the concerns with masculinities grew out of women's and feminist's complaints about heterosexual men's sexual, domestic and economic violence (Groombridge, 2001). Once again we can highlight that is has been feminist challenges to the conventional victimological agenda that have insisted on pursuing the 'woman question' that have made major achievements. They have been especially instrumental in bringing debates on masculinities, crime and victimisation into the arena of victim-centred research (Goodey, 2005: 83). Since these early applications, theoretical considerations around masculinity and notions of masculinities took on greater significance in the social sciences generally. Connell's (1987) work on a tripartite structure of gender relations and the gender order was particularly influential although Messerschmidt is credited with applying the concept of masculinities to the committing of crime by men and thereby importing the concept into criminology. Following this, masculinities emerged as a key theoretical concept in its own right (see McLaughlin and Muncie, 2001).

So far this section on men, masculinities and victimisation has considered some of the ways in which academic studies have considered men. It has discussed how there has been a shift from an over-riding concern with men as offenders and perpetrators, to a focus on the maleness of perpetrators of crime, that is, as male criminals, men who have masculine identities. These identities are some of the most salient of all gender identities. This section has also made brief reference to the influential body of work that has prompted the suggestion that violent crime in particular can be understood as a product of masculinities and of men 'doing-gender'. Masculinities have evolved in to not only a key theoretical concept and explanatory tool for understanding crime, but also it has proliferated to the extent that there are journals, degree modules and books dedicated to it as a subject area in its own right.

Masculinities sensitive victimology

So how might we think about the study of crime, criminal justice and victimisation from a masculinities perspective? How can we think about, or re-think, the 'man question'? A short quotation from Groombridge helps orient us in the right direction here. He suggests that we can now accept that 'whilst the problem may still be men, men still had problems' (Groombridge, 2001: 261). We can briefly summarise what we now understand the concept of masculinities to encompass and what the study of masculinities within victimology might properly need to include. A simple summary list can be compiled which includes an understanding of a number of key concepts and attributes. These include an understanding of:[1]

---

[1] As derived from the work of Connell, 1987, 1995; Jewkes, 2005b; Jefferson, 2001; Messerschmidt, 1993, 1997; Remy, 1990; Tolson, 1977; Walklate, 2004b 2007b; West and Zimmerman, 1987; West and Fenstermaker, 1995.

- essentialism;
- masculinism, 'manliness', the 'hyper masculine' and machismo;
- patriarchy, androcracy, fratriarchy;
- hierarchies of domination and status, ritual, symbolism, difference;
- hegemony and of male solidarity;
- culture, identity, self-image and reputation;
- manhood and male attributes, credentials and norms such as physical prowess, aggression, toughness and violence.

How all of these ingredients interact in very complex ways with femininity and sexuality might be particularly significant. Yet despite the recent emergence and fast growing proliferation of academic materials relating to masculinities, few have cared yet to import the concept into the study of victims and victimology and therefore what it is less easy to review in this chapter is how victimisation might be understood as a product of masculinity. Studies that are beginning to broach this question are very much in their infancy. However, there does appear to be some potential for making sense of some of the less visible forms of victimisation that some men experience and suffer from, especially those forms of victimisation that are perpetrated by other men.

So, having made these advances in terms of understanding how gender might facilitate our understanding of victims and victimology we might ask a further question. Can men now be victims? In the twenty-first century has the gender agenda fully incorporated men and masculinities? Is victimology up to the task of challenging established interpretations of who can be vulnerable, fearful and at risk? Clearly we do know, successive surveys have identified, (BCS, 1983; George, 1999) and qualitative studies have demonstrated, men can be, are and always have been victims of crime. Sometimes men suffer from victimisation whether it is murder, assault, sexual victimisation or stalking, from women and sometimes they suffer similar forms of victimisation from other men. Walklate reminds us 'it would be a mistake to presume that all the perpetrators of sexual violence are male and all its victims female' (Walklate, 2004). However, as Goodey (2005) has pointed out the 'taboo' subject of female on male domestic violence does have an empirical basis yet this has been downplayed (Gadd et al., 2003; Mirrlees-Black and Byron, 1999) and the real impact this has on men's lives remains under-researched.

Exceptionally within the criminological domain, Lees (1997) has undertaken consultancy research on male sexual assaults on men (with Lynn Ferguson the Director of the Channel 4 'Dispatches' programme on male rape, 1995). Two surveys were conducted in 1995, a survey of male victims of rape and the first ever survey of police recording practices of rape of men by men. The criminological and victimological analysis focuses on men's experiences of sexual violence in the context of masculinity (see Gregory and Lees, 1999: 112–33; Lees, 1997: 89–107). Lees presents a persuasive illustration of how hegemonic masculinity is a useful explanatory concept in this analysis:

> This chapter shows how this (hegemonic masculinity) seems to be the most feasible explanation for why sexual assaults on men are predominantly perpetrated by men who regard themselves as heterosexual in sexual orientation. It also explains why male rape so often takes place in all-male institutions such as prisons and the army. By sexually humiliating men who do not appear to live up to the dominant form of masculinity, the perpetrator's own masculinity is enhanced. (Lees, 1997: 13)

In this quotation Lees refers to a common and long known knowledge about experience peculiar to the imprisonment of men. Male rape and other experiences of mortification and brutality in men's prisons have been known about criminologically since the classic study by Sykes in 1958. Despit having been known about, this subject has been little cared about and victimologically men have not constituted real victims behind the closed doors of the prison. Men in prison who are subjected to aggression and violence are the victimological other twice removed or contradictorily in the case of the rapist and paedophile they are the deserving victim. Jewkes begins to shed light on the ways in which men behind bars do masculinity as an adaptation to imprisonment (2005b) although she does not discuss male rape as one of the overt manly or hyper masculine coping strategies used by inmates.

So, whilst some brave scholars have dared to put women in the frame as perpetrators of crime and victimisers, others have chosen to put men in the frame as victims. Such approaches are only beginning to uncover the implications of the maleness of victimisation.

Gender, risk-taking and risk-avoidance

This part of the chapter briefly notes an additional development to the complex gender dimensions to fear, risk and vulnerability to victimisation. One recently edited book entitled *Gendered Risks* (Hannah-Moffatt and O'Malley, 2007) has an explicit focus on the risk/gender nexus. Several parts of this book connect with matters concerning fear, risk and vulnerability to victimisation. Walklate for example focuses on gendered risk taking and how efforts to explore the fear of crime are often hampered by positivist domain assumptions (Walklate, 2007a, 2007b). This has been explored earlier in the chapter in relation to the problem of the positivist project of researching the fear of crime. However, several other chapters in this edited collection are relevant to a discussion about gendered risk taking practices and experiences. One, by Lyng and Matthews, considers contemporary forms of voluntary risk-taking and attempts to make sense of gendered risk taking and vulnerability to risk in the context of risk, edgework, and masculinities. These activities usually involve high risk of death or serious injury. Edgework is shown as seductive in terms of satisfying internal needs and providing opportunities for feelings of omnipotence and control in managing fear. The chapter's value here is in its contribution to new ways of thinking about gender differences in risk agency and new lines of research that challenge assumptions about males as risk takers and females as risk avoiders. Another chapter explores risk seeking young women in a context where they are more usually portrayed as risk avoiders and passive victims of risk rather than as active risk seekers. The author reports on young women involved in the same range of risky behaviours as young men, often for what seem like very similar reasons (namely, fun, excitement, self-respect and status) (Batchelor, 2007: 223) and thus this research shows female risk seeking is an important source of 'gender trouble'.

Summary conclusion

Together, Chapters 5 and 6 have explored feminist and other gendered perspectives in historical and contemporary understandings of the crime problem and of criminal victimisation in society. Both chapters have a strong theoretical strand to them and have been concerned with past, current and further shaping and influencing of, criminological and victimological debates with a view to provoking new theorising. Specific challenges in respect of the 'woman question' as well as the 'man question' have been highlighted as derived from focussing upon explaining and theorising offending and victimisation and issues surrounding fear, risk and vulnerability.

Chapter 6 has outlined key predictors and gendered findings from the researching fear project whilst engaging in a feminist inspired and critical critique of survey derived knowledges on fear, risk and vulnerability. It has done so providing examples and illustrations of hidden/invisible victimisations and the gender patterning to them. This chapter necessarily therefore explored men's 'gung-ho' lack of fearfulness and women's heightened fears of criminal victimisation. It explored developments around our understanding of women's fear of criminal victimisation as a result, at least in part, of serious forms of violence between intimate partners in the home but also due to other peripheral and hidden 'quasi-crimes'. The final substantive part of this chapter begins to rebalance the gender bias evident in inspirational theoretical work on crime and victimisation in society by steering the focus towards a masculinities sensitive perspective in victim studies in the hope of stimulating further gender based knowledges and theorising on the problems of crime and victimisation in society.

STUDY QUESTIONS/ACTIVITIES

- If you were asked to respond to questions about your own fears and worries about crime how would you respond in relation to property crime and in relation to crimes of violence?
- What are you most and least concerned about?
- How would your responses fit in terms of the findings from surveys and the patterns discussed early in this chapter?
- In a gendered crime, such as rape, why is there such a disparity between the reporting of rape, arrests for rape and prosecutions for rape? You may need to look again at Chapter 4 and Boxes 4.1 and 4.2 in order to provide a fuller explanation.

SUGGESTIONS FOR FURTHER READING

See various chapters in the edited collection by Hannah-Moffat, K. and O'Mally, P. (2007) (eds) *Gendered Risks*. Abingdon: RoutledgeCavendish. You may wish to start with the chapter by Sandra Walklate.

7

GENDER AND THE CRIMINAL JUSTICE SYSTEM: RESPONSES TO LAWBREAKERS

CONTENTS

GLOSSARY TERMS

Sexism   Double jeopardy
Social control   Equality (Equal rights, Equal treatment)
Gender roles/Social roles   'Doing-difference'
Gender-wise/Sensitive justice

CHAPTER AIMS

To examine:

- the concept of gender-wise justice
- how and why gender matters in responding to imprisoned lawbreakers
- gender-based needs in the prison environment
- how just responses to lawbreakers might be done through gender difference

Introduction

The previous chapter honed in upon some highly significant victimological concerns – feminist and gendered perspectives: on fear, risk and vulnerability to victimisation. In particular it explored developments around our understanding of women's fear of crime and of criminal victimisation as a result of serious forms of violence between intimate partners in the home. It took account of recent developments in the area of masculinities, crime and victimisation and did so with reference to gendered findings from surveys as well as knowledges emerging around risk including most notably those connected to gender, risk-taking and risk-avoidance. Some gender-related barriers to understanding more fully fear of crime, risk and vulnerability to victimisation were signposted in Chapter 6 and questions were raised about the potential that feminist victimology might hold for forging the way ahead.

Chapter 7 embarks upon a consideration of gender, crime and victimisation from a different starting point. The current chapter considers the criminal justice system's responses to lawbreakers through a gendered lens. Whilst there are continuities between fear, risk and vulnerability to victimisation, the major themes of the preceding chapter, there are various ways in which gender impacts upon our understanding of matters related to criminal justice, as well as justice for victims, that warrant a wider angled lens, with greater scope, to be used here. There are several ways of approaching this vast area of why, how and when gender might matter in the changing social and political climates of the twentieth and twenty-first centuries. Most commonly, feminist empirical work has examined how gender is significant in the process of doing justice in separate institutions of the criminal justice system, for example, police work and the policing of rape and domestic violence, in particular with regard to sexism, bias, leniency/harshness in the courts and in sentencing practices, the criminal and penal systems and amongst the legal profession more generally, in the Probation Service and in probation practice as well as the voluntary sector. More latterly, how gender issues emerge as key in the Youth Justice Board and youth justice dispensations are evident whilst data on gender patterns emanating from the National Offender Management System (NOMS) is a new development.

This chapter draws out the themes that remain relevant from this research as the aims of this chapter are to push these debates and controversies further forward. It proposes to do so through extending some of the most rigorous and promising gendered knowledges and considering the usefulness of these in one specific criminal justice context. Thus the chapter continues to consider the questions of how and when gender matters in understanding crime, its control and in the following chapter (Chapter 8) the experience and recovery from victimisation. Chapters 7 and 8 focus historically and contemporarily upon how the processes of crime and victimisation are gendered and thus how gender matters in respect of formal and informal social controls and responses to both offenders and victims. This chapter dwells especially upon the concept of gender-wise justice and considers the criminal and social justice potential of expanding upon a range of linked and useful conceptual and plausible arguments as explored in the literatures. In choosing to debate responses to lawbreakers under the conceptual framework of gender-wise justice, the chapter achieves depth of analysis by focussing especially upon issues surrounding women's and men's (but predominantly women's) imprisonment.

Key questions for Chapter 7

- Does the gender of offenders (and victims) influence their treatment by police, court, legal, probation, youth justice, voluntary and prison institutions and personnel?
- Are there gendered expectations connected to offenders' (and victims') interactions with, and treatment by, the criminal justice system?
- Does and should gender, influence the response of the criminal justice system to offenders (and victims of crime)?
- What is the interplay between gender and the criminal justice response to lawbreakers?
- How, why and when does gender affect the responses of the justice system to offenders (and victims)?

Doing gender-wise justice

First, what is meant by the phrase 'gender-wise' justice? This refers to whether or not treatment, provisions and interventions within and connected to the criminal justice system should be gender sensitive, that is, tailored to the gendered needs and specificities of the offender and victim.

This chapter focuses on lawbreakers and administering gender-wise justice with and for offenders. This part of the discussion is broken down into two subsections. The first explores the legacy and lessons learnt from those who posed questions and conducted research around the theme of (sexist) discrimination in the process of doing justice and in the separate institutions of the criminal justice system, police, courts, probation and prisons. The second explores the continued relevance of these narrow conceptualisations of gendered agendas in criminal justice institutions, processes and interventions into the twenty-first century and returns to debate, explain and illustrate in greater detail, what is meant by 'gender-wise' or gender-sensitive justice. It also raises some provocative questions about the ability and likelihood of this conceptual framework to offer insights and policy relevance. Can gender-sensitivity be invoked to address better interplays between the criminal justice system and offenders? Can this be used as an aspiration to deal more effectively with ingrained expectations and norms relating to offending by men and women alike? Can it help ascertain more precisely why, where and when gender matters?

Beyond sexism, discrimination, bias, leniency/harshness

Above, I refer to the concepts noted in this sub-heading – sexism, discrimination, bias – as being part of a rather narrow conceptualisation of gendered interplays, experiences and impacts in the criminal justice processes and systems. Certainly feminist inspired research and theoretical avenues have moved on and few would agree these in themselves are adequate explanations and accounts of what happens and why, to offenders caught in the criminal justice system. So why return to concepts and themes such as leniency and harshness? There are at least two very sound reasons. First, in order to be comprehensive in taking forward lessons from the past we need to tease out what themes were discovered as a result of finding answers to the questions this body of empirical research produced to its own sets of questions. Second, we need to take these themes on board as still relevant in any new theoretical and empirical inquiries as well as policy initiatives and topical developments that are hatching in terms of responding to lawbreakers.

So, those who posed questions and conducted copious empirical research to prove/disprove **sexism** and discrimination on other grounds, too, produced various answers and other avenues for further research and theoretical inquiry all of which remains useful and instructive in terms of more fully understanding and appreciating today how gender is significant in the process of doing justice in the criminal justice system and the connected institutions which are a part of it such as the police, courts, probation and prisons. And what were the various answers and other avenues for further research and theoretical inquiry that were produced? What are the themes that were discovered? Which of these themes remain more or less relevant today in terms of responding to lawbreakers? We now make an effort to delineate some of these.

In terms of the key questions posed at the beginning of this chapter, the first was,

> Does the gender of offenders (and victims) influence their treatment by police, court, legal, probation, youth justice, voluntary and prison institutions and personnel?

And, the set of inquires we are referring to did produce a range of findings on this, though the answers which were found were not always pointing in the same direction. A lecture given in 2006 given by B. Hale nicely captures the often contradictory and complex outcomes of such research on gender bias in the context of sentencing decisions. She uses the concept 'relevant difference' to explain that the situations and experiences of male and female offenders are typically so different that it would not generally be fair to treat female offenders as severely as male offenders even if they are legally and formally similar. However, it is the explanations for the often contradictory and always complex findings that are most useful to us here. It is this set of more detailed and nuanced knowledges and understandings that shed enormous light on the more recent and penetrative gender oriented questions that were also posed as key towards the start of this chapter:

- Are there gendered expectations connected to offenders' (and victims') interactions with, and treatment by, the criminal justice system?
- What is the interplay between gender and the criminal justice response to lawbreakers?

Wisdoms garnered were groundbreaking and an exciting period of feminist critique (as noted in Chapter 5), research and theorising was to follow. So, from the 1970s onwards there was a gradual extension of the feminist project to explore women's oppression in all areas of social life and as felt in their relationships, interactions and experiences of social institutions. Awareness dawned that these oppressions and subordinations were evident in the field of crime, deviance and criminology also, with the advent of feminist criminology and, with the concomitant empirical evidence all of these insights began to spawn explanatory wisdoms attesting to the criminal justice system's tendency to deal mainly with men and men's experiences.

Writers referred to in Chapter 5 such as Klein (1996 and Klein and Kress 1976), Heidensohn (1968), Smart (1976) all played a key part in developing a sustained feminist critique of accounts of crime and deviance and drew attention to the inherent sexism within them whether women and girls were included or not. So what are the most lasting legacies from this period of critique and the subsequent perspectives that were formulated? One of the neatest ways to summarise this is perhaps to turn our attention to some key concepts and constructs that herald from this body of work and which have withstood the test of several decades in remaining useful and insightful.

Some of the most significant of these concern the relationships between conformity and non-conformity and the importance of looking at the relationships between conformists and rule breakers, the non deviant (normal) and the deviant. As an illustration, the empirical work of Mary Eaton shows the ways in which informal and formal **social controls**, judicial and non-judicial, overt and covertly subtle processes operate. In particular she exemplifies the ways in which women are controlled through their domestic role, both within and beyond the criminal justice system. Her work used explanatory concepts such as **gender roles** and gender divisions and familial ideology to help explain the treatment of women defendants in magistrate's courts. Eaton concluded that summary justice in magistrates' courts, as evidenced in courtroom discourse, pronouncements from the bench, pleas of mitigation, and probation officer's reports, reveals a dominant familial ideology and domestic arrangements. She concludes in her study of women defendants,

> ... the court officials did more than describe a variety of domestic arrangements, they revealed their assumptions concerning the ways in which families should be organised, and their expectations concerning the results of such organisation ... By acting appropriately as a family member a man or women could demonstrate responsibility and respectability ... The family was also recognised as a site of social control ... The family was represented as an enduring unit which involves, primarily, a man and a women. Expectations concerning the division of labour between the man and the women were apparent ...The predominance of familial ideology in courtroom discourse is an acknowledgement of the role which the family plays in the socialisation and social control of members of society. (1986: 93–5)

The above might be used to typify broadly the results emerging from the prolific period of empirical work by feminist inspired research belonging to the 1980s. A number of key concepts that have proved lasting and enduring in terms of understanding female conformity and responses to those women who dare not to conform either originate from or were proven during this period of empirically informed theorising. The enduring value of concepts such as socialisation, social control and the significance of the division of labour and familial ideologies and discourse were all confirmed and affirmed by a range of scholarship that was conducted in the criminal justice arena. Others concepts can be added. Carlen for example has explored the way in which many criminal women found themselves in '**double jeopardy**' (Carlen, 1988, 1998; Carlen and Worrall, 2004) for stepping well outside their prescribed gender roles. All of these insights show, as Gelsthorpe (2007) has pointed out, how the sentencing of women has been overshadowed by faulty perceptions reflecting stereotypical concerns and a familial ideology of women's needs. She asserts:

> Accumulated research evidence suggests that sentencers treat women differently from men due to chivalry, paternalism, familial protection, or enforcement of gender appropriate behaviour. But what is also clear is that sentencers operate a bifurcated system of sentencing which distinguishes between those women who conform to gender stereotypes, and those who do not. (Gelsthorpe, 2002)

This all confirms neither leniency or harshness, or bias or discrimination, but suggests that gender related factors do mediate sentencing, not in a clear cut way, but these knowledges go some distance in explaining *why* difference occurs.

Gender-wise justice

Here I return to debate, explain and illustrate in greater detail, what is meant by 'gender-wise' or gender-sensitive' justice and to raise some provocative questions about the ability and likelihood of this conceptual framework to offer insights and policy relevance. As with other pioneering avenues of policy oriented provision, this debate about doing gender-wise justice heralded from a feminist perspective which saw the criminal justice system and social controls more generally, operating different norms, constraints and expectations about offending as seen from the brief illustration offered by Eaton earlier in this chapter. In essence the criminal justice system subjected masculine and feminine activities and behaviours, such as lawbreaking, to different norms and social rules (Lees and Gregory, 1996). Such arguments fit snugly with the more general feminist critique that the nature of criminal justice processes and interventions are 'male-centric', that is, designed for, and oriented to, the needs and offending experiences of men.

Contemporary scholarship then is suggesting that gender sensitive justice might be a useful way forward and these arguments have been proffered most strongly and illustratively in relation to women-wise penology and women wise justice. Furthering these debates, the following questions are currently pertinent:

• Can gender-sensitivity be invoked to address better interplays between the criminal justice system and offenders?
• Can this be used as an aspiration to deal more effectively with ingrained expectations and norms relating to offending by men and women alike?
• Can it help ascertain more precisely why, where and when gender matters?

As scholars and practitioners work more closely hand-in-hand, the research conducted in relation to these and similar questions, is beginning to show some promising criminal justice interventions and responses to lawbreakers. At various stages of women's criminal careers it seems there are pockets of good practice where interventions and responses to female offending are appropriately matched with women's criminogenic needs and risks as well as their personal circumstances. The aspirations of for example, a feminist/socialist policy agenda would translate, through a focus on gender-wise justice, from an unfriendly criminal justice system, into a female friendly set of criminal justice interventions and a feminist jurisprudence. Carlen (2002) has argued that a criminal justice system which is responsive to consideration of women's particular needs would be more progressive. Evans and Jamieson explain that such a system,

> ...would acknowledge that offenders should be treated differently depending on their particular situation, their familial responsibilities; any special needs they might have; the circumstances of their offending; their vulnerability and their history of prior victimisation. (2008: xxiii)

They continue:

> To incorporate sensitivity to difference within sentencing and treatment policies could also help to improve conditions for men, who can be similarly vulnerable and should be similarly individually assessed.

The latter part of the quotation above suggests that the criminal justice system is as yet far from being gender-sensitive – to men. Whilst the most developed theorising and policy oriented writing and literatures remain for the most part focussed on doing gender-wise justice for female offenders, several of these authors, as in the quotation from Evans and Jameson above, also acknowledge the importance of a criminal justice response, particularly in respect of imprisonment, being appropriate to men and women, that is fully gender-appropriate (see for example Gelsthorpe and Morris, 2002). This slant on gender-wise justice draws closer attention the importance of gender-matched provisions and even more explicitly, the expectation that there is likely to be a difference between what is appropriate for males and females. However, this debate is under-developed especially with regard to men-wise or an even more accurately matched set of responses and provisions that are masculinities wise.

As in earlier chapters, since the arguments are most thoroughly developed in relation to gender-wise justice – for female offenders, this chapter has a similar bias. There is a range of examples of best practice with women offenders across various jurisdictions together with commentaries on achieving woman-centred justice in various parts of the criminal justice system. One useful edited collection published in 2007 includes a comprehensive analysis of the issues relating to work with women offenders (Sheehan et al., 2007). This book contains a range of woman-wise knowledges about female offending, criminogenic and other needs during and after sentencing. These include knowledges related to offenders' transitional pathways (McIvor) and behaviour programmes (Pearce), sentencing, (Gelsthorpe), parole and probation (Trotter), risk (Severson, Berry, Postmus), drug and alcohol problems (Malloch and Loucks), health (Wolf, Silva, Knight and Javdani) and mental health needs (Ogloff and Tye), children (Sheehan and Flynn), and further knowledges related to three key stages in the criminal justice process: sentencing, during a prison sentence and post-release. One example of a woman-centred service is the 'Time Out' Centre or 218 service in Glasgow. Discussed to by Loucks et al. (2006) and Malloch and Loucks (2007) details of this service are provided in Box 7.1.

BOX 7.1

'TIME OUT' CENTRE

218 SERVICE

218 is a joint health and voluntary sector criminal justice service commissioned by Glasgow City Council to work with women offenders. 218 aims to address the root causes of their offending. It offers women offenders in Glasgow a person centred programme of care, support and development designed to stop women's offending by tackling substance misuse, the trauma and poverty that drive it. Women break the cycle of offending which results in the 'revolving door' syndrome that characterises many of their relationships with prison.

HOW IS THIS ACHIEVED?

By providing a holistic approach to the women who use the service by dealing with all the issues that arise in relation to their offending behaviour. The service delivers this through a social and health care model. A structured programme as well as one-to-one interventions facilitates this process.

WHO IS 218 FOR?

218 is for women living in or offending in Glasgow who are caught up in the criminal justice system. They may be in prison, have had a term of imprisonment, be on a current criminal justice order, or they may be facing prosecution. 218 is there to help.

REFERRALS:

Women can access the service from court, prison, community services or as part of a court order.

Anyone who is in contact with women offenders in Glasgow can refer. Referrers must be able to take on the care manager role. 218 is part of the professional tool box of:

1. The social work department
2. Criminal justice system including:

Police
Procurator Fiscal
Sheriff Principals
Stipendiary Magistrates
Solicitors and lawyers
Primary health care professionals and agencies
Addiction services

218 is not an easy option. It is not an accommodation service neither is it a scripting only service; although accommodation and prescribing can be part of a programme.

Contact details:

218

218 Bath Street

Glasgow

Adapted from: Loucks et al., 2006; Malloch and Loucks, 2007, Turning Point

New sets of questions are being generated during experiences of working within such gender-wise frameworks. These include matters concerning amel-iorative justice and questions that demand a clear gender-responsive policy agenda including the following:

- Can and should gender duty accommodate gender diversity?
- Can criminogenic needs be matched through gender diversity?
- What are gender-tailored and gender appropriate provisions?
- Can and should the criminal justice system be gender proofed?

The above outlines what kind of agenda can be achieved if due diversity and difference are recognised throughout the criminal justice process. Whilst such gender-specific interventions are expected to reduce the need to imprison the vast majority of criminal women, the next section focuses upon the prison environment and continues with this theme of gender-specific interventions in mind.

Doing gendered justice through imprisonment

This chapter has chosen to focus on the harsh end of lawbreaking, that offend-ing and those offenders whose behaviour is at the serious end of the gravity scale and where risk is a factor concerning their offending and thus imprison-ment appears to be warranted. I have also so far offered and continue to acknowledge a gender bias that is apparent throughout the volume for the most part (and this has been explained already and in greater depth in the introductory chapter) whereby feminist inspirations are highly foregrounded and a dominant focus on female crime and victimisation overshadows male crime and victimisation. To a large degree this section and the remainder of the chapter, follows a similar pattern whereby gender-wise justice for female offenders, women-centred or woman-wise jurisprudence is uppermost. This part of the chapter achieves greater depth to the analysis that is unfolding in terms of doing gendered justice through a focus on imprisonment. It commences with a sketch of the prison estate and this is followed by a series of bullet points highlighting a contemporary profile of men's and women's imprisonment this century. Then comes a consideration of the key issues that remain pertinent in terms of the futures for women's imprisonment. Here the work of Pat Carlen (1998) is relied upon to illustrate that these issues are longstanding and outstanding in the early twenty-first century.

The prison estate and gender separation

A snapshot of the prison estate sees 14 women's prisons in England, one in Scotland and none in Wales. There are 14 juvenile units four of which are purpose built, and there are seven mother and baby units (MBUs). Establishments in the prison services female estate are as follows:

Women's prisons

- Askham Grange open prison – includes a MBU
- Bronzefield – includes a MBU
- Downview
- Drake Hall
- East Sutton Park
- Eastwood Park – includes a MBU
- Foston Hall
- Holloway – includes a MBU
- Morton Hall
- Low Newton
- New Hall – includes a MBU
- Peterborough – includes a MBU and is the only prison which holds both men and women on the same site
- Send
- Styal – includes a MBU

Of the 139 jails in England and Wales, 83 are currently overcrowded. The ten most overcrowded adult male prisons are: Leicester, Preston, Dorchester, Exeter, Swansea, Shrewsbury, Usk, Leeds, Lincoln and Lancaster. There are 11 privately run prisons in England and Wales. Nine prisons have been financed, designed, built and are run by the private sector under PFI contracts (Dovegate, Altcourse, Ashfield, Forest Bank, Lowdham Grange, Parc, Rye Hill, Bronzefield and Peterborough).

Early twenty-first-century profile of men's and women's imprisonment

Women

- The prison population grew from 1,577 in 1992 to 4, 431 in March 2007.
- In 2002 the average female population in custody was 4,299 (an increase of 173 per cent since 1992).
- In 2005, a total of 12,275 women and girls were sent to prison.
- From September 2002 to March 2007 the female population in custody grew from 4,403 to 4,431 – an increase of less than 1 per cent.
- Ethnic minority women make up 36.3 per cent of the female prison population.
- 22.3 per cent of the female prison population consists of ethnic minority British women.
- 66 per cent of women in prison have dependent children under 18.
- Every year 18,000 children's mothers are sent to prison.
- 40 per cent of women in prison have received help for mental or emotional problems in the year prior to custody.
- Self-inflicted deaths have fallen from 14 in 2003 and 13 in 2004 to four in 2005 and three in 2006.
- 16 per cent of women in prison self-harm and more than half of all recorded incidents of self-harm occur in the female estate.
- Nearly one out of every five adult women in prison is on remand.
- More than one-third of women in prison have no previous convictions.
- 30 per cent of women in prison lose their accommodation while in prison.

Men

- The average population of males in custody increased by 50 per cent from 1992 to 2002.
- From September 2002 to March 2007 the male population in custody grew by 12 per cent.
- 3 per cent of men in prison self-harm.
- There are 50 per cent fewer men in prison than women with no previous conviction.
- Just over half (55 per cent) of male prisoners described themselves as living with a partner before imprisonment.
- 59 per cent of men in prison have dependent children under 18.

  (Compiled from Bromley Briefings, 2009; Fawcett Society, 2007; Home Office, 2006, 2007; Prison Reform Trust, 2009; Women in Prison, 2007, 2009.)

In Chapter 2 I described where information can be accessibly gleaned about the prison population in the UK and provided definitions of different measures that are used to describe and illustrate the contemporary profiles of (men's and women's imprisonment). As we also saw in Chapter 2, information can be gleaned from official sources and can be adapted to suit a gender based comparison which can then be used to draw out further points of comparison and difference. What are most striking of course are the differences in overall numbers of criminal men and criminal women. This was also illustrated in Chapter 2. It is also pertinent to note that the comparison and detailed breakdown of statistics by gender of those in detention, indeed statistics generally on men and women in the whole of the criminal justice system, as in Chapter 2 and here, are often incomplete and hard to access. As noted by the Fawcett Society in 2007 referring to the then most recent statistics (2004/05) published on women and the criminal justice system, these were 'incomplete, and there are no statistics on women in the criminal justice system scheduled for publication in 2007–8' (2007: 15). Thus the series of bullet points related to men's and women's imprisonment in the early twenty-first century has not been easy to compile. However, it lends weight to the arguments offered by Pat Carlen who, for over two decades now, has argued for the abolition of women's imprisonment. She wrote in 1998 that: 'Women's imprisonment in England and Wales at the end of the twentieth century is: excessively punitive; totally inappropriate to the needs of the women being sent to prison; and ripe for abolition in its present form' (1998: viii). She continued, 'the imprisonment of women is a penal sledgehammer which batters female offenders with an incremental and gendered punishment' (1998: 145). As probably the world's most committed, prolific and respected of authors on the subject of social and criminal justice and women, crime and imprisonment in particular, Carlen's overall arguments and conclusions on the subject of women's imprisonment at the close of the twentieth century were summarised in her publication *Sledgehammer* (1998). Although going back in time to a period when Carlen was writing about up to 1998, these issues remain pertinent, outstanding and are therefore longstanding. Her key arguments are reproduced below.

BOX 7.2

WOMEN'S IMPRISONMENT AT THE MILLENNIUM

1. Women's imprisonment at the end of the twentieth century incorporates and amplifies all the anti-social modes of control that oppress women outside prison, and it does so primarily because a coherent and holistic policy on women's imprisonment has never been developed.
2. A coherent and effective policy towards women in the criminal justice and penal systems will only be developed when the following are recognised: that women's

crimes are committed in different circumstances from men's; that women's law-breaking is, on the whole, qualitatively different from men's; and that therefore the response to both men and women lawbreakers should be in part gender-specific rather than merely crime and sentence specific.

3. The main components necessary to the development of a holistic policy towards women's imprisonment from outside the prison system would be: a ministry of social and criminal justice to co-ordinate all aspects of social policy in relation to social exclusion, including the monitoring of social exclusion via potentially anti-social modes of punishment such as prison regimes falling below minimum standards of decency and humanity; a sentencing council to monitor and regulate the sentencing of women offenders; and a women's prisons unit to monitor regimes in women's prisons.

4. All proposed prison regime innovations should be gender-tested and ethnicity-tested to assess their potential for differential impact on prisoners according to gender and/or ethnic minority affiliation.

5. Different regimes for men and women (or differential modes of rule implementation) can be justified on the principle of ameliorative justice – a principle that assumes that as women (and black women in particular), because of their different social roles and relationships and other cultural difference, are likely either to suffer more pains of imprisonment than men, or to suffer in different ways, the prison authorities are justified in running different regimes for women to make up for (or ameliorate) the differential pains of imprisonment attributable to gender or ethnic difference.

6. There are three possible futures for women's imprisonment – regressive, reformist and reductionist. If women's prisons are not to deteriorate, a principled approach combining reform and reduction must be adopted. If nothing is done, women's prisons will undoubtedly deteriorate still further. If there is merely piecemeal reform, the women's prison sector will remain in its usual pendulum state of reform and regression. Only a principled reform programme, combined with a commitment both to holism and reductionism is likely to avoid the regressive tendencies to which prisons (especially at times of political and economic conservatism and the heightened social anxieties associated with rapid social change) are prone.

7. The Prison Service should no longer bear the major portion of blame for the state of women's prisons. All the requisite materials for transforming the traditional forms of women's imprisonment into a much more rarely-used and (less wasteful) women's penal confinement are already available in the skills, commitment and creativity of good staff working for the Prison Service at all levels. What is now needed is a political commitment sufficient to ensure that those skills, together with the lives of women in prison, and their families, who might benefit from them, are not further wasted.

(Pat Carlen, 1998: 10–11)

Gender-wise justice in prisons: a gendered measure of pain

Gender based knowledges have been used to argue for, and in some cases to create, women-centred prison regimes (Hannah-Moffatt, 2001) and there are promising examples of innovations and practices across the globe from Scotland to Canada. These gender-based, gender-specific interventions are founded upon gender-based knowledges that recognise the importance of gender-matched provisions and even more explicitly, the expectation that there is likely to be a difference between what is appropriate for males and females. Here we are reminded that men and women have different pathways into crime and transitions through their lives which in turn generate different criminogenic needs. Above, gender-based needs were examined with specific reference to woman-centred justice. These illustrations offer promising prospects for achieving gender-matched justice.

At this point I return to a more holistic focus on gender issues as connected to responses to lawbreakers although I retain the use of the prison experience and men's and women's experiences of 'doing time' to do so. At a basic level this section simply pulls together some points of comparison between men's and women's imprisonment. Men's, and more latterly women's imprisonment, are often referred to as in 'crisis state' due to the sometimes steady and sometimes sharp increases in the numbers imprisoned and also due to the conditions of imprisonment. At a more sophisticated and critical level this section additionally explores questions concerning gendered measures of pain. So, though the whole of the penal estate might be 'in crisis', men and women experience this sometimes similarly and sometimes qualitatively differently. This section therefore compares and contrasts men's and women's prisoners' justice through imprisonment. At another level still, through this examination of gendered experiences of penalty, these pages of this chapter simply capture and highlight some interesting comparisons and nuances. These pages also point towards a theoretically informed policy agenda that might be translated into practice in the detention setting. In this regard, the aim is to push forward our more restricted understanding of masculinities, crime, victimisation and justice, as compared with femininities, crime, victimisation and justice. This ambition is best illustrated by posing some inter-related and yet also separately challenging, questions:

1 Can justice through prioritising gender-wise imprisonment be achieved?
2 Should gender equivalence for those imprisoned give way to 'gender difference' in matters concerning imprisonment?
3 Is a gendered agenda to criminogenic need justified and achievable?
4 Can a masculinities agenda be achieved here?

The main overall purpose remains steadfast to that of understanding ways of how best to advance our prospects of administering of gender-wise justice. Should 'gender equivalence' for lawbreakers give way to a relevant difference based on gender? First however, what of the shift in rhetoric from gender **equality, equal rights** and **equal treatment** towards gender-based duty?

Gender-duty

The Commission on Women and the Criminal Justice System as well as the Equal Opportunities Commission (EOC) has harboured concerns related to male domination in the prison service and prison environment more generally, not least for reasons of unlawful discrimination and sexual harassment (Fawcett Society, 2007). Whilst the 'gender duty' element of the Equality Act 2006 brings equality of treatment in prisons up to date and in line with the rest of the public sector, in theory it also promotes and facilitates the proper accommodation of gender diversity. Whether this can reconcile several 'contradictions of women's imprisonment' (Carlen, 1998) remains unclear. For example, the contradictory (feminist) concern to recognise the specific needs of women prisoners without denying them equal education, work and leisure opportunities to male prisoners, the state's preoccupation is that men and women prisoners suffer equal penal pain and concern about the damage done to the children of mothers in prison (Carlen, 1998). Corston recently reiterated this requirement to prioritise and accelerate the implementation of the gender equality duty. As she put it, equal outcomes for men and women require different approaches, such as 'the need for a distinct approach' to transform the way services are delivered for women (Corston, 2007: 3). There are now gender specific standards for women's prisons, published in 2008 and were due for implementation in 2009. Readers should keep a critical eye on this and note where the 'gender duty' rhetoric takes experiences of imprisonment in practice.

This chapter now confronts the question of 'gender difference' for lawbreakers head-on in the context of administering justice in prisons. The following section divides the analysis up looking first at what the key issues for women in prison appear to be and then looking at key issues for men in prison in the first decade of the twenty-first century.

Experiences of male and female prisoners
Issues for women in prison

A rather lengthy list of issues that impact particularly upon women's experiences of imprisonment has become evident in academic and policy related literature for over two decades now and other evidence of the appalling conditions of imprisonment and depredations of it emerges from a range of mediated sources including life stories of those women in prison, Nacro, the Prison Reform Trust, INQUEST, charities such as Women in Prison (WIP) and many others. It is worth noting two highly significant reports published in 2007 that serve as a useful inroad into the particular issues faced by women in prison. The first, of these is the *The Corston Report – A Review of Women with Particular Vulnerabilities in the Criminal Justice System*. The report's sub-title summarises Baroness Corston's findings: 'The need for a distinct, radically different, visibly-led, strategic, proportionate, holistic, women-centre, integrated approach'. The second report is one of three published by the Fawcett Society (2004, 2006, 2007) and it is entitled *Women and Justice: Third Annual Review of the Commission on Women and the Criminal Justice System*. The purpose of the unique Commission on Women and the Criminal Justice System, which began its investigation in 2002, was to carry out a thorough examination of women's experiences in the criminal justice system, as victims, as staff and as suspects, defendants and offenders. In 2004 it was reported that;

> women face systemic discrimination and severe disadvantages from being shoe-horned into a system designed by men for men and this remains the fundamental issue, the existing prison estate is geared towards meeting the needs of men. (Fawcett, 2007: 2 and 17)

Under the subheading 'male dominated' below, a few of the knock on effects of this latter point are outlined. In 2006 the *Second Annual Review of the Commission on Women and the Criminal Justice System* (Fawcett Society) added to the recommendations of the previous report in 2004 and made 35 recommendations to the criminal justice agencies many of which were related directly to issues concerning the detention and imprisonment of women. Here I draw especially upon the third report of 2007, as well as the Corston Report (2007) as together these publications bring together a wealth of information and evidence about the experiences women in prison endure and the conditions they live in. The issues listed below draw upon evidence from these and other sources. The list of sub-headings included here does not constitute an exhaustive list of the issues that contribute towards women-unfriendly penal provisions and gender-unfriendly responses to female lawbreakers. These issues are some of the end products of the cumulative and compounded process of unwise responses to all lawbreakers.

Male dominated

The prison service is male dominated throughout in terms of those employed within it and those imprisoned within it. This raises special pains of imprisonment for female inmates who are in the minority. Several critics of the imprisonment of women have drawn attention to the particular issues raised by the malestream service and provisions (Carlen, Heidensohn); to the different constituency of women prisoners' form as compared with their male counterparts and to their different and distinctive criminogenic needs (Carlen, 1998; Gelsthorpe, 2007; Gelsthorpe and McIvor, 2007; Hedderman, 2004). Amongst the issues are the problems that arise due to there being fewer women's prisons than men's and the widespread geographical distribution of these institutions across England, Scotland (where there is only one women's prison called Cornton Vale) and Wales (where there is no facility and women find themselves imprisoned away from their home areas often in Eastwood Park in Gloucestershire or Styal in Cheshire) and Northern Ireland. This in itself creates exacerbatory problems for those women in prison who are mothers of children, wives, partners, daughters and sisters who are highly likely to have been the primary nurturer's carers and familial lynchpins in their home towns. In the Northern Ireland there are further complications to the experiences of women in prison as a result of their political imprisonment (Corcoran, 2006) and their current predicament is confounded by their being housed in men's prisons (Scraton and Moore, 2008).

Whilst having fewer people in prison is the preferred option for many commentators, and there are clearly thousands fewer women in prison than men, it does not mean better experiences and conditions for women but different logistical problems which have routinely been poorly addressed. These 4,000 or so women's family links and supportive friendships are all likely to be strained and pressured by their having longer distances to travel for visits, which incur greater expenses in terms of transport and other means of communication. It also means there are far fewer female establishments, widely dispersed geographically and fewer detention facilities. As a consequence, female establishments can be odd hybrid facilities and have historically often been adjuncts to purpose built male establishments. In 2006 two women's prisons were converted into men's to deal with the crisis in the male estate. Indeed, converting men's jails into women's prisons at short notice was a key feature of early twenty-first-century penal policy. This has added to the difficulties women face in jails where most prison officers are men and women have increasingly found themselves even more distanced from their own homes and families. In 2007, around 800 women were held over 100 miles away from their homes (Bromley Briefings, 2009). This was also occurring against a backdrop of a huge rise or 'explosion' in the number of women being sent to prison which Nacro reported as a major concern in 2002. The prison population grew from 1,577 in 1992 to 4,431 in 2007. The women's prison population more than doubled in a decade and saw a rise of 126 per cent between June 1995 and June 2005 to approximately 6 per cent of the total prison population. In

2007–8 the number of women remanded in custody in Scotland stood at 2,235, more than twice the figure for 1998–9. Furthermore, over the ten year period 1998–2008 the average daily population increased by 87 per cent with a total of 371 women in Cornton Vale prison (Bromley Briefings, 2009). Whilst overcrowding, poor conditions of imprisonment and warehousing of men in prison has been part of the twentieth- and twenty-first-century 'crisis of imprisonment' saga, women offenders have largely been overlooked.

Over the last two decades the problems faced by female prisoners has become increasingly apparent with critics explaining the rise in the female prison population in terms of a 'carceral clawback' (Carlen 1998) and 'punitive turn' towards women (Gelsthorpe, 2007). Damning probation and prison inspectorate reports acknowledge all manner of problematic issues. Her Majesty's Inspectorate of prisons has been highly critical citing social exclusion, abuse and marginalisation. The conditions of imprisonment at Bullwood Hall were reported upon in 1998 where the prison's underlying problems were documented:

> 'can be traced to the deficiencies in the overall organisation and operational management of prisons holding female offenders'. Overall the prison service was not resourced to deal with the increased numbers of women prisoners, particularly female young offenders and juveniles: 'the tide of young women being received at the prison was remorseless' and ... there was 'very little, if any, flexibility to move prisoners around the estate to tackle specific offence focussed or rehabilitative needs'.

After a woman was found hanged in HMP Durham in August 2005 the women's unit at Durham was heavily criticised in a report a year later (Women in Prison, 2007).

Multiple problems and victims prior to imprisonment

Many women offenders are simultaneously victims and in prison constitute a category of women who are vulnerable. More than half of women in prison have experienced violence in childhood or as adult victims of domestic violence often by more than one perpetrator and a third have experienced sexual abuse (Fawcett Society, 2007). Many will have had chaotic childhoods and one in four have spent time in care as a child (Corston, 2007; Women in Prison, 2009). At least 50 per cent of women in prison report being victims of childhood abuse or domestic violence and one in three have experienced sexual abuse (Women in Prison, 2007, 2009). Many of these kinds of violence and abuses have a distinct gender pattern as described in Chapter 2. The victims are female, the perpetrators male. Women bring to prison a history of personal relationship problems which have often featured in their own pathways into crime.

Substance and/or alcohol abuse contributes towards many women's multiple problems both prior to and during their imprisonment. Alcohol and/or drugs might be an exacerbating factor linked to their close personal relationships with men who are violent and abusive. They might also be part of the multiplicity of problems personally experienced by the women themselves. Two thirds (66 per cent) of sentenced women prisoners have drug problems being either drug dependent or drinking hazardous levels before custody (Gelsthorpe, 2007; Women in Prison, 2009). Women tend to have a different type of drug use from men with higher levels of hard drug use (Ministry of Justice, 2009). In my own research with women in prison, as noted in Chapter 2, the majority of the women I interviewed in prison admitted to being addicted to drugs and some to alcohol. Others doing research with offending women have found similar chaotic lifestyles featuring drug addicted women (Carlen, 1988; Cusick et al., 2004; Daly, 1994; Maher, 1997; Surrat et al., 2004; Taylor, 1993). The hardships experienced prior to (abusive and exploitative relationships) and during imprisonment, by foreign national women (many are single mothers with different cultural norms and needs) who tend to serve long sentences for importing drugs make this an especially vulnerable and needy group who experience multiple problems.

Mothers, mothers to be, children, families and homes

As seen directly above, there is a host of issues which are markedly different for women in prison as compared to men. Many of these connect to their status as carers, and mothers. Women are normally the primary carers for elderly relatives and children. Women prisoners are much more likely to be solely responsible for the care of children than men, 66 per cent of female inmates are mothers (Women in Prison, 2009) and most have children below the age of 10 (Johnston, 2001). Around 55 per cent have a child under 16, 33 per cent a child under 5 and 20 per cent are lone parents (HM Prison Service, 2009). Eighteen thousand children are separated from their mothers by imprisonment every year (Corston, 2007). At least a third of mothers are lone parents before imprisonment and black and ethnic minority women are particularly likely to be single mothers (Bromley Briefings, 2009). Whilst imprisonment is likely to lead to the breakup of the family when the mother is incarcerated this is less likely when the father is incarcerated. As noted above, 30 per cent of women in prison lose their accommodation while in prison and some would argue this is a conservative figure which is more likely to be almost 40 per cent (Women in Prison, 2007). Women prisoners are much more likely to be solely responsible for the maintenance of a home than male prisoners. Just 5 per cent of women prisoner's children remain in their own home once their mother has been sentenced (Fawcett Society, 2007). Put another way, the living arrangements of at least 8,000 children a year are affected owing to their mother's imprisonment (Gelsthorpe, 2007). Half of all women on remand receive no visits from their family (Bromley Briefings, 2009). The children of women prisoners are likely to be more adversely affected than those of imprisoned men.

In my own research, interviews were conducted with 21 women in prison, the majority were in their twenties, although their ages ranged from 17 years to 46 years. Ten of the women had a total of twenty-one children between them with two of these same women pregnant again in prison. Eleven had a partner and the remainder described themselves as single. This is not dissimilar from the national profile that shows approximately two-thirds of women in prison have dependent children and a third had a child under five. The problems of looking after women in prison are compounded if they have young children (Johnston, 2001).

In 2004, 114 babies were born to mothers in prison when there were 80 places for babies in a prison estate encompassing 17 prisons. Between April 2005 and July 2008, 283 children were born to women prisoners, a rate of almost two births a week. Between April 2008 and June 2008, 49 women in prison gave birth, a rate of nearly four a week (Bromley Briefings, 2009). Mother and Baby Units (MBUs) have been a feature of the prison estate since the 1990s. There are now seven such units with 84 places. Two of these at New Hall and Holloway keep babies with their mothers up to the age of 9 months. Five others at Bronzefield, Peterborough, Styal, Eastwood Park and Askham Grange (the latter being the only open prison with an MBU) have facilities to accommodate babies with their mothers up to the age of 18 months. The young women's unit at Rainsbrook Secure Training Centre, which opened in 2006, houses a three bed mother and baby unit for under-18s. At the time of writing there are 39 children in mother and baby units. Caddle and Crisp (date) are amongst the few who have researched this controversial subject of babies in prison.

Suicide and deaths in custody

A shockingly high death rate in all detention settings is documented, monitored and analysed by INQUEST. INQUEST is a charity that supports those bereaved in connection with contentious deaths. It has a particular focus on deaths in detention settings and draws attention to the tragic deaths of vulnerable and troubled individuals that take place in Youth Offenders' Institutions (YOIs) and Secure Training Centres (STCs) which hold children and young people.

Deaths are also monitored in adult prisons and drawing upon INQUEST case-work women's deaths in prison was the subject of a report published in 2008 (Sandler and Coles, 2008) which documents inadequate treatment and neglect of women in prison.

As noted above, self-inflicted deaths fell from 14 in 2003 and 13 in 2004 (amounting to 27 self-inflicted deaths in 2003/04) to four in 2005 and three in 2006. However, two women died in prison during the first 10 days of May 2006 (Women in Prison, 2007) and by the time of the publication of the Fawcett Report in June 2007, five women had already taken their own lives. Two women died within the first fortnight of 2007 (Women in Prison, 2007). There are particularly high levels of attempted suicide amongst female remand prisoners where nearly two thirds of the women there suffer from depression (Bromley Briefings, 2009).

Mental health

There are various ways in which mental health issues connect with both men's and women's imprisonment. Mentally disturbed offenders should normally receive care and support from health and social services rather than being imprisoned. However, many such offenders end up in prison. Women's experiences of imprisonment link closely to their own mental condition whilst other's mental health can be impacted upon negatively when their caring womenfolk are incarcerated. Women, as noted throughout this text often bear the burden of familial caring responsibilities and this often includes extremely vulnerable dependents who would suffer if their carer were incarcerated.

There are high levels of mental health problems as well as self-harming in women's prisons. As noted above, 40 per cent of women in prison have received help for a mental or emotional problem in the year prior to custody (Fawcett, 2007). Seventy per cent of women prisoners have two or more diagnosed mental health problems and of all women who are sent to prison, 37 per cent report having attempted suicide during their life (Women in Prison, 2009). Four out of five women going to Cornton Vale, the prison for women in Scotland, have mental health problems and seven out of ten disclose a history of abuse or trauma (Bromley Briefings, 2009). As noted above there are high levels of psychiatric morbidity among women prisoners and the prevalence of this is greater among women prisoners than among male prisoners as well as being far higher than levels in the general population.

As noted above, 16 per cent of women in prison self-harm and more than half of all recorded incidents of self-harm occur in the female estate. Rates of self-harm or injury rose 48 per cent between 2003 and 2007 (Women in Prison, 2009). The Fawcett Report (2007) states this is totally unacceptable and sympathetic commentators agree. In the context of women's and girl's imprisonment in Northern Ireland, Scraton and Moore have observed complacency and 'institutionalised indifference towards self harm and suicide' (2008: 32). Furthermore, in October 2009, there were 72 women serving indeterminate sentences for public protection (IPP). Nearly 80 per cent were for offences of arson, which is often an indicator of serious mental illness or self-harm (Bromley Briefings, 2009). In addition to self-harm there are other low self-esteem indicators that are significant issues for many imprisoned women including substance misuse and eating disorders (Corston, 2007).

A tidy summary of the issues faced by women in prison is not possible. Different women have different priorities of problems and this gives rise to the question of whether femininities-wise imprisonment is on the distant horizon. Nevertheless, as is evident here, there is a rather lengthy list of issues with growing robust evidence amassed over a number of years in the UK and elsewhere that testify to the special pains of imprisonment felt by women prisoners. The US Bureau of Justice statistics shows a similar picture with 'increasing numbers, increasing controversy' (Pollock, 2002) and in some jurisdictions there are particular issues faced by women on death row. The rate of imprisonment for women is increasing across western jurisdictions (England and Wales, Scotland, the United States, Australia, Canada, New Zealand) and across the world since the early 1990s there have been sharp increases in the prison population of women. Several have cogently argued that the effects of imprisonment on women are far more damaging than they are on men; indeed that prison causes damage and disruption to the lives of vulnerable women. The implications for policy are clear. As Nacro put it

> The importance of recognising that women offenders as a group have different and separate needs from those of male offenders is now being appreciated. Strategies specifically aimed at women offenders are beginning to be developed. (Nacro, 2002)

So whilst some imprisonment issues are common and qualitatively similar for men and women, and research indicates that some needs of men and women may be similar, other issues and needs are qualitatively different. The above suggests that women are especially vulnerable to the male dominated prison environment that prison impacts disproportionately harshly on many women prisoners and causes serious disruption to the lives of their children. Whilst legislative changes might herald new hopes of reconciling apparent contradictions of women's and girls' imprisonment, recent research suggests that in Mourne House, Northern Ireland this is not happening. Anticipating improvements and reforms researchers found no gender-specific strategies or policies and no gender-oriented training (Scraton and Moore, 2008).

None of the above should be taken to imply that men don't also suffer from the effects of imprisonment and that they might also suffer in ways that are peculiar to men. It is some of these issues that are considered below.

Issues for men in prison

Some of the issues that affect men's experiences of imprisonment are clearly highly similar to those of women. Whether male or female, the vast majority of those admitted to prison suffer mental health disorders and test positive for class A drugs and report a drink problem (Bromley Briefings, 2009). More than three quarters of men on remand suffer from a personality disorder. One in ten has a functional psychosis and more than half experience depression (Bromley Briefings, 2009).

Similar percentages of prisoners in the male (27 per cent) and female (28 per cent) estate are from ethnic minorities. On 30 June 2008, 22,406 prisoners were from a minority ethnic group and the aging population of men and women is growing. The number of sentenced prisoners aged 60 and over rose by 142 per cent between 1998 and 2008 (Bromley Briefings, 2009). For all of these minorities in prison there are particular criminogenic and personal needs.

Male dominated

The issue of male domination impacts rather differently upon men as compared to women. For men in prison, overcrowding and its associated problems have long been fundamental to the conditions that many incarcerated men endure in prison. For men, the degradations of imprisonment, which in the none too distant past have included and sometimes continue to include slopping out, have often been linked to over occupancy of cells and pressures on some parts of the prison establishment most notably the old, local remand centres and prisons.

As noted above, from 1992 to 2002 the average population of males in custody increased by 50 per cent. From September 2002 to March 2007 the male population in custody grew by 12 per cent. As the Ministry of Justice Prison Population and Accommodation Briefing for 9 October 2009 shows (see Chapter 2) the male prison population stood at 80,264, an increase of 1,497 on the population on the corresponding Friday 12 months previously. The problem of prison overcrowding does focus itself most predominantly upon the male estate. The ten most overcrowded prisons in England and Wales in September 2009 can be seen in Table 2.2 shown in Chapter 2 with overcrowding ranging from 153 per cent at Bedford to 179 per cent overcrowding at

Leicester (Bromley Briefings, 2009). The male population is made up of a particularly toxic mix of prisoners. As shown on Chapter 2 men are primarily detained for offences of violence against the person, drug offences, robbery, sexual offences and burglary.

Fathers, children and families

Some information on children, families and homes has been noted above in relation to women in prison and the implications of one or other of a child's parents being imprisoned are far reaching. When we add in the data on fathers in prison this is clearly evident. Seven per cent of all children in England and Wales, at some point in their school years, will experience their father's imprisonment and there are 160,000 children with a parent in prison each year (Prison Reform Trust, 2009). Twenty-five per cent of young men in YOIs are fathers (Bromley Briefings, 2009). One in four men on remand receives no visits from their family and like women, men are often held in prison over 50 miles away from their normal place of residence (Bromley Briefings, 2009).

Rape and bullying

Deaths and risks to various types of violence, including rape, abuse, bullying, assault, suicide and self-harm all occur with worrying frequency in some parts of the prison estate as do other forms of suffering including psychological distress and poor health amongst inmates (Harvey, 2007; HM Chief Inspector, 2005; Hudson, 1998; Liebling, 1994, 1999, 2007; O' Brien et al., 2001; Singleton et al., 1998). Self-harm, deaths and suicides for men in prison are considered in more detail below.

There is robust criminological knowledge on most of these matters including gender sensitive knowledge yet much of this remains suppressed, publicly ignored (Jewkes, 2005b) and immune from community safety interventions. Male rape and other experiences of mortification and brutality in men's prisons have been long been publicly known about. Although known about however, this subject has been little cared about and victimologically, men have not constituted real victims behind the closed doors of the prison. Men in prison who are subjected to aggression and violence are the victimological other twice removed (Davies, 2007a).

Self-harm

Lower incidents of self harm are recorded in the male estate than the women's. According to the Fawcett Society 3 per cent of men in prison self-harm

(Fawcett). The Prison Service states that since 2003, approximately 30 per cent of prisoners self-injured each year compared to 6 per cent of males (2009). The proportions are higher for young offenders where life inside can be very grim as exposed by Harvey (2007), see Box 7.3.

BOX 7.3

YOUNG MEN IN PRISON

YOUNG MEN IN PRISON. SURVIVING AND ADAPTING TO LIFE INSIDE

JOEL HARVEY (2007) CULLOMPTON: WILLAN

This book helps to expose what life as a prisoner is really like. As the title suggests, it sheds light on the immediate and short-term experiences of male inmates aged 18–21 who are either on remand, convicted and awaiting sentence or are sentenced at Feltham Young Offenders Institution.

The research strategy has 'an embedded multi-method approach'. Data triangulation is achieved using different sources including semi-structured interviews, quantitative measures, social network analyses and observations.

The book provides a detailed breakdown of the psychosocial state of a sample of young inmates. Chapter 2 discusses the transition phase of imprisonment and psychological distress factors on entering prison and during the first three days. Chapter 3 continues to focus on what contributes to young men's psychological distress in their first month of confinement. Chapter 4 examines sources and types of support between staff and prisoners whilst Chapter 5 explores peer interactions and social support networks in different parts of the prison. Chapter 6 looks at the methods and experiences of, as well as the protective mechanisms connected to, self-harming. Chapter 7 provides some broader theoretical conclusions on transition, adaptation and attachment.

The key concept used to understand these experiences is that of adaptation. Adaptation is defined as 'a process whereby people move towards reaching a cognitive, emotional and behavioural equilibrium' (10). Practical, social and psychological factors each contribute to this process. Practical adaptation to life inside, social interactions with staff and fellow prisoners and problem and emotion based coping factors interact with one another in a complex and dynamic rather than linear process, such that 'a certain level of psychological adaptation was needed *first* before an individual could adapt practically and socially; social and practical adaptation, in turn, assisted psychological adaptation' (58). However, there are three stages on a continuum that stretch towards a cognitive, emotional and behavioural equilibrium: first, liminality, which is an ambiguous and limbo-like phase; second, is acceptance: third equilibrium which is a stage not apparent for any of the young men before the end of first month. Moreover, once achieved, equilibrium can be lost again.

(Continued)

(Continued)

There are useful insights in respect of improving regimes; physical and social environments; staff-prisoner-peer transactions; interactions and relationships. Ways of reducing physical harms and protections from harm and victimisation and in particular the provision of support for the most vulnerable inmates who are least likely to seek support for themselves might also materialise.

Suicide and deaths in custody

As noted above in relation to women's suicides and deaths in prison, there are worryingly high death rates in all detention settings (Coles and Shaw, 2008). There have been over 30 deaths of children in detention since 1990 the majority being boys. The following which includes boys taking their own life as well as being killed is illustrative of this:

- 16-year-old Joseph Scholes hanged himself at Stoke Heath Young Offender Institution (YOI) in 2002.
- 15-year-old Gareth Myatt was killed at a secure training centre (SCT) in April 2004 following the use of restraint.
- 14-year-old Adam Rickwood was found hanged in his room at a secure training centre in August 2004.
- 15-year-old boy hanged himself at HMYOI Lancaster Farms in 2008 (Coles and Shaw, 2008: 30–1).
- More than a quarter of men on remand have attempted suicide at some stage in their life (Bromley Briefings, 2009).

As was summarised in connection with the particular issues faced by women in prison, a tidy summary of the issues faced by women and men in prison is not possible. Women have sometimes similar and sometimes different priority issues from those of men in prison. Women undergotheir own special tortures of imprisonment and men have their own sufferings that are peculiar to them. Furthermore, different women and different men have different priorities of problems and as indicated above, this gives rise to the question of whether femininities-wise imprisonment and also following the above, whether masculinities-wise imprisonment is on the distant horizon or not. Nevertheless, the pains of imprisonment are acutely felt by male and female prisoners.

The issues covered in the various sub-headings belonging to this section do not provide an exhaustive list of issues affecting men and women. There are many more. For example, learning disabilities and difficulties are rife amongst people in prison. Similar percentages of men (47 per cent) to women (50 per cent) sentenced prisoners ran away from home as a child as compared with 11 per cent of the general population. Similarly large percentages of the prison population were taken into care as a child (27 per cent), regularly truanted from school (30 per cent), were excluded from school (49 per cent of male and 33 per cent of female sentenced prisoners), had no qualifications (52 per cent of men and 71 per cent of women), were unemployed before prison (67 per cent) (Bromley Briefings, 2009). During their sentence 45 per cent of people lose contact with their families and many separate from their partners yet Home Office research has found that maintaining family contact is associated with successful resettlement. All of the above are likely to impact upon men's and women's experiences as offenders before the criminal justice system and their respective responses to imprisonment.

Other issues which have been superficially alluded to or glossed over here include those relating to security. The characteristics of the female prison population as compared with the male population are quantitatively as well as qualitatively different. This chapter and Chapter 2 have noted the difference in terms of numbers of men as compared with women in prison. It has also noted the difference in terms of offending patterns. In sum, women commit less crime, less often than men and they commit less serious crimes than men. Almost a third of women in prison have no previous convictions and the majority (64 per cent) of sentenced female prisoners are held for minor, non-violent offences. It follows that women generally pose a lower level of risk to the public, present lower risks of harm and have lower risks in terms of reoffending than men. Women serve shorter prison sentences than men and for less serious offences. Sixteen per cent of the female prison population are serving sentences of six months or under (Bromley Briefings, 2009). Levels of security in prison were put in place to stop men escaping (Corston, 2007). Women have suffered disproportionately to the risk they pose having had higher levels of security imposed upon them because of the higher threat men pose and the need to impose the same level of security upon the whole of the prison population where there has been a 'punitive turn' generally (Garland, 2001).

Summary conclusion – justice through gender

This main focus of this chapter has been to explore gender matters, and in particular how and why gender matters, in responding to (imprisoned) lawbreakers. The overall purpose has been to explain and provide an understanding of how best to advance our prospects of doing gender-wise justice. Can justice be done through gender? Should ambitions to achieve sameness or 'gender equivalence' for lawbreakers facing the criminal justice system give way to **'gender difference'** for lawbreakers (at least between men and women but perhaps between different women and different men)? Should we be searching for similarities or differences in the ways in which men and women offend; their offending patterns, their reasons for offending, the way in which they are criminalised, in remand and mode of trial, in sentencing and penal policy and, as explored in this chapter, in matters concerning imprisonment?

This chapter has examined the concept of gender-wise justice, how and why gender matters in responding to imprisoned lawbreakers, gender-based needs in the prison environment and has explored how just responses to lawbreakers might be done through gender difference.

It has furthered the arguments that suggest gender should usefully be fore-grounded. It has raised further questions about problematising and prioritising masculinity/ies to achieve a better response to male lawbreakers. If prisons were man- or, masculinity-wise would imprisonment work better for all men? What would be the gendered way forward for women? What would happen if femininity were prioritised not problematised? These latter questions fall neatly within a gendered agenda whereby a relevant 'gender-duty' can be achieved and whereby gender difference is accommodated.

The lack of strategic planning generally seen within the prison service could adopt wholesale the ambition of gender-wise justice as explored in this chapter. Many of the issues discussed above suggest men and women have particular needs and moreover, needs that can sensibly and meaningfully be separated on gender grounds. Men and women experience criminal justice agencies – police, courts, prison in different ways. We know they have been controlled and treated according to faulty perceptions and stereotypical concerns. We also know now there are distinct criminogenic and other needs at key stages of the criminal justice process; sentencing, in prison and post-release. The review of issues affecting men's and women's experiences of imprisonment provided here, together with the factual overview of imprisonment in the early twenty-first century, raises the question of whether or not more harm is being done than justice for offenders and their communities of care. Whether or not increased victimisation and injustice is being directly experienced by offenders and indi-rectly experienced by their families and friends. These are just some issues that we shall take up again in the next chapter.

STUDY QUESTIONS/ACTIVITIES

- From your reading of this chapter and your accumulated knowledge from Chapter 2 onwards, compile a list of the similarities and differences between men and women in terms of criminogenic needs.

- Does this list lend weight to a justice through gender approach whereby gender equivalence should give way to gender difference in order to achieve gender-wise justice?

SUGGESTIONS FOR FURTHER READING

Corston, J. (2007) *Corston Report.* London: Home Office.

Eaton, M. (1986) 'Magistrates talk', Chapter 6 in M. Eaton (ed.) *Justice for Women? Family, Court and Social Control.* Milton Keynes: Open University Press.

Fawcett Society (2007) *Women and Justice: Third Annual Review of the Commission on Women and the Criminal Justice System.*

Your are also encouraged to visit a range of different web based resources belonging to and linked to the Ministry of Justice, pressure groups and charitable organisations. These include:

- The Howard League for Penal Reform
- The Prison Reform Trust
- Women in Prison
- NACRO

8

GENDER AND RESPONSES TO VICTIMISATION

CONTENTS

GLOSSARY TERMS

Victim movement/Unofficial victim movement

Social justice

Witness

Victim-witness

Vulnerable victim/witnesses

Victim focussed/oriented

Social harm

Sexual violence

Secondary victimisation

Re-victimisation

Witness support

CHAPTER AIMS

- Outline the gender agenda to victimisation
- Engage in a gendered critique of responses to victimisation

- Examine how and why gender matters in responding to victimisation
- Explore victims needs through a gender lens
- Consider gender-wise and gender different responses to victimisation

Introduction

This chapter focuses on victim related public policies and social support practices. It considers political, formal and informal policies and strategies which together represent societal responses to victims of crime. An overview of gendered knowledges pertinent to the subject of responding to victimisation is offered and some key gender-related issues that emerge from the changing role of the (visible) victim in criminal justice are outlined. In looking at various state and other responses to victimisation generally and to specific victims, through a gendered lens, this chapter explores demands upon political and policy response to victims of crime. A number of questions frame the broad organising parameters for the chapter. Looking through a gendered lens these questions are:

- How appropriate are the various responses to victimisation?
- What has been the political and policy response to specific victims of crime?
- How do victims experience criminal justice systems and processes?

These are questions which build upon gendered knowledges of the past and present yet offer forward looking options for a gender agenda for responding to victimisation in the future.

The scope of the examination of gender and responses to victimisation undertaken here is wide. It is not restricted to an analysis of the state response, nor does it confine itself to victims who have been criminally victimised. It adopts an inclusive definition of the term victim, one that includes those who feel victimised or who have experienced something similar to a crime or where something akin to victimisation has taken place. It includes therefore injustices and social harms as well as criminal victimisation. The chapter therefore moves between a narrow field of vision where a detailed examination of a selection of the key gender related issues are examined to a much more open and expansive territory in the search for a gender driven agenda in support of all victims.

The substantive part of this chapter commences by contextualising responses to victimisation generally. It then moves on to consider victim specific provisions and gendered assistance and support. The chapter makes use of some well established victimological concepts namely secondary and repeat victimisation and the notion of invisible victims in order to illustrate and exemplify a changing range of responses to victims of crime and other victims of social harm. The chapter focuses in some detail on the question of compensating victims of violent crime as a way of illustrating how through lessons from gendered knowledges, improved support might be achieved. The final part of the chapter remarks upon victims, gender and unmet needs before putting a spotlight on women victims and support for men as victims and gender-sensitive support for all victims.

Key questions for Chapter 8

- How can gender-based insights help shape what counts as victimisation?
- Does a victim's gender influence the way in which they are supported and responded to by state, voluntary and other bodies as well as significant others?
- Are there gendered expectations connected to the victim's role in criminal justice and does gender mediate victim's ability to access services and find support?
- How, why, when and should, gender matter most in responding to victimisation?
- How does a gendered lens shed light on the extent and seriousness of 'secondary victimisation'?
- How can gender sensitive research: help challenge domain assumptions on the victim of crime; reveal gender-relevant and sensitive victims needs; inform the political and policy agenda for supporting and assisting victims in their recoveries?

Contextualising responses to victimisation

The social and historical context of responses to victimisation generally are necessarily but rather sketchily summarised here. Several have argued that the criminal justice system has largely overlooked the victim of crime and given little attention to any rights or needs that they may have (Doak, 2007; Goodey, 2005; Hall, 2009; Rock, 2004; Spalek, 2006). Given the functional importance of victims of crime to the operation of the criminal justice process in England and Wales, it is interesting to note that by 1945 there was no real sense in which victims of crime had a voice in the political or policy arenas. It was during the post-war period, and the construction of the welfare state that mechanisms were introduced allowing for the introduction of the criminal injuries scheme and over the last four decades numerous developments relating to victims; policy and practice have taken place.

In international jurisdictions, too, the official **victim movement** gathered pace over the last 50 years (Mawby, 2007). A range of supportive provisions and victim assistance schemes can now be identified in most social systems across the world, all of which will have differing relationships to their respective criminal justice systems. Some victim services are at arm's length or fully independent of the government and criminal justice system; some are provided under statute, and others by voluntary groups and charities. Many have had a positive impact, especially in terms of changing the status of the victim. Some measures have significantly improved victims' experiences in connection with help in their efforts to achieve **social justice**. Other developments have been helpful in meeting victims' needs in the short, medium and longer term.

In England and Wales, there has been a proliferation of different victimagogic activities. For a detailed list of landmarks connected to the support and assistance of victims generally in the UK 1964–2006 see Davies, (2007c: 259–61). The impetus for putting the victim 'centre stage' gained particular momentum in the 1990s after the publication of the ambitiously sub-titled *Victims Charter: A Statement of the Rights of Victims of Crime* (Home Office, 1990). New Labour claims to have placed victims at the heart of the criminal justice system in the wake of a period of increased marketisation of public services. Certainly in recent years, better support and assistance for victims of crime has featured on the official policy making agenda and improving the experiences of victims, **witnesses** and **victim-witnesses** is a key priority for the UK Ministry of Justice.

Continuing in the contextual vein, forms of support for victims are variegated and heterogeneous and cover a wide range of provisions, services and schemes. Some support comes in the form of practical advice and help such as 'target hardening' assistance; other support might be information and communication about compensation and insurance for example. Some supportive groups' core ideology prioritises personal support through 'good neighbour' and 'listening ear' approaches. Some stretch to counselling whilst others prioritise advocacy, explore victim entitlements and are more legalistic in nature than others. Some groups and organisations offer a variety of types of support and focus on short to medium term help and support whilst others focus on medium to long term support and campaigning.

In sum, support can come in a variety of forms and a generic description of 'support' is increasingly difficult to pin down. Support can also be provided by various people, groups and via a range of institutions. It can be informal, local and highly personal through to formal, distanced, professional and official. Some receive support from multiple sources whilst others receive none.

There is more political attention focussed on the victim in criminal justice matters than ever before and the roles of the state and voluntary sectors have both been instrumental in this repositioning of the victim. The proliferation of different victimagogic activities has resulted in a blurring of the boundaries of whether help and assistance is public, private or voluntary and whether it is offered as of right. Moreover, victimological scholarship has critiqued the apparent politicisation of some service provision (Phipps, 1988). Similarly it has challenged the extent to which support and assistance, in the form of initiatives, schemes, special measures, pilot and proper, and in particular the court experience of **vulnerable victims**, have been introduced as efficiency measures and for value for money (National Audit Office, 2002) reasons. Whether or not some administrative changes to the process of achieving justice are in the interests of the victim first and foremost, i.e. **victim focussed/oriented**, or in the interests of the smooth running of the criminal justice system, i.e. system focussed, remains a contested issue. Thus since the 1990s, findings from survey research, as well as information derived from monitoring of services, attests to the continued difficulties in matching victims' needs with support and services. These are issues that are grappled with throughout the ensuing pages of this chapter.

At the more focussed level of analysis adopted in this chapter, it is clear that gender-related issues in connection to criminal victimisation have been deeply neglected. The social relations of gender in the study of victims have slowly been exposed during the last 30 to 40 years or so. In the UK, one of the ways in which this can be appreciated is in the context of feminism and voluntarism. The confluence of feminism and voluntarism was particularly evident in the 1970s when feminist pressure groups together with pro-victim lobbies within the voluntary sector shared a number of ideals and principles. Against this backdrop, political impetus was provided to the victim movement producing practical responses to the problems faced by women victims of violent crime and abuse. This in turn provided much space for empirical research, methodological and epistemological developments. It is evident then, that certain time periods correspond with specific social groups achieving victimological recognition. Prior to the emergence of the second wave of feminism and the impact of the women's movement in the 1970s in the US and the UK, for example, there was virtually no acknowledgment of women's victimisation in the home. This movement was enormously influential in the development of services for victims of rape, sexual assault and domestic violence. Legislative landmarks and statutory obligations featured in both the 1970s and 2000s relating to domestic violence. Some of these issues are explored in further detail later in this chapter.

Gendered knowledges on supporting victims

One useful starting point in a chapter such as this is to ask what can be learnt from the history of academic research. Lessons about women in the comparatively youthful sub-discipline of victimology are inextricably linked to the feminist critique of criminology which Carol Smart contributed to significantly in the 1970s (Smart, 1976). Pioneering work followed throughout the 1980s that had major implications in terms of understanding women as victims of violent and sexual abuse from men (see, for example, Dobash and Dobash, 1979; Hanmer and Maynard, 1987; Hanmer and Saunders, 1984; Kelly and Radford, 1987; Stanko, 1985, 1987, 1988). These are issues which were summarised in Chapter 7. Interestingly, this era of work from the late twentieth century also shaped our understanding of criminal women so that their criminality has been for the most part explained in terms of social and economic marginalisation and dependency. This has tended to have the effect of reframing criminal women as suffering at the expense of unjust, sexist, bias and patriarchal systems and institutions (see, for example, Carlen, 1983, 1985, 1988; Carlen and Worrall, 1987; Eaton, 1986; Gelsthorpe, 1989). In turn this has encouraged views of women as vulnerable and socially and culturally victimised. Thus criminal women might have been thoroughly explained as gendered economic victims (see Carlen, 1983, 1985, 1988; Carlen and Worrall, 1987) but not as comprehensively as perpetrators of economic crimes (Davies, 2003a, 2003b) and as perpetrators of violent interpersonal crimes (Batchelor et al., 2001). All of this has had an impact upon how a gendered perspective has been incorporated in the victimological enterprise, upon how victim research has been conducted and upon the choice of subject matter under investigation. Some of the consequences of this have already been explored in this book and more are considered below.

In terms of the history of gendered victim policies, the second wave of feminism and the political climate in the United States and later in the United Kingdom fuelled radical and left unrest and activism. Radical and left realist scholarship was simultaneously published throughout the 1970s, and 1980s reflecting criminologically this changing political mood. This body of work challenged and critiqued conventional and traditional definitions of the crime problem and positivistic victimology. It also offered an alternative focus for the crime problem focussing upon the role of the state and also upon women's roles and experiences in public and private and in some cases a strong policy agenda for placing previously marginalised victims more firmly centre stage. This critique and the aims to incorporate lessons of feminism, together with political activities and initiatives, many of which were specifically aimed at providing a response to women's unmet needs, resulted in the formation of Women's Aid and Refuge provisions for female victims only of domestic abuse, rape crisis interventions and later rape suites, all of which helped put women victims at least, firmly onto the victimological agenda. In addition to a whole variety of different social harms and injustices being highlighted, for a select few scholars, (see, for example, Pearce and Snider, 1995; Perry and Dawson, 1985; Szyockyi and Fox, 1996) their victims became worthy of studyworthy and are only sometimes included within the parameters of victimological study.

The purpose of the above was to provide an insight into how questions tangentially related to gender issues have shaped the way in which the study of the victims of crime, victimology, has developed. What then are some of the key features of the positivist legacy and how has a gendered perspective been incorporated into the victimological enterprise and with what consequences? Within the study of victimology, women were originally characterised as victim-prone, indeed women were generally ascribed ideal victim status (Christie, 1984). Some women however, for example, those with risky lifestyles such as prostitution, were seen as culpable and precipitous victims. Women and particularly female children have tended to be visible and classically fragile and vulnerable as well as often passive victims (but only in public spaces and places). There has also been a presumption that all the victims of **sexual violence** are female and all perpetrators of it male and that all women are always fearful. However, the impact of feminism has been significant in that it has become clearer for example that the private domain of the home as a potential site for criminal victimisation has been obscured as have the risks of serious violence and abuse, particularly to those women and children who spend much of their time at home with those they know and often trust the most.

In contrast to this characterisation of women, are men. However, women are not simply the opposite of men; they are hierarchically subordinated to men. In particular white, heterosexual, men were the norm or 'gold standard' against whom the (irrational, fearful, victim prone female) victim could be compared. Men have been largely exempt from victim status and have been rendered invisible as victims. Men and males are fearless criminals and there has been a presumption that all the perpetrators of sexual violence are male and all its victims, female. These caricatures, myths and stereotypes, have persisted despite clear and consistent evidence from survey based research such as the British Crime Survey dating back to the early 1980s, that men are most at risk from almost all forms of criminal victimisation but especially those serious forms of inter-personal violence that occur on the streets and in public spaces. However whilst risky places have been defined as those where men are, men have apparently refused to be fearful. And despite the feminist exposé of serious forms of victimisation behind closed doors, risky places tend not to be defined as those where women are frequently harmed. This has impacted upon the pace, standard, quality and availability of support for victims and upon appropriately gendered provisions in particular. Clearly this is not a neat and tidy picture where lessons for the gendering of victimology are concerned. Our victimological knowledge is fraught with stubborn and persistent legacies, unequal equations and paradoxes and contradictory sets of discourses. Unacknowledged experiences of victimisations remain in hidden locations and settings and between individuals and groups.

Changing responses to visible victims

Provided above is a solid range of knowledges on gender and victimisation which builds especially upon the themes identified in Chapters 2 and 6. However, these knowledges are incomplete and there are huge gaps in our knowledge as also already noted, especially surrounding men's victimisation. Our limited toolkit of research techniques and methodological inadequacies are part of the barrier to achieving more gender relevant information and detail. Elsewhere I have suggested that the nature and extent of our knowledge of women as victims is generally hampered by 'invisibility' (Davies, 2007b: 170). Victims of crime who appear in the public arena usually do so because they have made contact with the police. These individuals form a small minority of the total number of crime victims. They are a selective category of crime victim. They have become separated from other victims because they have become part of the political and policy process and thus, in relative terms, are who we might call 'visible victims'. These are the men and women whose victimisations have come to official notice and some will present themselves or be pulled into the criminal justice system to seek or help 'do justice'. Their experiences are officially known about and they may qualify for assistance and support. This highly selective group of victims have had a changing role in criminal justice and incrementally their status has been moved towards centre stage. This known about select group are those discussed first below.

Secondary victimisation

For the small minority of crime victims who do seek, or help achieve justice through the criminal justice process many will find this experience unproblematic. For others, there may be unintended consequences which may incur further harm. Sometimes the hard to achieve balance between doing justice/ achieving victimisation, of promoting harmony/incurring harm leaves the victim/witness feeling further victimised.

In terms of **secondary victimisation** let us focus for a moment on the serious crime of rape. In the UK, the adversarial system assumes innocence on the part of the accused and attempts to establish guilt. In terms of police interviewing of rape victims Roger Graef's pioneering 'fly on the wall' *Police* film in 1982 of Thames Valley Police's treatment of women reporting rape was to force a change in police practice as their treatment of women accusing men of rape was so poor. Whilst the adversarial system might appear to encourage this form of **re-victimisation** as might hostile police interrogations and similar approaches from defence solicitors and barristers and members of the judiciary whose questioning, cross-examinations and judgements assume the woman is an 'alleged victim', this does not excuse the treatment some women have been subjected to by the various institutions and personnel of the criminal justice system. Thus the reality of the rape victim's experience in court is that she has often been forced to relive her ordeal in the witness box – almost as if to prove her innocence in the crime (see, for example, *R v Allen 1982, Ipswich Rape Case*) or as in 1989 the judge has suggested that she precipitated or caused her rape. Following immediate survival of the ordeal of rape and other forms of sexual victimisation women and girls must cope with the longer-term aftermath and this includes psychological damage and the suffering of stigmatisation and ostracisation (Human Rights Watch, 2004).

Repeat victimisation

This concept has already been explained and exemplified and is similar to that of serial victimisation. In terms of repeat victimisations, for women domestic violence is the most obvious example and for female (and male) children, sexual abuse. In relation to domestic violence, victim blaming is also in evidence. Gilchrist and Blisset (2002) report victims being blamed for the perpetrator's behaviour in the courts. Additionally for women, multiple or serial victimisation is often a feature of their overall experience of victimisation.

Invisible victims

Some victims remain either relatively or completely invisible to officialdom. Evidence suggests, for example, that victims of mundane and less serious crimes including car crime victims are excluded and their needs are consequently rendered invisible yet some victims of such crimes have very distinct needs which an objective Victim Support policy to supporting victims in a climate of stretched and finite resources renders invisible (Simmonds, forthcoming). Others draw attention to the neglect of the needs of white-collar and corporate crime victims (Croall, 2007b; Spalek and King, 1999; Tombs and Whyte, 2007), honour-based violence (Tucker, 2009) and despite the revelation of domestic violence as a seriously violent crime there is still ignorance here too, rendering many seriously victimised women and children's needs obscured. Thus there is still a serious under counting of the 'true' extent of this crime type. Victims of some of these, but more routinely other types of crimes where the victim mirrors the ideal victim, are more readily ascribed victim status. In significant numbers then, victims' needs are not satisfactorily met or are not met at all. The latter group could be a shockingly large number depending on how victimisation is defined and depending also upon if you are male or female.

Compensating victims of violent crime

The case of England and Wales – Criminal Injuries Compensation (CIC)

The CIC scheme originated in the 1960s and has since developed into a statutory, tariff-based scheme for victims of unlawful violence. There are several contentious issues related to this form of state compensation. First, there are fundamental concerns connected to key features of the scheme's 'rules' and 'eligibility' criteria. Controversial issues surrounding inappropriate applicant biography and undeserving victims as distinct from blameless and innocent victim applicants are reviewed below.

When is a victim not a victim?

According to the rules and eligibility criteria of the CICS there are victims who deserve (but do not have a right to) compensation and there are others who can be discriminated against and can be denied their application for a variety of reasons. Some of these reasons are related to keeping down the cost of the scheme (the minimum and maximum payments and the tariff-based approach). Some appear to punish and even re-victimise those who have failed to help in the criminal justice process and there are other 'disentitling conditions' (Goodey, 2005). Boxes 8.1 and 8.2 summarise the assumptions that are implicit within the CICS and illustrate when a victim is not a victim. The historically complex rules and eligibility criteria continue to apply in the twenty-first century and also to result in uneven distribution of criminal injuries compensation awards. Victims of non-violent crimes are excluded. Those with greater financial resources as well as those with very little economic power continue to be subjected to penalty point deductions. Those whose injuries do not meet the lower threshold of compensation are excluded entirely from the scheme. The scheme has been modified at irregular intervals since its creation, indeed award limits have remained under regular review.

BOX 8.1

WHEN A VICTIM IS NOT A VICTIM

Not a (CICS deserving) victim if: undeserving, blameworthy, culpable, partially responsible, contributed to the attack/injury, participated in the violence, attracted, incited, precipitated the injury/assault/attack, engaged in provocative behaviour, was the author of own misfortune, brought the suffering on own head, fraudulent, the criminal is likely to gain from any payment, in collusion with the offender, no violence was involved, behaviour before, during or after the criminal event disqualifies you, involved in excessive risk taking, failed to co-operate with the authorities, refused to make a statement, refused to go to court, refused or failed to report the incident without delay, refused or failed to co-operate with the police, refused to go on an identity parade, the injuries were received abroad, do not qualify for the minimum award, have previous (unspent) criminal convictions, suffered from a minor assault, suffered from the effects of a non-violent crime, don't know of the existence of the CICS.

BOX 8.2

REAL VICTIMS

Is a (CICS) victim, if blameless, innocent, not at fault, a worthy victim (i.e. are an ideal victim), suffering physical and mental pain and injury due to criminal injury (a physical attack, an assault, wounding or sexual attack, arson, death of a close relative) but are none of the above in Box 8.1.

These explicit and implicit value judgements about 'undeserving' and 'real' victims and the CICS emphasis on moral desert as opposed to moral complicity (Rock, 2004) can be made sense of victimologically. Walklate (2007a) has explained how these types of assumptions about victims within victimology are connected to 'domain assumptions'. Domain assumptions are deep seated, taken for granted beliefs that originated in the work of the founders of the discipline in the 1940s and 1950s. Von Hentig and Mendelsohn, for example, were concerned with identifying and differentiating victim characteristics and non-victim characteristics and with identifying victim traits in their attempt to understand the victim-offender relationship. The typologies they developed have been clearly described in the context of positivist victimology elsewhere (see Davies et al., 2003, 2007; Mawby and Walklate, 1994) and the world views dominating victimological discourse have proved a powerful legacy in subsequent research practices and theorising as well as in policy and practice responses connected to crime victims. Notions of victim proneness, victim precipitation, victim-blaming and victim provocation, victim culpability and lifestyle as compared and contrasted with the ideal victim are deeply embedded in the dominant ways of thinking about victimhood and the study of victims more generally. Such assumptions are core to the discipline of victimology and fit very comfortably alongside the domain assumptions that are at the heart of positivist criminology.

Gendered unfairness

For feminist commentators in particular the legacy of the above domain assumptions, with their stereotypical implications about women and men as variously deserving/undeserving victims and their inherent sexism is particularly evident and troublesome. Victimologically, feminism provoked a very strong and effective grass roots response to female victims and survivors of domestic violence and sexual abuse from men. Rock and Reeves have suggested that responses other than the state compensation scheme and responses that seek to address needs that are met other than financially have been under resourced by the state as they are in the shadow of the state compensation scheme – the main plank of the government's response to victims of crime (Rock, 1990). The needs of women and children and the victimisation that occurs behind the closed and private doors of the home, for example, have been neglected by the state. It is largely the feminist movement and the voluntary sector that has attempted to breach this gap. Even where the state has recognised domestic violence there have been special eligibility considerations attached (the CICS was only amended in 1979, 15 years after the scheme was first created to allow victims of violence within the family to make claims, the lower threshold for CICS awards was generally £400 in 1983 but was £500 in the case of intra-family violence). These are just some of the real implications and consequences of the domain assumption problems which reflect a very male view of who real victims are and where victimisation happens and this centring of maleness is also reflected in terms of who gets what help. The rules and eligibility criteria for state criminal injuries compensation therefore tend to embody the fundamental assumptions of the discipline of victimology.

The Criminal Injuries Compensation Scheme (2001) booklet listed and described 14 injuries in its tariff (Home Office, 2001: 25). It also listed 25 levels of compensation (Home Office, 2001: 21). If we were to read the tariff from a feminist perspective and ask what it does for women, the tariff notes 'loss of foetus' – level 10, standard amount £5,500. Other women-specific victimisations in the tariff fall within the three categories: 'Physical abuse of adults', 'Sexual assault/abuse of victims (if not already compensated as a child)' and 'Sexual assault /abuse – additional awards'. However, many of the harms and hazards and criminal victimisations including the compounded nature of women's victimisations fail to be adequately recognised in these formulaic, strict and rigid categorisations of harms. The Criminal Injuries Compensation Scheme not only fails to deal with the gendered nature of victimisation as it specifically harms and impacts upon women but also in some instances it may inflict further harm, adding insult to injury and re-victimisation (Dignan, 2005).

Victims and others have occasionally been outspoken about the impact of the scheme. Experiences of secondary victimisation over and above their efforts to survive extremely violent types of criminal victimisation are additionally injurious to women victims in particular.

One rape victim expressed concern about the surreal procedures followed by the CICA which she claims has delayed her recovery (Davies, 2007b; Stewart, 2004). Merlyn Nuttall wrote a book length account of her abduction, violent sexual assault and attempted murder where she especially focuses on 'the absurdity of the legislation the Home Secretary had tried to introduce in April 1994 to compensate the victims of violent crime' (1998: 114). She refers to the proposals for a tariff-based scheme where for example rape would attract the same set amount of £7,500 compensation as a broken kneecap. Whilst her claim eventually came under the 'old scheme' which was not restricted to a low level tariff rate, she described 'her scheme' as 'sluggish, inordinately bureaucratic and out of touch' (1998: 114). In a Foreword to the same book, Helena Kennedy also focuses in detail upon the issue of criminal injuries compensation. Fuelled by her own frustrations at the tariff-based scheme at the time, Kennedy was already sympathetic towards rape victim claimants due to the extra difficulties placed in their way by the regulations, the refusal of the CICB to accept psychological suffering as evidence in support of applications and the lack of generosity to such victims. Kennedy offered to argue the case before the CICB and became heavily involved in the criminal injuries application. Several short extracts from the Foreword illustrate the variety of problems and concerns concerning the ethos, rationale, administration and impact of the CICS and the CICB. The following extracts and phrases describe how Helena Kennedy and Merlyn Nuttall experienced the processing of this case:

> I was conscious of the appalling irony: that Merlyn's efforts towards her own recovery would reduce the award she would finally receive. (Kennedy xvi)

Rape victim applicants 'cannot claim the cost of legal representation' and there is often 'a delay in getting the case heard which is enormously stressful. The process can also be quite humiliating ...' (Kennedy xiii).

The procedures and discretionary rules of the CICB have been called into question on several occasions (see Davies, 2007; Mullin, 1995; Stewart, 2004; WAR, 1998) and are variously described by Nuttall, Kennedy and others as 'absurd', 'byzantine and unsympathetic', 'peculiar', 'demanding', 'inadequate', 'stressful', 'humiliating', 'variable', 'morally prejudiced', 'sexist' and 'deeply unjust'.

Compensating victims of crime generally can be gender unjust as seen above. However, it can also disadvantage less affluent victims as also noted above. Croall (2007a) has also suggested it can discriminate against the rich and the poor.

Victimisation and need: state and voluntary services

Gender and unmet needs

The notion of victims needs is a controversial one (Zedner, 2003) yet useful in terms of searching for ways in which improved support might be achieved for victims. If we combine useful feminist inspirations and knowledges about what victims want with the concept of victims' needs, lessons for the policy agenda are signposted. Victims' needs ought to be paramount on such agendas. Defining victims' needs remains a challenge (Walklate, 2007b) and perhaps the most insightful way of unpacking victims needs is to do so through a gender-sensitive approach. However, the challenges are slightly broader than those of identifying appropriate gender-sensitive needs. There is also the problem of matching victims' needs with support and services.

This complex area, in particular the sub-section pertaining to how victims' needs can be met by the state, has been of academic interest for some time (see Maguire and Pointing, 1988; Miers, 1978, 1983). There are several ways of gauging whether or not victims harbour any unmet needs. Two inter-related research questions are relevant. One relates to the match between victims and support and the second relates to the match between needs and services:

1 The match between victims and support – are those victims who are in most need more likely than other victims to be contacted /offered services?
2 The match between needs and services – do those who are helped receive the sort of assistance they require? (Mawby, 2001)

Evaluations are now commonplace and research has shown how successful Victim Support (VS) are in terms of meeting the needs of crime victims, contacting those most in need and providing an adequate service. Evidence of good matching seems to point in the right direction but there is room for a better fit.

Amongst the clientele that do avail themselves of support from under-resourced services, there are unmet needs and further obstacles to full service provision (Corbett and Maguire, 1988). From the outset, helping certain groups of victims was a priority for VS and the elderly as well as victims of burglary received a disproportionate amount of attention (Mawby and Walklate, 1994). Despite efforts to widen their service to victims of more serious crimes, including victims of serious sexual assault, rape, hate crimes as well as bereaved families, Victim Support's work in Britain – unlike victim assistance programmes across the world – tends still to be dominated by its support to victims of burglary.

An evaluation of VS in Plymouth (Simmonds and Mawby, 2000) found that victims of crime contacted in person by a VS volunteer were very positive about the service they received. However, this research also uncovered two points worth further scrutiny. First, those victims who were not contacted by VS registered levels of need and a desire for support that exceeded those anticipated and second, those who were visited but not seen clearly rated priority, but were less satisfied with the contact they received than those successfully visited or sent a letter. Evidence from the 2002/2003 British Crime Survey (Ringham and Salisbury, 2004) shows that between 2001 and 2003 awareness of Victim Support has been constant with 80 per cent of adults having heard of the organisation. Men and women under the age of 30 and over 59 as well as Asian and Black respondents and those on small incomes were far less likely to have heard of Victim Support.

In Maguire and Kynch's (2000) extracted findings from the 1998 British Crime Survey they report that there is high public awareness and knowledge of Victim Support. They also report findings on differential satisfaction levels according to the nature and timeliness of the contact and type of support. Well over 70 per cent of victims wanting practical help and advice did not receive it. They also report the emotional impact of crime and needs tends to be greater among some victim populations many of which have low contact rates with Victim Support. Victims of burglary want security advice. Victims of violence and threats want protection, so needs vary between offence types. Many victims receive help from unofficial volunteers such as family and friends but almost 40 per cent expressed needs which were not met from any source.

Another important survey, the first of its kind in England and Wales, was the Witness Satisfaction Survey 2000 which looked at levels of satisfaction of witnesses with their treatment by the police, the CPS/prosecution lawyers, defence lawyers, court staff, judges and magistrates, Victim Support and the Witness Service. It found that 76 per cent of prosecution and defence witnesses were satisfied with their overall experience (Whitehead, 2001). Furthermore, the individual agencies of the criminal justice system that rely heavily on volunteers had high satisfaction levels; for example, the Witness Service scored 97 per cent and judges and magistrates 95 per cent. At the time that the survey was conducted, however, the Witness Service did not yet cover all criminal courts and half of all witnesses had no contact and over a third (37 per cent) of these witnesses would have liked some support. There were significant levels of dissatisfaction linked to four key areas: intimidation, information, facilities and waiting times.

Whilst there is evidence to suggest Victim Support is reaching out to victims of all types of crime, yet targeting resources at those most in need, there are low contact rates for some groups which report higher levels of impact and needs. Similarly within the narrower remit of the Witness Satisfaction Survey, findings suggest satisfaction levels are high, yet there are areas where improvements could lessen the irritations and anxieties experienced by some witnesses. Whilst there are special measures to assist child witnesses to give best evidence, the Department of Health involvement on the Victims' Advisory Panel has recently suggested that children's needs for support are not currently being met (Victims' Advisory Panel, 2004). Such findings, that dig deeper into the mismatch of service provision, suggest there are issues to be confronted regarding service provision and what victims *want* and what victims *need*. This connects to a broader debate concerning whether 'need' is an objective, universal and fixed measure or a relative and dynamic measure (Simmonds, forthcoming). Victims' needs might be linked to a complex variety and combination of impacts that include anger, shock, fear, upset, difficulty sleeping and financial distress, all of which implies a relative set of needs. The question for the service then becomes, 'How does a service such as VS, with objective need at its core, meet the relative needs of its potential pool of service users? Can men's and women's needs, whether or not they are black or white, old or young, rich or poor, be met?

There are then still gaps in service provision arising from a non-existent or poor match between victims and support and/or between needs and services, all giving rise to unmet needs. Some victims' experiences fall totally outside the governing and community safety agenda. Some victims falling outside this agenda might find support from voluntary organisations. However, there are still voids and gaps especially where the nature of the victimisation is diffuse or relatively hidden as it takes place in private and invisible locations (Davies, 2008). For certain victims then there is no provision.

Quantitative statistical data collected by national, regional and local level service providers all points towards the strain upon many provisions provided in the main from the voluntary sector. Qualitative research findings also evidence pressures upon overstretched services and point towards the under resourcing of provisions all impacting upon the availability and level of support offered to victims. In addition to the evidence reported upon above, further research has uncovered some interesting anomalies between urban and rural demands upon services provided under the umbrella of Women's Aid

(Davies et al., 2001). This points towards the unmet needs of many hundreds of women and children across the country every year. Collectively, the needs of women and children in violent households and relationships amount to an enormous and continuing demand for refuge places and other services. There is a clear requirement to develop services in line with those needs. There is no doubt that women's immediate and longer-term needs in surviving domestic violence include the need for safe accommodation and refuge provision and these women's needs are surely amongst the more serious unmet needs amongst victim groups.

Women victims and support

As defendants and victims in contact with the CJS and facing the courts particularly, women present a complex paradox for feminists. Conforming to the ideal-type female victim presents a double-bind situation. There are positive connotations attached to the term victim as well as negative ones. Women can capitalise on these associations or they can suffer from them. In terms of surviving victimisation, on the one hand it is important for women not to accept, collude and through surrendering to victimhood help reproduce gendered stereotypes of femininity and prescriptive notions of the victim. On the other hand if women fail to toe the line of doing-gender through victimisation in traditional CJS settings, if we appear to resist and deny labels and victimhood as understood by the justice system that judges us all, we risk incurring harsher treatment and penalties, and in the case of victims, 'rough justice' (Davies, 2007c).

Goodey has stated 'feminist research has done much to recast women outside the stereotype of passive victims of male aggression' (Goodey, 2005:83). Perhaps most significantly, by employing the concept of 'survivor' rather than 'victim', (London Rape Crisis Centre, 1984) feminists have made several points about the gendered nature of victimisation and its impact and about gender issues in the recovery from victimisation. The concept of 'survivor' challenges the ideologies and scientific basis of positivist victimologies and in particular public perceptions of the female victim as passive, helpless, powerless, blameworthy or victim-prone. Moreover, the concept carries with it positive connotations and is forward looking. It signifies all of the negotiating and coping strategies women employ to live their daily lives.

There are several levels from which we might approach the problem of women suffering harms and victimisations and several ways of tackling the problems they face in the short, medium and longer terms. At one level, women actively and routinely engage with and negotiate their own safety in their daily social life (Stanko, 1990b). At another level they have recourse to formal and legal remedies and there are also provisions and assistance generally available to crime victims, and some very specifically offered to women, from the voluntary sector.

The level at which women 'do it for themselves' by negotiating their own safety in 'climates of unsafety' (Stanko) and minimising risks, connects strongly to the ways in which victimisation, fear and risk are mediated through gender. As was shown in Chapter 6 virtually all of 'fear of crime' surveys and other research on fearfulness has found women as more fearful of crime and victimisation than men. We are reminded also, that women can be fearless (Gilchrist et al., 1998), protect themselves in all manner of rational ways from domestic violence and also contribute towards the stabilising of relationships in communities (Mooney, 2000; Pearce and Stanko, 2000; Walklate, 2004a). The latter point leads us to consider also, how women often form a reserve army for helping protect others. The ways in which women help others and other women in particular is evident in the voluntary and mutual support work which they have previously carried out under the auspices of Women's Aid.

The first UK Women's Aid refuge was set up in Chiswick, London in 1972. Since then the charity has co-ordinated and supported local projects, provided over 500 refuges, run helplines and outreach services. Women and children's use of all the services offered by Women's Aid grew year on year with demand outstripping available provision producing significant strains on services at local levels and being particularly felt in rural areas (see Davies, 2007b).

Support for men as victims

Whilst men as victims of crime can avail themselves of the help and support offered by Victim and **Witness Support** services and as victims of violent crime they can apply for criminal injuries compensation, in terms of masculinities and the policy agenda there is very little to review to date. Having unearthed statistical data attesting to men's experiences of domestic violence, the Home Office, in 2003 asked for views on how it should respond to the needs of this population (Home Office, 2003). Few programmes or initiatives can be listed as appropriately gendered provisions for supporting men as victims in the same way as they can for women. However, conversely, a number of programmes can be cited as suitable for men only as perpetrators and these are often connected to anger management and zero-tolerance towards domestic violence suffered by women.

Whilst there are few provisions in existence specifically for men as victims we do have some interesting flags as to how men cope with and respond to their own victimisation, especially sexual victimisation. This information derives from a very small number of research studies and surveys that have been conducted with men to develop our understanding of men, masculinities and sexual victimisation. As we saw in Chapter 6, the stigma of male rape for example and men's fears that they will be considered to be homosexual and myths regarding the promiscuity of gay men all conspire to prevent both heterosexual and gay men from reporting their experiences to the police (Gregory and Lees, 1999) and to men's needs in respect of personal and violent crime and victimisation remaining undisclosed.

For a succinct review of three studies that take a different position of these issues and represent three quite different ways of researching them see Walklate, 2007a where she outlines the work conducted by Coxell et al. (1999), Allen (2002) and Jefferson (1996). Her developing argument suggests that men as victims are constrained by hegemonic masculinity. Walklate (2007a) and Allen (2002) both draw attention to the 'uneasy relationship that exists between being male and being a victim' and Walklate continues 'In making sense of the tensions in this relationship, men who experience victimisation clearly engage in different kinds of coping to keep their sense of themselves as men whole' (Walklate, 2007a: 159). Sexual crimes pose a huge challenge to men's sense of their masculinity (Allen, 2002). This is interesting in that this is not something that women subject themselves to and this is an instance where difference in terms of victims' need and in terms of responding supportively is implied.

Knowledges about crime, criminal justice and victimisation from a masculinities perspective are growing apace. Yet as Groombridge points out we are slow in recognising that men have problems (Groombridge, 2001: 261). Appreciating masculinities knowledges in devising well matched support and services for victims of violent crime includes an understanding of at the very least, masculinities (Connell, 1995; Goodey, 1997; Jewkes, 2005b; Messerschmidt, 1993, 1997; Stanko and Hobdell, 1993), 'hegemonic masculinities' (Hearn, 2004; Jefferson, 2001) and hierarchies of masculinities. By allowing such knowledges to come to the fore, the victim policy agenda can respond to those victimisations that might be a product of masculinity. These gendered perspectives have the potential for making sense of some of the less visible forms of victimisation that some men experience and suffer from, especially those forms of victimisation that are perpetrated by other men.

As noted earlier in this chapter, compensatory arrangements for victims of crime can be unjust on gender grounds at the same time as discriminating against the rich and the poor. Thus not everything may be explicable by reference to gender. When is gender the key variable over and above class? An additional point highlighted by Walklate, about Jefferson's (1996) works on Mike Tyson the boxer, is that toughness and masculinity was intertwined with Tyson also being black and from a deprived neighbourhood. Thus not everything in this instance may be explicable by reference to masculinity. When is masculinity the key variable over and above race and/or class?

Summary conclusion – gender-sensitive support for all victims

This chapter has explored tangible ways of improving support for victims of crime with a specific focus on victims of violent crime. It has problematised who gets to be and counts as a victim of crime, what support constitutes, where support might come from and what types of services and assistance exists. It has recognised the blurred and fuzzy boundaries of where victim care comes from. It has stressed that locations for victimisation as well as support are important and that the timing is also significant. The useful influence of feminist inspirations in the policy domain has been demonstrated leading to the conclusion that gendered knowledges should be drawn upon to improve support and services for all victims. Thus in the context of responses to victimisation, 'gender' matters. Irrespective of what 'sector' – public, private or voluntary – support for victims comes from, gendered knowledges are applicable and relevant.

This conclusion makes three further substantive conclusions. First, is the insistence that victim's needs are paramount. Victim's needs are neither simple, nor necessarily singular. Different victims have different needs and some victims will be affected by crime more than others within the same offence type. Not all victims of violent crime will have a need for support and/or assistance but there is a distinct message arising from this chapter that the policy agenda should take seriously the need for defining victim's needs and there are pointers as to how this can effectively be achieved.

Second, the notion of sameness and difference has been a thread throughout this chapter as it was in the previous chapter. In Chapter 7 conclusions suggested that just responses to lawbreakers might be achieved through gender difference. In concluding this chapter also, it is clear that understanding gender differences and similarities in responses to victimisation is important. This chapter can similarly propose an item for the gender agenda whereby responses to victimisation and supportive provisions for victims accommodate a relevant 'gender-duty' as well as gender difference.

Third, this chapter has resurrected the knotty and complex question of how and when does gender matter. Moreover, when does gender matter more than race, or class or in combination with other intersections that make our individual biographies? When might other variables be more or less important?

This is one of the key questions that are addressed in the next and final chapter which pulls together this and an additional range of continuity threads which run throughout the pages of this book so far.

STUDY QUESTIONS/ACTIVITIES

- Look again at Boxes 8.1 and 8.2. What stereotypes are reproduced, myths perpetuated and patterns of victimisation are reinforced by such policies? Remind yourself of the themes and case studies that were explored in Chapters 2 and 3 when you do this activity.
- Trace the potential for secondary victimisation to occur throughout a victim's journey through from their direct experience of victimisation to an appearance as a victim-witness in court.

SUGGESTIONS FOR FURTHER READING

Cape, E. (2004) (ed.) contains a number of excellent, short pieces on UK government policy towards victims, including several by academic lawyers concerned about the drift of government policy.

Rock, P. (2004) *Constructing Victims' Rights*. Rock's insider research gave him a unique position to explain where victim policy comes from.

9

CHALLENGES TO UNDERSTANDING CRIME AND VICTIMISATION THROUGH GENDER

Introduction

The purpose of this final and concluding chapter is to do three things. First, it serves as a reminder of the overall vision of the book. In doing this it restates the key foci that form the spinal threads. Second, it consolidates the arguments arising from these established focal points by drawing together the prominent arguments derived from each substantive chapter. This involves revisiting your thoughts on the seven provocative and highly controversial questions, as posed in Chapter 1.Third, this final chapter concludes on the major questions, 'Does gender deserve priority?' 'Why does gender matter and when and where should it be privileged?' – whilst looking forward to where to go from here. The chapter will achieve these three things by considering them under three appropriate headings:

- Crime, victimisation and gender
- Researching gender
- Safety and justice

Thus this final chapter reviews the arguments that have been gathering momentum throughout the remainder of the book in respect of research, theory and policy issues connected to the study of gender, crime and victimisation. It reviews how crime is gendered, and how gender impacts upon and influences the experiences and recovery from crime and victimisation in society. It underscores a number of themes, most notably the legacies of 'domain' assumptions within criminology and similar 'world views' in the study of crime victims and the impact and influence of feminisms and developments around masculinities.

Crime, victimisation and gender

What has formed the overall vision of this book? What have been the key foci that form the backbone to it? Here, in summary form only, we remind ourselves and reinforce the main thrust of the book: to contribute further to knowledge on gender, crime and victimisation in society.

First the overall vision has been steered by a concern to bring together the concepts of gender, crime and victimisation and to firmly establish the overall relevance, significance and lasting importance of the gender/crime/victimisation nexus, thus to justify the very title of the book itself. Introduced in the early pages of Chapter 1, the pivot of gender, crime and victimisation was set out. From there on, the book has set out on a promise to draw upon, combine, compare and contrast perspectives and knowledges from criminology with those from its sub-discipline victimology with a view to opening up research, theory and policy agendas to new and developing ideas and possibilities. The book consequently set itself two major frames of reference which were: gender and crime and gender and victimisation. The book has developed both of these themes, occasionally in parallel and often in tandem, giving both roughly equal weight and attention throughout. This has produced a number of problematics and sometimes rather confusing outcomes in terms of research findings, theorising and policy considerations. Many of these have been left hanging in the air awaiting further debate and rigorous scholarly attention. However, what has been firmly established is that:

- Crime is a gendered phenomenon – it occurs on a gendered terrain.
- Gender impacts upon and influences experiences and recovery from victimisation, which is also gendered.
- We understand more about crime and risks to criminal victimisation as well as other forms of harm that are not criminalised through gendered learning.
- We also understand more about crime and victimisation in society generally having appreciated the influence of feminism and feminist perspectives, including all varieties of feminisms.

- We further understand that the problem of crime and victimisation is not simply a problem of men but a problem of masculinity.
- Further still, we understand through emerging developments and new theorising within masculinity, the significance of masculinities.

This is by no means an exhaustive list of the certainties we know about gender, crime and victimisation. It is however, a convincing set of points which justify giving each and every topic which comprise the contents of the chapters within this book a detailed scrutiny in order to provoke further stimulating developments within the disciplines of criminology and victimology.

Researching gender

One of the main features running throughout this book has been its sustained use of past, present and emerging research developments and findings. How this research has been conducted and what has influenced this research has also been highlighted. Research that has a specific gender agenda to it has been exemplified and sources of information from which gendered data can be derived have also featured. How to conduct gender sensitive research has been considered as well as gaps in our research inquiries and our research capabilities. In this part of the concluding chapter we consolidate the arguments arising from the established focal points noted in the section above by drawing together the spinal arguments derived from the various research knowledges and wisdoms that have been covered in each substantive chapter. In this section you are also asked to revisit your thoughts on the seven provocative and highly controversial research questions, as posed in Chapter 1.

Let us now draw together some of the key signals emerging from these gendered themes. What stand out as the major and minor themes, continuities and what are the discontinuities? For the most part these are summarised and concluded upon at the end of each substantive chapter. Some conclusions however, have necessarily been reserved for the section after this to consider.

Chapter 2 clearly argued for these to be mapped out as accurately as possible and understood in all of their nuanced detail. In doing so it began to illustrate how a gendered scrutiny of crime and victimisation might be activated. Primarily it concerned itself with two important questions about gender, crime and victimisation – the *levels* of crime and victimisation and the *correlates* of crime and victimisation. It also summarised our gendered knowledges as amassed from a variety of different sources of information. This chapter, in problematising some of the issues around finding information on levels and correlates of crime and victimisation, made it clear there are two further important questions – the *dynamics* of crime and victimisation and – the *consequences* of criminal victimisation. These were the signals from Chapter 1. All four of these questions have a strong bearing on the extent of our knowledges; they demand and merit our research attention.

Chapter 3 covered much ground and made use of a number of case studies to exemplify its main messages. The notion of crime, criminals and victims being cultural constructions was explored and some of the key concepts that are signalled as useful include, folk devils, ideal type constructions, gender-blindness and bias, stereotypes, newsworthiness and news values as well as signal crimes.

To re-cap, crime news reporting and media images have an overall tendency to reproduce myths and stereotypes of crime, criminals and victims and we are provided with an exaggerated picture of violence in society and sex crimes. This has very real consequences and impacts upon some individuals and some groups and in some places. Some are labelled and ostracised as part of a problem category whilst others are left well alone. Similarly with victims, some are singled out and supported; some types of crime are tackled whilst others have been left out in the cold, as invisible, their victims neglected. All of this was related to the notion of media partiality and at this point the continued significance of well worn concepts such as stereotypes were deemed lastingly useful. More recent theoretical constructs now used in criminology were also noted as having explanatory value – the notion of 'otherness' for example, in particular, the '*Criminal Other*' – for women criminals, and the '*Victimological Other*' – for men as victims.

This chapter also, through its focus on case study critique addressed the underlying concern that gender is not always and necessarily the main or only structural variable contributing to people's experiences of crime and victimisation and to how they are represented in the media. Finally also, the nexus between structural and locational bias was shown as worthy of research attention. The principles that underpinned the critical approach adopted for the deconstruction of media representations of crime and victimisation as adopted and encouraged in Chapter 3 are ones that were further developed in the following chapter.

Chapter 4 operated on two levels relating to both ideology and practice. The chapter was organised around two substantive areas. First of all it focussed on the 'legacy of positivism', demonstrating the positivist underpinnings to criminological and victimological knowledges and outlining feminisms as they relate to the sub-discipline of victimology. As in other chapters this one too provided examples of feminist knowledges and showed how these can be used to critique other (mediated) knowledges and public policy in order to develop further feminist inspired research methodologies and gendered theoretical knowledge. The case study approach adopted throughout this book was exploited to the full in this chapter which then went on to consider a detailed research case study: 'Interviewing Female Offenders'. The chapter thus wedded together the two substantive areas in order to especially exemplify and illustrate gender and other connected and salient 'power' issues connected to doing criminological and victimological research – themes that were introduced in Chapters 2 and 3.

Chapters 5 and 6 variously explored feminist and other gendered perspectives in historical and contemporary understandings of the crime problem and of criminal victimisation. The first of these two chapters entitled 'Explaining and Theorising Offending and Victimisation', outlined the origins and development of feminist influences in criminology and albeit to a lesser extent, in victimology too. It considered the backdrop to the feminist critique of criminology, the critique itself and its lasting impact which are worth drawing attention to once again in terms of pioneering work and feminist influences in understanding crime and victimisation. In doing all of this, Chapter 5 focussed on a range of key social and criminological concepts including those of patriarchy, marginalisation, oppression, social control, male domination and sexism. All of these, like the well worn concept of a 'stereotype' noted above, remain useful and instructive. They also serve as a reminder of the significant interplays between crime, victimisation and not only gender, but also, the broader social division nexus – how class/race/age/gender variously combine as 'intersecting, interlocking and contingent' (Daly, 1997: 33).

However, more significantly in terms of future research agendas to gender, crime and victimisation, several messages are derived from the primary case study flagged in Chapter 1 'Women and Crime for Economic Gain'. This case study, as in the previous chapter, is heavily drawn upon in Chapter 5 too. Hence the subject of women's criminality formed a substantial part of this chapter and there was a detailed examination of the way in which women's criminality has been explored criminologically. One key signal in terms of future research agendas arising from this case study concerns theoretical scholarship on women and crime for economic gain and the 'explanatory gap' in the literature. One particular question springs to mind: 'Do women only ever steel for need or can women be greedy?' This question in itself generates a further reminder of the need to explore more sophisticated and nuanced sets of knowledges about the relevance of gender-class intersections. The research questions around the committing of economic crime however have even broader implications for gendered scholarship which can be summed up by the question: 'Can crime by men and women be similarly explained or do men's crimes warrant a different explanation from women's?' As stressed, this was particularly examined with regard to economic crime but could be widened to include violent, sexual and abuse crimes. Furthermore it could be applied also to different locations for crime where different modus operandi are used by different classes of offenders who have different types of opportunities open to them, as considered in

Chapter 3. In addition to these gendered research questions, the messages that I would put foremost from this particular Chapter (5) comprise of a tripartite set of challenges which are consistent with the themes of both this chapter and the book as a whole. These are equivalent to the throwing down of a 'gendered gauntlet' that seeks to: reconcile women offenders as victims with women as real offenders and they were expressed in terms of acknowledging three caveats. These three caveats were fully explained in Chapter 5 and you are reminded of the subsequent direction that was offered to you there for exploring these issues in more detail.

As a brief memory jogger, but at risk of oversimplification, these caveats relate to

- whether or not women criminals are more 'sinned against than sinning';
- whether or not men are always to be cast as offenders and women as victims;
- whether or not we will ever take women seriously as real offenders.

There are then specific challenges in respect of the 'woman question' as well as the 'man question'.

As already noted, Chapters 5 and 6 were both devoted to exploring feminist and other gendered perspectives in historical and contemporary understandings of the crime problem and of criminal victimisation. Where Chapter 5 focussed for the most part on the committing of crime, and on victims to a lesser extent, Chapter 6 homed in on some highly significant (mainly) victimological concerns – fear, risk and vulnerability. Both chapters have a strong theoretical strand to them and are concerned with past, current and the further shaping and influencing of, criminological and victimological debates with a view to provoking new theorising. Specific challenges in respect of the 'woman question' as well as the 'man question' are derived from issues surrounding fear, risk and vulnerability as well as from the host of issues to be taken forward on the gendered research agenda from the accompanying Chapter 5. Chapter 6 has outlined key predictors and gendered findings from the researching fear project whilst engaging in a feminist inspired and critical critique of survey derived knowledges on fear, risk and vulnerability. From this, and for the future, we identify young men's apparent 'gung-ho' attitude to violent attacks on them, their apparent lack of fearfulness, women's heightened fears of criminal victimisation as all requiring more detailed research in order to understand better the mis-match, indeed near inverse relationship, between some of these attitudes and fears and the likelihood of them coming to fruition.

Chapter 7 considered the criminal justice system's responses to lawbreakers through a gendered lens. Following the case study approach consistently adopted throughout the book, and in order to achieve depth of analysis it focussed upon one specific criminal justice context: women and men's (but predominantly women's) imprisonment. The chapter looked historically and contemporarily at how the processes of crime and victimisation are gendered and thus how gender matters in respect of formal and informal social controls and responses to both offenders and victims. The chapter debated responses to these lawbreakers within the conceptual framework of gender-wise justice, specifically addressing how and why gender matters in responding to imprisoned lawbreakers through a focus on gender-based needs in the prison environment.

As such this particular chapter considered whether or not justice can be done through gender and under this ambit it considered 'gender equivalence' in opposition to 'gender difference' for lawbreakers. That is, should sameness and the drive towards equality of treatment between men and women give way to diversity between men and women? By implication, the chapter therefore raised questions about problematising and prioritising masculinity/ies to achieve a better response to male lawbreakers. If prisons were man- or, masculinity-wise would imprisonment work better for all men? What of the gendered way forward for women? What if femininity were prioritised not problematised? Would a movement from one to the other on all the above counts avoid 'rough justice' for more and achieve greater justice for all? Furthermore, the above provokes the question of whether or not, difference be applicable to different women and to different men? Ultimately, when broadened out, should we be searching for similarities or differences in the ways in which men and women as offenders and victims are responded to in order to maximise justice? These latter questions fall neatly within a gendered agenda for research whereby a relevant 'gender-duty' might be achieved incorporating gender difference.

Chapter 8 essentially engaged in a critical review in a search for gender-sensitive support for all victims. It did so through an exploration of tangible ways of improving support for victims of crime with a specific focus on victims of violent crime. It problematised who gets to be and counts as a victim of crime, what constitutes support, where support might come from and what types of services and assistance exist. It recognised the blurred and fuzzy boundaries of where victim care comes from. It stressed that locations for victimisation as well as support are important and that the timing is also significant. The useful influence of feminist inspirations in the policy domain was demonstrated leading to the conclusion that gendered knowledges should be drawn upon to improve support and services for all victims. Thus in the context of responses to victimisation, 'gender' matters. Irrespective of what 'sector' – public, private or voluntary, support for victims comes from, gendered knowledges are applicable and relevant.

It concluded with three clear messages that gender sensitive research should take account of. First, is the insistence that the policy agenda should take seriously victim's needs and ensure they are paramount. However, different victims have different needs and some victims will be affected by crime more than others within the same offence type. This leads us to the second message which harks back to the notion of sameness and difference – a thread which recurred throughout Chapters 7 and 8. On this point, the message emanating from Chapter 7 was that just responses to lawbreakers might be achieved through 'relevant gender difference'. In relation to victims also, the starting point should therefore be 'different victims'. In connection with both of these chapters, in research terms the theoretical construct 'doing-gender' (West and Zimmerman, 1987; West and Fenstermaker 1995) and variations on this theme might be revisited as a useful theoretical referent. Whilst arguments put forward in Chapter 5 show reservations about pursuing 'doing-gender' for understanding girls' and women's offending, in respect of men and boys it seems there is still mileage to be gained from further exploiting this. It may be that, in light of very recent developments around masculinities the new understanding of 'difference' where crime is viewed as an ongoing interactional accomplishment (Lorber, 1994; Simpson and Elis, 1996; West and Fenstermaker; 1995, West and Zimmerman, 1987) might hold more hope for understanding both crime and victimisation. Third, Chapter 8, like Chapter 7, proposed an item for the gendered agenda for research whereby responses to victimisation and supportive provisions for victims accommodate a relevant 'gender-duty' as well as gender difference.

So, there are whole array of issues that can be drawn together from the substantive topics covered in each chapter of this book. Here these arguments have largely been consolidated but some have been pushed further forward and made even more provocative to ensure they remain on the gendered agenda for research on crime and victimisation. There are some matters that have arisen directly from all of the chapters that have not yet been fully revisited or concluded upon however. One matter concerns methodology and criminologists and victimologists toolkits. In 1994 Mawby and Walklate, writing in support of critical victimology, insisted upon the use of a plurality of research methods and Walklate has since explained the need to go beyond the victimisation survey so that research involves comparison, triangulation of method and longitudinal studies (Walklate, 2003). According to the research reviewed throughout the research for this book, it would seem that there remains a tendency to rely upon and revert to traditional tools of our trades which often cause us to slip back into positivist modes of data collection and empirical work. This point is as much about our research capacity and our imaginative modes of inquiry as it is about our research imaginations. In one respect this is a call for a reinvention of our research designs and a plea for scholars to elucidate more transparently their research methodologies and to publicly reflect upon their methodological choices.

The other matter that is yet to be concluded upon is the question that is likely to provoke the most consternation about the title and content of the book more generally – the question of gender salience and whether or not gender deserves priority. Chapters 7 and 8 have moved us much closer to a firm conclusion on this and the conclusions on this major question – why gender – will shortly be considered in the next section safety and justice.

As a final plea in this section on researching gender as linked to crime and victimisation in society, the seven provocative and highly controversial research questions, as posed in Chapter 1 are reproduced below. Having read the pages in between, you are encouraged to revisit your thoughts on these and compare them with your earlier notes. To entice you into following up some of these themes and others your may have latched onto, you may also wish to add your own 'big' and subsidiary questions to the list as a bump start or foil to your own gender sensitive research inquiries.

1   Are there any well established gender patterns to crime and victimisation in society which cannot be challenges by new knowledges?
2   What do media and cultural constructions of crime, criminals and victims look like and how can they be challenged?
3   How might you do gender sensitive research in your chosen area of study?
4   If crime is gendered, can it be universally explained?
5   Why might an understanding of 'victimological otherness', combined with an understanding of masculinities, be useful in tackling crime and victimisation in society?
6   Are lawbreakers victims or offenders?
7   Whose responsibility is it to tackle victimisation and who can help and how in the recovery from it?

Safety and justice

As promised above, this final and concluding chapter and section will conclude on the major questions. Does gender deserve priority? Why does gender matter and when and where should it be privileged? It does so in a broader context and that is of safety and justice and thus the chapter hopes to close on a forward looking note which clearly demarcates where to go from here – not exclusively in terms of a gender agenda fit for crime and victimisation but in terms of an agenda, thoroughly informed by gender sensitivity which is safe and just. In many ways, the safety and justice context is self explanatory. Surely the aim of most scholars of criminology and victimology is to make the societies we live in safer, more secure and crime and victimisation free at the same time as making them more equitable, fair and just societies? As a concluding section to this book, this sub-title is a fitting one for additional reasons. As you may have noticed directly above, in relation to Chapters 7 and 8 in particular, a discourse touching upon matters concerning *justice* is discernable. This denotes not only criminal justice but justice for all whether as an offender or a victim, whether criminally victimised or otherwise harmed, injured, abused, unfairly or unjustly treated. Indeed this theme was evident throughout the preceding chapters too, if not articulated as a specific discourse. In these and other chapters some parts of the discussions hinged more closely around matters concerning *safety* and these were marked out by their preoccupation with risk, fear, vulnerability, protection. Thus safety and justice have been undulating themes throughout the full measure of the book and merit bringing together under this final section.

Ultimately then, why gender? Sceptics and critics of this book will pounce on why this particular socio-structural component from amongst several other potentially equally or more significant and weighty ones has been plucked out and foregrounded. As I have acknowledged above, this is the question that is likely to provoke the most consternation about the title and content of the book more generally. From those with a research interest in race – the question will remain why is this a minor and not equal or more significant linchpin for considering crime and victimisation? For those with keener concern about class, economic marginalisation and power, there will be similar questions. These questions will no doubt be repeated for those who have other priorities such as age. The critique will no doubt be exaggerated by those who feel we should be able to articulate better the relevance of gender/class intersections or to expand further, the gender/class/race/age intersectionalities to crime and victimisation.

Let us recall how this was broached in the introduction to this book where a specific section focussed exclusively upon what was called the 'Crime, victimisation/social division nexus'. Some considerable space was devoted to this and it is acknowledged and re-iterated here that social divisions as categories are not static, but rather dynamic and change over time, space and place; they are situated historically, culturally, economically, and politically. From the outset and throughout I have been at pains to stress formulations that emphasise this for example 'doing-gender' (West and Zimmerman, 1987; West and Fenstermaker 1995), later extended to 'doing race' and 'class' (Daly, 1993, 1997). In the introductory chapter also, 'gender salience' featured and clearly as noted there, others have focussed exclusively on the 'risk/gender nexus' (see Hannah-Moffatt and O'Malley, 2007: 7). They, others and I have expressed concerns about whether it is ever or always the key variable.

In respect of the research example threaded throughout this text as the main case study, what are the conclusions? In terms of women's motivations for committing economic crime, need and/or greed were certainly inextricably bound to these women's structural and cultural positions *as women*. Yet as women they were inextricably pushed and pulled into economic crimes whether they were initially, overridingly or sometimes comitted for either need or greed. It did not seem possible to sufficiently disentangle their womanhood from their economic power. Gender unquestionably matters, but it does not appear in this case study, and therefore my own conclusions adhere closely to these findings, that it should always and necessarily take precedence over economic and class explanations. What about the arguments developed throughout the remainder of the chapters in this book? Certainly, in examining the concept of gender-wise justice, Chapter 7 specifically addressed the questions of how and why gender matters in responding to imprisoned lawbreakers, and furthered the arguments that suggest gender should usefully be foregrounded. Even more explicitly, Chapter 8 resurrected the questions of how and when gender matters, when gender matters more than race, or class or in combination with other intersections that make our individual biographies. The main case study is unable to offer any original sentiments on race as the sample included only white women. Data and other literature however, would tend to point in the direction of race being highly significant in terms of women's and young men's offending.

Hoping not to close this discussion on a weak note, it is perhaps worth noting how cumbersome and difficult it is to comment upon such complex matrices and interplays without having a rich source of data on which to draw. This point makes the case for further qualitative, in-depth and ethnographic studies in order to capture these intricate interlocking social structural elements as they cut across and along individuals' lives and biographies.

Summary conclusion

This book has covered much ground. It has faced up to a range of historical and contemporary debates and controversies all connected to gender, crime and victimisation in society. It has picked out which of these have been most illuminating, which are likely to endure and which are worth devoting much more imaginative research efforts and time to if, as criminologists and victimologists, we are interested in knowing more about the subject matters that come within our areas of interest and expertise, and if we are motivated to keep our disciplines alive, making impacts upon the real world.

In Chapter 5 a quotation was used to stimulate thoughts around the discipline's ability to carry forward some of the theoretical and policy challenges laid out there. By now you will have been thinking more about the progressive potential that is open to us within the confines of our, albeit interdisciplinary, discipline. Is criminology interdisciplinary enough? Can it adapt and adopt some of the areas that call out for us to engage in our research agendas? Are we sufficiently well equipped to move beyond and outside some of our more comfortable zones of study and subject matters for inquiry? As tutors we are quick to criticise students who wish to study the psychological minds of serial killers and psychopaths. We point out the dearth of research in areas of financial and economic crime, health and safety crimes and child abuse yet we leave this research in the hands and power of others. These are all criminologically and victimologically areas that are worthy of our attention and all of these areas have been touched upon within the covers of this book. If our discipline recoils from the challenges such as those set out in Chapter 5 which are re-iterated above, perhaps these challenges are beyond the ability of criminology to cope with and sadly then 'criminology becomes largely a redundant source of explanation' (Wykes and Welsh, 2009: 65). Let us not let this happen.

Glossary

Agency – the capacity of individuals to act in a self-directed independent manner out of a sense of moral choice and purposeful free will, as opposed to being 'acted upon' by social forces and structures.

Androgynous – to be androgynous is for individuals to be non-gendered beings, for example a structurally neutral image of a crime victim. There is some degree of similarity if something is described as **gender-free** or **gender-neutral** or an individual or group is described as **androgynous** or gender-blind. Each of these concepts are closely related and associated although each concept can be slightly differentiated from one another.

Classicism – an approach to the study of crime and victimisation which is underpinned by the notion of rational action and free will. Classicist penal beliefs maintain that offenders should be held responsible for their actions as they contend people can choose how to act. Often classicism is pitched against positivism which has a more determined view on behaviour.

Crime survey – see **Victim survey**.

Crime victim – see **Victim**.

Criminological other – a phrase used to denote who is normally included and excluded from criminological attention.

Critical criminology/victimology – an approach to the study of criminology/victimology which examines deficiencies and closures in existing theories and concepts, and which highlights the social origins and the influence of these theories and concepts.

Cultural construction – the social context and processes by which discourses are produced and sustained and that helps shape and create events and phenomena within any culture.

Discrimination – the unfavourable treatment based on a person's colour, age, sexuality, gender or ethnicity.

Doing-difference – a theoretical construct formulated in the wake of 'Doing-gender' by West and Fenstermaker (1995) and adopted by others to denote how crime and other actions can be used to make distinctions from peers and social groups and to accomplish gender difference.

Doing-gender – a theoretical construct as formulated by West and colleagues (1987). The construct postulates that crime is one of the resources that men and boys in particular call upon to accomplish and demonstrate their masculinity.

Double jeopardy – used in the context of the criminal justice process and imprisonment, Pat Carlen for example, has argued that women in particular find themselves doubly judged and doubly punished.

Equality, equal rights, equal treatment – typifies a liberal feminist approach to achieving criminal and social justice. Equality based arguments are based on the belief that parity is seen to result from men and women for example being treated the same. This is one approach to avoiding discrimination. It is close to a human rights concern that all people should be treated equally, fairly and with dignity.

Fear of crime – the fear of crime is generally taken to mean the personal worry about becoming a crime victim, although it is sometimes seen more vaguely as the feeling of being unsafe, particularly when out alone at night (Ditton, 2008).

Feminisation of poverty – is where women represent an increasing proportion of the poor in society.

Feminism/feminist – at a simple definitional level feminism is concerned with advocating the claims of women and with bringing a woman centred or 'feminist' perspective or theory to analyses. There are many different varieties of feminisms however, and these are more fully explored in Chapter 4.

Folk devil – a term predominantly associated with Cohen (1972) to describe a person or group defined as a threat to societal values and interests.

Gender – is a cultural concept relating to the social classification of masculine and feminine. It refers to the differences between men and women that are socially constructed and sustained.

Gender bias – the antithesis to the associated concepts **gender freedom** and **gender-neutrality**. Where **gender-bias** or **gender specificity** is evident such work or research will have a very definite and specific masculinist or feminist orientation to it.

Gender-blind – sometimes also referred to as **gender myopia**, normally refers to a failure to consider gender at all and so the masculine and feminine as well as males and females are indistinguishable.

Gender differences – these have their source in culture; they are socially generated and sustained by socialisation. Gender difference is not pre-given by nature.

Gender freedom – see **gender-neutral**.

Gender myopia – see **gender-blind**.

Gender neutral – or **gender free** – suggests that the woman and /or man question is absent. In the context of policy issues gender-neutrality is wedded to equality based feminist positions whilst gender-specific policy advocates are wedded to difference based perspectives (Daly, 1994). Philosophically feminists have warned that gender-neutrality simply equates to the male standard where masculinity and maleness are the yardsticks against which judgements of others are made (MacKinnon, 1987).

Gender ratio and gender gap – these concepts are related but have different applications. In simple terms the gender ratio refers to the large quantitative disparity between the volumes of crime committed by men (large) as compared with the volume done by women (small). The gender gap is sometimes referred to as this difference but it also connotes differences in quality and type of offending as well as motivations for offending.

Gender/social roles – these are roles played by men and women that are socially generated or learnt and are therefore culturally constructed.

Gender-wise/gender-sensitive justice – this refers to measures usually meted out to offenders that meet their needs as gendered beings. It is another way of alluding to gender relevant, or gender appropriate interventions.

Hegemonic masculinity – 'hegemony' was a term coined by Antonio Grasci (1978). Hegemonic masculinity is a particular and often damaging and criminal way of achieving, or 'doing', manhood.

Hierarchy of victimisation – the terms 'primary', 'secondary' and 'tertiary' victimisation suggest that there is a hierarchy in the level of suffering experienced. However, it cannot be assumed that secondary and tertiary victims necessarily suffer fewer traumas than primary victims, since secondary and tertiary victims can also face significant physical, psychological and emotional pain (Spalek, 2006: 13).

Ideal type – Weber's term for an abstract statement or model of the essential characteristics of any social phenomenon.

Ideal victim – a term coined by Christie (1986) to denote the major attributes belonging to a model crime victim. It is a contentious term suggesting an 'innocent', victim where the victim has played no part in their own victimisation and fits the stereotyped view of a victim who deserves help. Such victims need to be vulnerable, innocent, incapable of fighting back against an assailant, previously unacquainted with the offender, with no offending history of their own. Often this term is linked to an 'ideal offender' who is evil and entirely blameworthy.

Indirect victimisation – the impact that crime has on those not directly involved in the particular event concerned.

Masculine, masculinity, masculinities – pertaining to men and the socially constructed and ascribed attributes belonging to manhood and being a man. Masculinities denote the diversity of masculine subjectivity.

News values – the professional, yet informal, codes used in the selection, construction and presentation of news stories. The more news values a potential story conforms to, the more newsworthy it is perceived to be.

Newsworthiness – a term that encapsulates the perceived 'public appeal' or 'public interest' of any potential news story – determined by **news values**.

Positivism – an approach to the study of crime and victimisation which is underpinned by the empirical methods of the natural sciences. Scientific inquiry relies on observations and measurements of social reality (crime and victimisation in society) and deductive reasoning to explain, theorise, predict and test hypotheses.

Primary victimisation – the impact of crime on the victim.

Primary victims – those who experience harm directly.

Qualitative research – research that investigates aspects of social life which are not amenable to quantitative measurement. Associated with a variety of theoretical perspectives, qualitative research uses a range of methods to focus on the meanings and interpretation of social phenomena and social processes in the particular contexts in which they occur (Sumner, 2006).

Quantitative research – involves the collection of data in numerical form for quantitative analysis. The numerical data can be durations, scores, counts of incidents, ratings, or scales. Quantitative data can be collected in either controlled or naturalistic environments, in laboratories or field studies, from special populations or from samples of the general population. The defining factor is that numbers result from the process, whether the initial data collection produced numerical values, or whether non-numerical values were subsequently converted to numbers as part of the analysis process, as in content analysis. (Garwood, 2006).

Radical criminology and radical victimology – see **victim perspectives**.

Reflexivity – is a style of research that considers how the researcher is part of the research process and how the researcher contributes to the construction of meaning on the research questions being investigated. In reflexive research the researcher's own beliefs and objectives are made clear.

Repeat victimisation – occurs when the same person, place, vehicle or target suffers the same criminal victimisation repeatedly over a specified period of time. In relation to some offences the repeated vulnerability of particular individuals is self evident – domestic violence is the most obvious example, so too are child abuse and racial attacks. Repeat victimisation can also be linked to 'lifestyle' and 'routine activities'.

Revictimisation – occurs when people are literally or metaphorically victimised again. Typically, someone who has suffered criminal victimisation suffers another similar incident (but this is more commonly called repeat victimisation). Metaphorically, it refers to events or attitudes which make the victim feel as though they are undergoing another victimisation (see also **secondary victimisation**).

Secondary victimisation – there are two distinct meanings of secondary victimisation in general use. One refers to those who are indirectly harmed for example the significant others of murder or rape victims. The other more accurate meaning is similar to being **re-victimised**. In this sense secondary victimisation occurs at the hands of criminal justice system staff or anyone else responding to an offence. Secondary victimisation exacerbates feelings of victimisation and results from the insensitive treatment of victims of crime – often inadvertently – by the criminal justice system (or by friends and acquaintances). Barristers, jurors, police officers may be a cause of secondary victimisation or, being amongst those and others who regularly attend crime scenes or hear grisly details of offences, may suffer indirect or secondary victimisation.

Sex – refers to the biological differences between men and women mainly in terms of differences in procreative function.

Sexism – oppressive attitudes and behaviours directed towards either sex.

Sexual violence – is a term used to signify any bodily harms or violation that have a sexual component and that may (or may not) be recognised in law or statute. Sexual violence is therefore a broader term than that of **sexual offences.**

Signal crimes – are criminal incidents which act as warning signals to people and therefore impact not only on the immediate participants (victims, offenders, witnesses), but also are a broader threat to security and wider society. They tend to have a disproportionate impact on the way people think, feel or act.

Social control – a sociological approach to understanding the methods and processes through which social conformity and obedience to rules is achieved. The focus is on the ability of strong social ties in society and social institutions including the family, parents, peer groups education and employment, to restrain human behaviour.

Social harm – is closely associated with criminal victimisation and immorality but is more inclusive of injury or damage as harmful and as inflicted on individuals, societies and social institutions.

Social justice – is similar to natural justice and insists on the notion of fairness in relation to the distribution of opportunities, rewards and responsibilities in society. Proponents of such perspectives argue that criminal justice should take account of social justice.

Stereotype – a schematic portrayal achieved by a process of categorising and classifying people in caricature-like ways. The process leads to condensed, over-simplified and over generalised assumptions about 'types' of people, their values, behaviours and lifestyles. Stereotypes often serve to demonise certain groups in society.

Stigma – a sign assigned to individuals or social groups that is one of disgrace and a means of marking them out as negatively different, deviant or criminal.

Survivor – this term, as opposed to that of victim, acknowledges victims' agency, and active resistance. This label challenges the notion of victim passivity, and in particular it is often used by feminists in connection with women's resistance to their apparent structural powerlessness and potential victimisation.

Tertiary victimisation – this includes a wider circle of 'victims' who may have been affected by a particularly shocking event. For example, the rescue and medical personnel involved in some kind of traumatic incident (Spalek, 2006: 12).

Unofficial victim movement – victim action and support groups who campaign for a number of different issues including greater recognition as victims with specific needs arising from harms experienced.

Victim – the label 'victim' is contingent, complex and dynamic. Rock (2002) suggests 'victim' is an identity and a social artefact that is constructed by different actors in different contexts. It is usually now associated with crime but also relates to someone suffering some kind of misfortune.

Victim blaming – an emotively charged term closely associated with the phrase '**victim-proneness**'. Victim blaming can result from attempts to understand how people become victims of crime. Early writers about victims created a tradition of victim-blaming by putting the victims of particular types of crime into a variety of categories, partly according to how blameworthy they appeared to be. They focussed on the individual victim's conduct and the victim's relationship with the offender (see for example the work of von Hentig and Mendelsohn).

Victim culpability – closely associated with the concept of '**victim precipitation**', victim culpability refers to the extent to which the victim can be held to be responsible for what has happened to them.

Victim focussed – in the policy context this refers to putting the victim 'centre stage'. Sometimes policies claim to be victim-oriented rather than offender – or, the smooth running of the criminal justice system – focussed. A real victim focus does not amount to political gimmicks aimed at wooing voters which are not necessarily in victims' interests, even if they are publicised as such.

Victim impact statement or victim personal statement – is a written statement by a victim of crime to the courts and other criminal justice agencies. It can be a pro forma or free-form victim-information statement where victims are invited to formally detail what physical, financial, psychological, social or emotional effects the offence had on them and the wider impact of the crime including upon their family.

Victim movement – similar to the **unofficial victim movement** in its aspirations to support victims. The victim movement includes a range of well known voluntary bodies and charities who engage in campaigns for a number of different issues including greater recognition of victims with specific needs.

Victimological other – a phrase used to refer to the way in which victimology makes some groups of people more likely to be included as victims rather than others.

Victimology – a sub-discipline of criminology that is concerned with the study of victims of crime and other social harms. It is also concerned with exploring the causes, nature, extent and impact of victimisation in society and the dynamics of relationships between victims, offenders and the spatial and social structural environments in which they occur.

Victim oriented – see **Victim focussed**.

Victim perspectives – refers to different ways of viewing the victim of crime. Sometimes called theoretical perspectives, these approaches differ as to how they approach the study of the victim of crime including who counts as a victim, how research is conducted and how policies might be developed. The main three are: positivist perspectives, radical perspectives and critical perspectives.

Victim precipitation – closely associated with the concept of **victim culpability**, this concept draws attention to what it was that the victim did that resulted in their victimisation.

Victim proneness – the notion that there are some people, by virtue of their structural characteristics, who are much more likely to be victims of crime than other people. It is a small step from victim-proneness to 'victim-blaming'.

Victim provocation – see **Victim precipitation**.

Victim support (VS) – in the English and Welsh context, this refers to a large number of locally based Victim Support schemes that operate according to the same guidelines and common principles as laid down nationally. The schemes provide sympathetic advice and support as well as practical assistance for victims. It is a also a strong campaigning and lobbying group.

Victim/crime survey – originally referred to as a crime survey but more latterly referred to as a victim survey – these terms are often used interchangeably. Such surveys are specifically designed to collect data about the incidence, patterning and experiences of victimisation. They typically take a representative sample from a general population and use structured interviews to gather information on individuals' experiences of a wide range of victimisation over a given period of time whether or not they reported it to the police and if not, why not. They therefore go some way to uncovering the so-called 'dark figure' of unreported or unrecorded crime.

Victim typologies – used in connection with the early scholars of the subject of victimology who were interested in victim-offender relationships and the extent to which victims of crime contributed to crime and their own victimisation. Several of these scholars (Garofalo, Gottfredson, Hindelang, Mendelsohn, Von Hentig) identified different victim characteristics. The classification schemes they devised are referred to as victim typologies and help show what different types of victims have in common and how they differ from others.

Victim-witness – see also **Witness**. A victim-witness is the person who directly experienced the victimisation as a direct result of the crime.

Victims' rights – a term used in relation the policy agenda for victims of crime. Some views of victim's rights are more like intentional commitments whilst others view victims' rights in a more legal manner.

Victimology – often described as a sub-discipline of criminology this area of scholarship involves the study of victimisation, including its causes and reduction. In particular it seeks to theorise about events and disasters, whether legal or illegal, criminal or non-criminal that incur victimisation in society.

Vulnerable witness – a witness who is entitled to 'special measures' as are intimidated witnesses. All child witnesses are defined as vulnerable, and in practice the special measures also apply to victims of sexual and violent offences and witnesses with a range of special needs.

Witness – a witness to crime is a person who might report a crime to the police or tell the police about what they know. They may stand up in court to state what they know about the crime after taking an oath to tell the truth.

Witness care/service/support – witness support is usually provided by Victim Support. There are volunteers in all courts, who can show nervous witnesses and victims around an empty court room, explain procedures and give moral support during a hearing. There growing numbers of **Witness care units** across England and Wales that are jointly staffed by the police and the Crown Prosecution Service. They provide a single point of contact for Victims and Witnesses, minimising the stress of attending court and keeping victims and witnesses up to date with any news in a way that is relevant to them.

References

Adler, F. (1975a) 'The rise of the female crook', *Psychology Today*, 9: 42–6, 112–14.

Adler, F. (1975b) *Sisters in Crime.* New York: McGraw-Hill.

Akers, R.L., La Greca, A.J., Sellers, C. and Cochran, J. (1987) 'Fear of crime and victimization among the elderly in different types of communities', *Criminology,* 25 (3): 487–505.

Allen, S. (2002) 'Male victims of rape: responses to a perceived threat to masculinity', in C. Hoyle and R. Young (eds), *New Visions of Crime Victims.* Oxford: Hart Publishing.

Askin, K.D. (1997) *War Crimes Against Women: Prosecution in International War Crimes Tribunals.* The Hague: Kluwer.

Babcock, J.C., Miller, S.A. and Siard, C. (2003) 'Toward a typology of abusive women: differences between partner-only and generally violent women in the use of violence', *Psychology of Women Quarterly,* 27: 153–61.

Bacon, B. (2004) 'Women's Violence Towards Intimate Partners: Intergenerational Explanations and Policy Considerations', paper presented at the British Criminology Conference July, Portsmouth.

Bagshaw, D. and Chung, D. (2000) *Women, Men and Domestic Violence.* Canberra: Commonwealth of Australia.

Batchelor, S. (2007) 'Getting mad wi' it': risk seeking by young women' in K. Hannah-Moffat and P. O'Mally (eds), *Gendered Risks.* Abingdon: RoutledgeCavendish.

Batchelor, S., Burman, M. and Brown, J. (2001) 'Discussing violence: let's hear it from the girls', *Probation Journal*, 48 (2): 125–34.

Batty, D. (2005) 'Complaints cause doctors to shun child protection' *Guardian (Society).*

Bennett, T. and Wright, R. (1984) *Burglars on Burglary: Prevention and the Offender.* Aldershot: Gower.

Bennetto, J. and Judd, T. (2004) 'Murder cases under review to identify "honour killings"', http://news.independent.co.uk/uk/crime/story.jsp?story=534253.

Best, S. (2005) *Understanding Social Divisions.* London: Sage.

Bishop, P. (2001) 'Bosnian Serbs jailed for rape and sexual slavery', *The Daily Telegraph* 23.02.2001.

Bracchi, P. (2008) 'The feral Sex: the terrifying rise of violent girl gangs', 16 May MailOnline, accessed 14/04/2009.

Bradley, K. (2009) *The Bradley Report: Lord Bradley's Review of People with Mental Health Problems or Learning Disabilities in the Criminal Justice System.* London: DH.

Broadhurst, K. (2007) 'Sure Start and the 're-authorisation' of Section 47 child protection polices', *Critical Social Policy*, 27 (4): 443–61.

Bromley Briefings (2009) *Bromley Briefings Prison Factfile.* London: Prison Reform Trust.

Brown, P. (1999) 'Companies to face naming and shaming for emission of cancer-causing chemicals', *The Guardian,* 8.02.1999.

Brown, S. (1998) *Understanding Youth and Crime: Listening to Youth?* Buckingham: Open University Press.

Budd, T. and Mattinson, J. (2000) *The extent and nature of stalking: findings from the 1998 British Crime Survey*. Home Office Research Study 210. London: Home Office.

Caddle, D. and Crisp, D. (1997) *Mothers in Prison. Home Office Research Findings 38*. London: Home Office.

Caiazza, A. (2001) 'Why gender matters in understanding September 11: women, militarism, and violence', *Institute for Women's Policy Research Briefing*, Paper no. 1908.

Cain, M. (1990) 'Realist philosophy and standpoint epistemologies or feminst criminology as a successor science?', in L. Gelsthorpe and A. Morris (eds), *Feminist Perspectives in Criminology*. Milton Keynes: Open University Press.

Campbell, A. (1991) *The Girls in the Gang,* second edition. New York: Basil Blackwell.

Campbell, A. (2005) 'Keeping the "lady" safe: the regulation of femininity through crime prevention literature', *Critical Criminology*, 13: 119–40.

Campbell, B. (1993) *Goliath: Britain's Dangerous Places*. London: Virago.

Cape, E. (2004) (ed.) *Reconcilable Rights? Analysing the Tension between Victims and Defendants*. London: Legal Action Group.

Carlen, P. (1988) *Women, Crime and Poverty*. Buckingham: Open University Press.

Carlen, P. (1990) *Alternatives to Women's Imprisonment*. Milton Keynes: Oxford University Press.

Carlen, P. (1994) 'Why study women's imprisonment? Or anyone else's?', in R. King and M. Maguire (eds), *Prisons in Context*. Oxford: Clarendon Press.

Carlen, P. (1998) *Sledgehammer Women's Imprisonment at the Millennium*. Basingstoke: Macmillan.

Carlen, P. (ed.) (2002) *Women and Punishment: The Struggle for Justice*. Cullompton: Willan.

Carlen, P. and Worrall, A. (eds) (1987) *Gender, Crime and Justice*. Buckingham: Open University Press.

Carlen, P. and Worrall, A. (2004) *Analysing Women's Imprisonment*. Cullompton: Willan.

Carlen, P., Christina, D., Hicks, J., O'Dwyer, J. and Tchaikovsky, C. (1985) *Criminal Women*. Cambridge: Polity Press.

Carrabine, E., Iganski, P., Lee, M., Plummer, K. and South, N. (2004) 'Victims and victimisation' in *Criminology: A Sociological Introduction*. London: Routledge.

Chan, W. and Rigakos, G.S. (2002) 'Risk, crime and gender', *British Journal of Criminology*, 42: 743–61.

Chibnall, S. (1977) *Law and Order News: An Analysis of Crime Reporting in the British Press*. London: Tavistock.

Chigwada-Bailey, R. (2003) *Black Women's Experiences of Criminal Justice: Race, Gender and Class: A Discourse in Disadvantage*. Winchester: Waterside Press.

Christie, N. (1986) 'The ideal victim', in E.A. Fattah (ed.) *From Crime Policy to Victim Policy*. London: Macmillan.

Cloward, R. and Ohlin, E.L. (1960) *Delinquency and Opportunity: A Theory of Delinquent Gangs*. New York: Free Press.

Cohen, A.K. (1955) *Delinquent Boys. The Culture of the Gang*. New York: Free Press.

Cohen, S. (1972/2002) *Folk Devils and Moral Panics: The Creation of Mods and Rockers* (2nd edition with revised Introduction). Oxford: Martin Robertson.

Cohen, S. (2002) *States of Denial: Knowing about Atrocities and Suffering*. Cambridge: Polity Press.

Coles, D. and Shaw, H. (2008) 'Deaths in detention', *Criminal Justice Matters*, 71: 30–1.

Collier, R. (1998) *Masculinities, Crime and Criminology*. London: Sage.

Connell, R.W. (1987) *Gender and Power*. Oxford: Polity.

Connell, R.W. (1995) *Masculinities*. Oxford: Polity.

Corbett, C. and Maguire, M. (1988) 'Volunteer-based services to rape victims: some recent developments', in M. Maguire and J. Pointing (eds), *Victims of Crime: A New Deal?* Milton Keynes: Open University Press.

Corby, B. (2000) *Child Abuse: Towards a Knowledge Base, second edition*. Buckingham: Open University Press.

Corcoran, M. (2006) *Out of Order: The Political Imprisonment of Women in Northern Ireland 1972–1998*. Cullompton: Willan.

Corporate Watch (2004a) Nestle SA http://www.corporatewatch.org.uk/profiles/food-supermarkets/nestle/nestle1.html.

Corporate Watch (2004b) Monsanto Corporate Crimes http://www.corporatewatch.org.uk/profiles/biotech/Monsanto/monsanto5.html.

Corston, J. (2007) *The Corston Report Executive Summary*. London: Home Office.

Cowie, J., Cowie, V. and Slater, E. (1968) *Delinquency in Girls*. London: Heineman.

Coxell, A., King, M., Mezey, G. and Gordon, D. (1999) 'Lifetime prevalence, characteristics and associated problems of non-consensual sex in men: cross sectional survey', *British Medical Journal*, 318, 27 March.

Crawford, A., Jones, T., Woodhouse, T. and Young, J. (1990) *Second Islington Crime Survey*. London: Middlesex Polytechnic.

Croall, H. (1995) 'Target women: women's victimisation from white-collar crime', in R. Dobash and L. Noaks (eds), *Gender and Crime*. Cardiff: Cardiff University Press.

Croall, H. (1998) *Crime and Society in Britain*. London: Longman.

Croall, H. (2007a) 'Social class, social exclusion, victims and crime', in P. Davies, P. Francis and C. Greer (eds), *Victims, Crime and Society*. London: Sage.

Croall, H. (2007b) 'Victims of white-collar and corporate crime', in P. Davies, P. Francis and C. Greer (eds), *Victims, Crime and Society*. London: Sage.

Cusick, L., Martin, A. and May, T. (2004) 'Vulnerability and involvement in drug use and sex work', *Research Study 268*. London: Home Office.

CWASU (2002) *Information on Trafficking in Women and Children for Sexual Exploitation*. http://www.cwasu.org/factsontrafficking1.htm.

Daily Mail 'Menace of the violent girls', 31.07.08.

Daily Mail 'The ladette louts', 21.07.08.

Daly, K. (1993) 'Class-race-gender: sloganeering in search of meaning', *Social Justice*, 20 (1–2): 56–71.

Daly, K. (1994) *Gender, Crime, and Punishment*. London: Yale University Press.

Daly, K. (1997) 'Different ways of conceptualising sex/gender in feminist theory and their implications for criminology', *Theoretical Criminology*, 1 (1): 25–51.

Davies, P. (1999) 'Women crime and an informal economy: female offending and crime for Gain', *British Criminology Conferences; Selected Proceedings Volume*, http;//www.lboro.ac.uk/departments/ss/bsc/bccsp/vol02//01davie.htm.

Davies, P. (2000) 'Doing Interviews with female offenders', in Jupp, V., Davies, P. and Francis, P. (eds), *Doing Criminological Research*. London: Sage.

Davies, P. (2003a) 'Is economic crime a man's game?', *Feminist Theory*, 4 (3): 283–303.

Davies, P. (2003b) 'Women and crime: doing it for the kids?', *Criminal Justice Matters*, 50.

Davies, P. (2005) 'Women and crime for economic gain', PhD Thesis Newcastle-upon-Tyne: University of Northumbria.

Davies, P. (2006) 'Consultant accused mother of killing child', *The Daily Telegraph*, 15 November.

Davies, P. (2007a) 'Lessons from the gender agenda', in S. Walklate (ed.), *The Handbook of Victims and Victimology*. Cullompton: Willan.

Davies, P. (2007b) 'Women, victims and crime', in P. Davies, P. Francis and C. Greer (eds), *Victims, Crime and Society*. London: Sage.

Davies, P. (2007c) 'Criminal (In)justice for victims?', in P. Davies, P. Francis and C. Greer (eds), *Victims, Crime and Society*. London: Sage.

Davies, P. (2008) 'Looking out of a broken old window: community safety, Gendered crimes and Victimisations', *Crime Prevention and Community Safety: An International Journal*, 10 (4).

Davies, P. (2010) 'Doing Interviews in prison', in P. Davies, P. Francis and V. Jupp (eds), *Doing Criminological Research* (2nd edn). London: Sage.

Davies, P. and Jupp, V. (1999) 'Crime-work connections: exploring the invisibility of workplace crime', in P. Davies, P. Francis and V. Jupp (eds), *Invisible Crimes: Their Victims and Their Regulation*. Basingstoke: Macmillan Press.

Davies, P., Francis, P. and Jupp, V. (eds) (1999) *Invisible Crimes: Their Victims and Their Regulation*. Basingstoke: Macmillan Press.

Davies, P., Francis, P. and Jupp, V. (2003) *Victimisation: Theory Research and Policy*. Basingstoke: Palgrave Macmillan.

Davies, P., Francis, P. and Greer, C. (eds) (2007) *Victims, Crime and Society*. London: Sage.

Davies, P., Clark, A., Francis, P. and Thompson, J. (2001) *Domestic Violence in Rural Northumberland*. Newcastle-upon-Tyne: University of Northumbria.

Department of Health (2001) *Changing the Outlook – A Strategy for Developing and Modernising Mental Health Services in Prisons*. London: DH.

Dignan, J. (2005) *Understanding Victims and Restorative Justice*. Berkshire: Open University Press.

Ditton, J. (2008) 'Fear of crime', in T. Newburn and P. Neyroud (eds), *Dictionary of Policing*. Cullompton: Willan.

Doak, J. (2008) *Victims' Rights, Human Rights and Criminal Justice. Reconceiving the Role of Third Parties*. Oxford: Hart.

Dobash, R.E. and Dobash, R.P. (1979) *Violence Against Wives: A Case Against Patriarchy*. Shepton Mallet: Open Books.

Dobash, R.P. and Dobash, R.E. (1998) *Rethinking Violence Against Women*. London: Sage.

Dobash, R.P. and Dobash, R.E. (2008) 'Women's violence to men in intimate relationships: working on the puzzle', in K. Evans and J. Jamieson (eds), *Gender and Crime: A Reader* Maidenhead: Open University Press.

Dobash, R., Dobash, R. and Gutteridge, S. (1986) *The Imprisonment of Women*. Oxford: Blackwell.

Durcan, G. (2008) *From the Inside: Experiences of Prison Mental Health Care*. London: Centre for Mental Health.

Eaton, M. (1986) *Justice for Women? Family, Court and Social Control*. Milton Keynes: Open University Press.

Eaton, M. (1993) *Women After Prison*. Buckingham: Open University Press.

Enarson, E. and Hearn Marrow, B. (1998) (eds) *The Gendered Terrain of Disaster.* Florida Laboratory for Social and Behavioural Research: Florida International University.

Evans, K. and Jamieson, J. (2008) (eds) *Gender and Crime: A Reader.* Buckingham: Open University Press.

Fawcett Society (2004) *Report on Women Working in the Criminal Justice System.* Commission on Women and the Criminal Justice System.

Fawcett Society (2006) *Justice and Equality: Second Annual Review of the Commission on Women and the Criminal Justice System.* London: Fawcett Society.

Fawcett Society (2007) *Women and Justice: Third Annual Review of the Commission on Women and the Criminal Justice System.*

Feminist Majority Foundation (2001) 'Feminists Against Sweatshops' www.feminist.org/other/sweatshops/sweatfaq.html

Finlay, L.M. (1996) 'The pharmaceutical industry and women's health', in E. Szockyi and J.G. Fox (eds), *Corporate Victimisation of Women.* Boston: Northeastern University Press.

Fisher, B.S. and Gunnison, E. (2001) 'Violence in the workplace: gender similarities and differences', *Journal of Criminal Justice*, 29 (2): 145–55.

Folbre, N. (1994) *Who Pays for the Kids? Gender and the Structure of Constraint.* Routledge: London.

Folbre, N. (2001) *The Invisible Heart: Economics and Family Values.* New York: The New Press.

Fox Keller, E. (1985) *Reflections on Gender and Science.* London: Yale University Press.

Francis, P. (2007) 'Young people, victims and crime', in P. Davies, P. Francis and C. Greer (eds), *Victims, Crime and Society.* London: Sage.

Gadd, D., Farrall, S., Dallimore, D. and Lombard, N. (2003) 'Victims of domestic violence', *Criminal Justice Matters*, 53: 16–17.

Galtung, J. and Ruge, M. (1965) 'Structuring and selecting news', in S. Cohen and J. Young (eds) (1981) *The Manufacture of News: Deviance Social Problems and the Mass Media*, revised edition. London: Constable.

Garland, (2001) *The Culture of Control: Crime and Social Order in Contemporary Society.* Oxford: Oxford University Press.

Gelsthorpe, L. (1989) *Sexism and the Female Offender.* Aldershot: Gower.

Gelsthorpe, L. (2002) 'Feminism and criminology', in M. Maguire, R. Morgan and R. Reiner (eds), *The Oxford Handbook of Criminology*, third edition. Oxford: Clarendon Press.

Gelsthorpe, L. (2007) 'Women and criminal justice under labour', *Criminal Justice Matters*, 67: 22–3.

Gelsthorpe, L. and Morris, A. (1994) *Feminist Perspectives in Criminology.* Milton Keynes: Open University Press.

Gelsthorpe, L. and Morris, A. (2002) 'Women's imprisonment in England and Wales: a penal paradox', *Criminal Justice*, 2 (3): 277–301.

Gelsthorpe, L. and McIvor, G. (2007) 'Difference and diversity in probation', in L. Gelsthorpe and R. Morgan (eds), *Handbook of Probation*. Cullompton: Willan.

George, M.J. (1999) 'A victimisation survey of female-perpetrated assaults in the United Kingdom', *Aggressive Behaviour*, 25 (1): 67–79.

Gerber, J. and Weekes, S.L. (1992) 'Women as victims of corporate crime: a call for research on a neglected topic', *Deviant Behaviour*, 13: 325–47.

Gilchrist, E. and Blisset, J. (2002) 'Magistrates' attitudes towards domestic violence and sentencing', *Howard Journal of Criminal Justice*, 41: 4.

Gilchrist, E., Bannister, J., Ditton, J. and Farrall, S. (1998) 'Women and the fear of crime: challenging the accepted steroetype', *British Journal of Criminology*, 38 (2): 283–98.

Gilchrist, E. Bannister, J., Ditton, J. and Farrall, S. (2008) 'Women and the "fear of crime": challenging the accepted stereotype' in K. Evans and J. Jamieson (eds), *Gender and Crime: A Reader*. Maidenhead: Open University Press.

Gilligan, C. (1982) *In a Different Voice: Psychological Theory and Women's Development*. Cambridge, MA: Harvard University Press.

Glaser, B. and Strauss, A. (1967) *The Discovery of Grounded Theory*. Chicago: Aldine.

Goodey, J. (1997) 'Boys don't cry: masculinities, fear of crime and fearlessness', *British Journal of Criminology*, 37 (3): 401–18.

Goodey, J. (2004) 'Sex trafficking in women from Central and East European countries: promoting a "victim-centred" and "woman-centred" approach to criminal justice intervention', *Feminist Review*, 76: 26–45.

Goodey, J. (2005) *Victims and Victimology: Research, Policy and Practice*. London: Longman.

Gramsci, A. (1978) *Selections from Political Writings 1921–1926*. London: Lawrence & Wishart.

Greer, C. (2003) *Sex Crime and the Media: Sex Offending and the Press in a Divided Society*. Cullompton: Willan.

Greer, C. (2007) 'News media, victims and crime', in P. Davies, P. Francis and C. Greer (eds), *Victims, Crime and Society*. London: Sage.

Gregory, J. and Lees, S. (1999) *Policing Sexual Assault*. London: Routledge.

Groombridge, N. (2001) 'Sexuality', in E. McLaughlin and J. Muncie (eds), *The Sage Dictionary of Criminology*. London: Sage.

Hall, M. (2009) *Victims of Crime. Policy and Practice in Criminal Justice*. Cullompton: Willan.

Hall, R.E. (1985) *Ask Any Woman*. Bristol: Falling Wall Press.

Hall, S. (2002) 'Daubing the drudges of fury: men, violence and the piety of the hegemonic masculinity thesis', *Theoretical Criminology* 6(1): 35–71.

Hanmer, J. and Maynard, M. (eds) (1987) *Women, Violence and Social Control*. London: Macmillan.

Hanmer, J. and Saunders, S. (1984) *Well Founded Fear: A Community Study of Violence to Women*. London: Hutchinson.

Hannah-Moffat, K. (2001) *Punishment in Disguise: Penal Governance and Federal Imprisonment of Women in Canada*. Toronto: University of Toronto Press.

Hannah-Moffat, K. and O'Mally, P. (2007) (eds) *Gendered Risks*. Abingdon: RoutledgeCavendish.

Harding, S. (ed.) (1987) *Feminism and Methodology*. Milton Keynes: Open University Press.

Harvey, J. (2007) *Young Men in Prison Surviving and Adapting to Life Inside*. Cullompton: Willan.

Hearn, J. (2004) 'From hegemonic masculinity to the hegemony of men', *Feminist Theory*, 5 (1): 48–72.

Hedderman, C. (2004) 'The criminogenic needs of women offenders', in G. McIvor (ed.), *Women Who Offend*. London: Jessica Kingsley.

Hedderman, C. and Gelsthorpe, L. (1997) *Understanding the Sentencing of Women*. Home Office Research Study 170. London: HMSO.

Heidensohn, F. (1968) 'The deviance of women: a critique and an enquiry', *British Journal of Sociology*, 19: 160–75.

Heidensohn, F. (1985) *Women and Crime*. London: Macmillan.

Heidensohn, F. (1989) *Crime and Society*. London: Macmillan.

Heidensohn, F. (1996) *Women and Crime,* second edition. London: Macmillan.

Heidensohn, F. (1997) 'Gender and crime', in M. Maguire, R. Morgan and R. Reiner (eds), *The Oxford Handbook of Criminology,* second edition. Oxford: Clarendon Press.

Heidensohn, F. (2002) 'Gender and crime' in M. Maguire, R. Morgan and R. Reiner (eds), *The Oxford Handbook of Criminology,* third edition. Oxford: Clarendon Press.

Heidensohn, F. (2003) 'Gender and policing', in T. Newburn (ed.), *Handbook of Policing*. Cullompton: Willan.

Heidensohn, F. (2006) *Gender and Justice*. Cullompton: Willan.

Heidensohn, F. and Gelsthorpe, L. (2007) 'Gender and crime', in M. Maguire, R. Morgan and R. Reiner (eds), *The Oxford Handbook of Criminology*, fourth edition, Oxford: Oxford University Press.

Herbert, I. (2007) 'Kate McCann: from anguished parent, to grieving mother, to suspect', 8 September, accessed 13/08/2007.

Hindelang, M.J., Gottfredson, M.R. and Garofalo, J. (1978) *Victims of Personal Crime: An Empirical Foundation for a Theory of Personal Victimisation*. Cambridge, MA: Ballinger.

Holgate, A. (1989) 'Sexual harassment as a determinant of women's fear of rape', *Australian Journal of Sex, Marriage & Family,* 10: 21–8.

Home Office (1990) *The Victims Charter: A Statement of Rights for Victims of Crime*. London: Home Office.

Home Office (2001) *The Criminal Injuries Compensation Scheme.* Criminal Injuries Compensation Authority. London: Home Office.

Home Office (2003) *Safety and Justice: The Government's Proposals on Domestic Violence*. Cm5874. London: Home Office.

Home Office (2004) http://www.crimereduction.gov.uk/domesticviolence42.htm

Hough, J.M. and Mayhew, P. (1983) *The British Crime Survey: First Report. Home Office Research Study No. 76*. London: HMSO.

Hudson, A. (1994) 'Elusive subjects: researching young women in trouble', in L. Gelsthorpe and A. Morris (eds), *Feminist Perspectives in Criminology*. Milton Keynes: Open University Press.

Hudson, B. (1998) 'Restorative justice: the challenge of racial and sexual violence', *Journal of Law and Society,* 25: 237–56.

Hudson, B. (2000) 'Critical reflection as research methodology', in V. Jupp, P. Davies and P. Francis (eds), *Doing Criminological Research.* London: Sage.

Hudson, B. (2002) 'Gender issues in penal policy and penal theory', in P. Carlen (ed.), *Women and Punishment: The Struggle for Justice.* Cullompton: Willan.

Hughes, D.M. and Denisova, T. (2002) 'Trafficking in women from Ukraine', http://www.ncjrs.org/pdffiles1nij/grants/203275.pdf.

Independent (1999) 'Mothers Who Kill: Not as Rare as We Think'.

Innes, M. (2003) 'Signal crimes: detective work, mass media and constructing collective memory', in P. Mason (ed.), *Criminal Visions: Representations of Criminal Justice.* Cullompton: Willan.

Innes, M. (2004) 'Signal crimes and signal disorders: notes on deviance as communicative action', *British Journal of Sociology*, 55 (3): 335–55.

Jamieson, R. (1998) 'Towards a criminology of war in Europe', in V. Ruggiero, N. South and I. Taylor (eds), *The New European Criminology: Crime and Social Order in Europe.* Routledge: London.

Jardine, C. (2006) ' A system that abuses the whole family', *Daily Telegraph,* Thursday October 19.

Jefferson, T. (1998) '"Muscle", "hard men" and "iron" Mike Tyson: reflections on desire, anxiety and the embodiment of masculinity', *Body and Society,* 4 (1): 77–98.

Jefferson, T. (2001) 'Hegemonic masculinity', in E. McLaughlin and J. Muncie (eds), *The Sage Dictionary of Criminology.* London: Sage.

Jewkes, Y. (2005a) *Media and Crime.* London: Sage.

Jewkes, Y. (2005b) 'Men behind bars: "doing" masculinity as an adaptation to imprisonment', *Men and Masculinities,* 8 (1): 44–63.

Joe Laidler, K. and Hunt, G. (2001) 'Accomplishing femininity among the girls in the gang', *British Journal of Criminology,* 41: 656–78.

Johnston, P. (2001) 'Too many women are sent to jail, judges are told', *Daily Telegraph,* 27.11.201:16.

Jones, T., Maclean, B. and Young, J. (1986) *The Islington Crime Survey: Crime, Victimisation and Policing in Inner-City London.* London: Gower.

Jupp, V. (1989) *Methods of Criminological Research.* London: Allen and Unwin.

Jupp, V. Davies, P. and Francis, P. (2000) (eds) *Doing Criminological Research.* London Sage.

Kahn, A.S., Jackson, J., Kully, C., Badger, K. and Halvorsen, J. (2003) 'Calling it rape: differences in experiences of women who do or do not label their sexual assault as rape', *Psychology of Women Quarterly,* 27(3): 233–42.

Kahn, J.S. (2009) *An Introduction to Masculinities.* Chichester: Wiley-Blackwell.

Kelly, L. and Radford, J. (1987) 'The problem of men: feminist perspectives on sexual violence', in P. Scraton (ed.), *Law, Order and the Authoritarian State: Readings in Critical Criminology.* Milton Keynes: Open University Press.

Kershaw, C., Chivite-Matthews, N., Thomas, C. and Aust, R. (2001) *The 2001 British Crime Survey: First Results, England and Wales.* London: Home Office.

Klein, D. (1996) 'The etiology of female crime', in J. Muncie, E. McLaughlin and M. Langan (eds), *Criminological Perspectives: A Reader.* London: Sage in association with The Open University.

Klein, D. and Kress, J. (1976) 'Any woman's blues: a critical overview of women, crime and the criminal justice system', *Crime and Social Justice,* 5: 34.

Knowsley, J. (1994) 'Earrings, bracelets and baseball bats', *Sunday Telegraph*, 27.11. 4: 3.

Laming, Lord (2003) *The Victoria Climbie Inquiry. Report of an Inquiry by Lord Laming*. London: Health and Home Department.

Lees, S. (1997a) *Ruling Passions: Sexual Violence, Reputation and the Law*. London: Sage.

Lees, S. (1997b) *Carnal Knowledge: Rape on Trial*. Harmondsworth: Penguin.

Leonard, M. (1994) *Informal Economic Activity in Belfast*. Aldershot: Avebury.

Levi, M. (1994) 'Masculinities and white collar crime', in T. Newburn and E. Stanko (eds), *Just Boys Doing Business?* London: Routledge.

Liebling, A. (2007) 'Prison suicide and its prevention', in Y. Jewkes (ed.), *Handbook on Prisons*. Cullompton: Willan.

Liebling, A. (1994) 'Suicides amongst women prisoners', *Howard Journal*, 33: 1–9.

Liebling, A. (1999) 'Prisoner suicide and prisoner coping', in M. Tonry and J. Petersilia (eds), *Crime and Justice: A Review of Research*, 26. Chicago: University of Chicago Press.

Lombroso, C. and Ferrero, G. (1893) *Criminal Woman, the Prostitute and the Normal Woman* (trans.). Durham: Duke University Press.

London Rape Crisis Centre (1984) *Sexual Violence: The Reality for Women*. London: LRCC.

Lorber, J. (1994) *Paradoxes of Gender*. New Haven, CT: Yale University Press.

Loucks, N., Malloch, M., McIvor, G. and Gelsthorpe, L. (2006) *Evaluation of the 218 Centre*. Edinburgh: Scottish Executive.

Lynch, M.J. and Stretesky, P. (2001) 'Toxic crimes: examining corporate victimization of the general public employing medical and epidemiological evidence', *Critical Criminology*, 10: 153–72.

Maguire, M. and Pointing, J. (1988) (eds) *Victims of Crime. A New Deal* Milton Keynes: Open University Press.

Maguire, M., Morgan, R. and Reiner, R. (2002) (eds) *The Oxford Handbook of Criminology* (3rd edn). Oxford: Oxford University Press.

McCrea, R., Shyy, T.-K., Western, J., and Stimson, R.J. (2005) 'Fear of crime in Brisbane: individual, social, and neighborhood factors in perspective', *Journal of Sociology*, 41 (1): 7–27.

McIntosh, M. (1975) *The Organisation of Crime*. London: Macmillan.

McLaughlin, E. and Muncie, J. (2001) (eds) *The Sage Dictionary of Criminology*. London: Sage.

McLeod, E. (1982) *Women Working: Prostitution Now*. London: Croom Helm.

Macionis and Plummer (1998) *Sociology A Global Introduction*. London: Prentice Hall.

MacKinnon, C. (1989) *Towards a Feminist Theory of the State*. Harvard: Harvard University Press.

Maguire, M. (1982) *Burglary in a Dwelling: The Offence, the Offender and the Victim*. Cambridge Studies in Criminology. London: Heinemann.

Maguire, M. and Kynch, J. (2000) *Public Perceptions and Victims' Experiences of Victim Support: Findings from the 1998 British Crime Survey*. London: Home Office.

Maher, L. (1997) *Sexed Work. Gender, Race and Resistance in a Brooklyn Drug Market*. Oxford: Clarendon Press.

Malloch, M. and Loucks, N. (2007) 'Responding to drug and alcohol problems: innovations and effectiveness in treatment programmes for women', in R. Sheehan, G. McIvor and C. Trotter (eds), *What Works with Women Offenders*. Cullompton: Willan.

Marsh, I., with J. Cochrane and G. Melville (2004) *Criminal Justice: An Introduction to Philosophies, Theories and Practice.* London: Routledge.

Martin, C. (2000) 'Doing research in a prison setting', in V. Jupp, P. Davies and P. Francis (eds), *Doing Criminological Research.* London: Sage.

Mawby, R.C. (forthcoming) 'Using the media to understand crime and criminal justice', in P. Davies and P. Francis (eds), *Doing Criminological Research,* second edition. London: Sage.

Mawby, R.I. (2007) 'Public sector services and the victim of crime', in S. Walklate (ed.), *Handbook of Victims and Victimology.* Cullompton: Willan.

Mawby, R.I. and Walklate, S. (1994) *Critical Victimology.* London: Sage.

Maynard, M. and Purvis, J. (eds) (1994) *Researching Women's Lives from a Feminist Perspective.* London: Taylor and Francis.

Mays, J.B. (1954) *Growing up in the City: A Study of Juvenile Delinquency in an Urban Neighbourhood.* Liverpool: Liverpool University Press.

Medlicott, D. (2007) 'Women in prison', in Y. Jewkes (ed.), *Handbook on Prisons.* Cullompton: Willan.

Mellor, M. (1992) *Breaking the Boundaries: Towards a Feminist Green Socialism.* London: Virago Press.

Mellor, M. (1997) *Feminism and Ecology.* Cambridge: Polity.

Mendelsohn, B. (1940) 'Rape in criminology', trans. and cited in S. Shafer (1968), *The Victim and his Criminal.* New York: Random House.

Mendelsohn, B. (1956) 'A new branch of bio-psychosocial science: la victimology', *Revue Internationale de Criminologie et de Police Technique,* 2.

Mendelsohn, B. (1974) 'The origins of the doctrine of victimology', in I. Drapkin and E. Viano (eds), *Victimology.* Lexington, MA: Lexington Books.

Merton, R. (1938) 'Social structure and anomie', *American Sociological Review,* 3: 672–82.

Merton, R.K. (1968) *Social Theory and Social Structure.* New York: Free Press.

Messerschmidt, J.W. (1993) *Masculinities and Crime.* Lanham, MD: Rowman & Littlefield.

Messerschmidt, J.W. (1994) 'Schooling, masculinities and youth crime by white boys', in Messerschmidt, J.W. (1995) 'From patriarchy to gender: feminist theory, criminology and the challenge of diversity', in N. Hahn Rafter and F. Heidensohn (eds), *International Feminist Perspectives in Criminology: Engendering a Discipline.* Philadelphia: Open University Press.

Messerschmidt, J.W. (1997) *Crime as Structured Action.* Thousand Oaks, CA: Sage.

Messerschmidt, J. (1998) 'Men victimizing men: the case of lynching, 1865–1900', in L. Bowker (ed.), *Masculinities and Violence.* London: Sage.

Messerschmidt, J.W. (2004) *Flesh and Blood: Adolescent Gender Diversity and Violence.* Lanham, MD: Rowman and Littlefield.

Messerschmidt, J. (2009) 'Hegemonic and subordinated masculinities', in T. Newburn (ed.), *Key Readings in Criminology.* Cullompton: Willan.

Miers, D. (1978) *Responses to Victimisation.* Abingdon: Professional.

Miers, D. (1983) 'Compensation and conceptions of victims of crime', *Victimology,* 8: 204–12.

Miers, D. (1989) 'Positivist victimology: a critique', *International Review of Victimology,* 1 (2): 3–22.

Miller, J. (1998) 'Up it up: gender and the accomplishment of street robbery', *Criminology* 36 (1).

Miller, J. (2001) *One of The Guys: Girls, Gangs and Gender.* New York: Oxford University Press.

Miller, J. (2002) 'The strengths and limits of "doing-gender" for understanding street crime', *Theoretical Criminology,* 6 (4): 433–60.

Mintz, M. (1985) *At Any Cost: Corporate Greed, Women, and the Dalkon Shield.* New York: Pantheon Books.

Ministry of Justice (2009) *Prison Population and Accommodation Briefing, 9th October 2009.* London: Ministry of Justice.

Mirrlees-Black, C. and Byron, C. (1999) *Domestic Violence: Findings from the BCS Self-Completion Questionnaire,* Home Office Research Findings 83. London: Home Office.

Mooney, J. (2000) *Gender, Violence and the Social Order.* London: Macmillan.

Moore, S. and Shepherd, J. (2007) 'The elements and prevalence of fear', *The British Journal of Criminology,* 47 (1): 154–62.

Morash, M. (2006) *Understanding Gender, Crime and Justice.* London: Sage.

Morris, T.P. (1957) *The Criminal Area: A Study in Social Ecology.* London: Routledge & Kegan Paul.

Morley, R. and Mullender, A. (1994) *Preventing Domestic Violence to Women.* Crime Prevention Unit, Paper 48 London: Home Office Police Department.

Mullin, J. (1995) 'When crime doesn't pay', The *Guardian* 2 November.

Muncie, J. (2004) *Youth and Crime.* second edition. London: Sage.

Muncie, J. and McLoughlin, E. (2001) *The Problem of Crime,* second edition. London and Buckingham: Sage in association with the Open University.

Munro, E. (2004) 'Common errors of reasoning in child Protection work', *Child Abuse and Neglect,* 23: 745–58.

Naffine, N. (1997) *Feminism and Criminology.* Cambridge: Polity Press.

National Audit Office (2002) *Helping Victims and Witnesses: The Work of Victim Support* (Report by the Comptroller and Auditor General, House of Commons Session1212, 2001–2002, 23 October 2002). London: The Stationery Office.

Nelson, J.A. (1996) *Feminism, Objectivity and Economics.* London: Routledge.

Newburn, T. (2007) *Criminology.* Cullompton: Willan.

Newburn, T. and Stanko, E. (1994) (eds) *Just Boys Doing Business: Men, Masculinities and Crime.* London: Routledge.

Nuttall, M. with Sharon Morrison (1998) *It Could Have Been You.* London: Virago.

Osborne, R. (2002) *Megawords.* London: Sage.

Pain, R. (2001) 'Gender, race, age and fear in the city', *Urban Studies,* 38 (5–6): 899–913.

Parton, N. (1997) *Child Protection and Family Support.* London: Routledge.

Parton, N. (2006) *Safeguarding Childhood: Early Intervention and Surveillance in a Late Modern Society.* Palgrave Macmillan, Basingstoke.

Pearce, F. and Snider, L. (1995) (eds) *Corporate Crime: Contemporary Debates.* Toronto: University of Toronto Press.

Pearce, F. and Tombs, S. (1997) 'Hazards, law and class: contextualising the regulation of corporate crime', *Social & Legal Studies,* 6 (1):79–10.

Pearce, F. and Tombs, S. (1998) *Toxic Capitalism: Corporate Crime and the Chemical Industry.* Aldershot: Ashgate.

Pearce, J. and Stanko, E. (2000) 'Young women and community safety', *Youth and Policy,* 66: 1–18.

Peppin, J. (1995) 'Feminism, law and the pharmaceutical industry', in F. Pearce, and L. Snider (eds), *Corporate Crime: Contemporary Debates*. Toronto: University of Toronto Press.

Perry, S. and Dawson, J. (1985) *Nightmare: Women and the Dalkon Shield*. New York: Macmillan.

Phipps, A. (1988) 'Ideologies, political parties and victims of crime', in M. Maguire, and J. Pointing (eds), *Victims of Crime: A New Deal?*, Milton Keynes: Open University Press.

Police Criminal Statistics (2006) Wiesbaden: Germany.

Pollock, J.M. (2002) *Women Prison and Crime*, second edition. London: Thomson.

Pollack, O. (1961) *The Criminality of Women*. New York: A.S. Barnes.

Prison Reform Trust (2010) *Women in Prison*. London: PRT.

Raj, A. and Silverman, J. (2002) 'Violence against immigrant women', *Violence Against Women*, 8/3: 367.

Radford, J. (1987) 'Policing male violence', in J. Hanmer and M. Maynard (eds), *Women, Violence and Social Control*. London: Macmillan.

Redner, P. and Duncan, S. (2004) 'Making the most of the Victoria Climbie inquiry report', *Child Abuse Review*, 13: 95–114.

Reiner, R. (2002) 'Media made criminality: the representation of crime in the mass media', in M. Maguire, R. Morgan and R. Reiner (eds), *The Oxford Handbook of Criminology*, third edition. Oxford: Oxford University Press.

Remy, J. (1990) 'Patriarchy and fratriarchy as forms of androcracy', in J. Hearn and D. Morgan (eds), *Men, Masculinity and Social Theory*. London: Allen & Unwin.

Ringham, L. and Salisbury, H. (2004) *Support for Victims of Crime: Findings from the 2002/2003 British Crime Survey*. London: Home Office.

Ristanovic, V. (1999) (ed.) *Women, Violence and War: Wartime Victimisation of Refugees in the Balkans*. Budapest: Central European University Press.

Ristanovic, V. (2004) War victimisation of women http://www.penelopes.org/Anglais/xarticle.php3?id-article=302

Rock, P. (1990) *Helping Victims of Crime: The Home Office and the Rise of Victim Support in England and Wales*. Oxford: Oxford University Press.

Rock, P. (2002) 'On becoming a victim', in C. Hoyle and R. Young (eds), *New Visions of Crime Victims*. Oxford: Hart.

Rock, P. (2004) *Constructing Victims' Rights. The Home Office, New Labour, and Victims*. Oxford: Oxford University Press.

Ruggiero, V., South, N. and Taylor, I. (1998) *The New European Criminology*. London: Routledge.

Sandler, M. and Coles, D. (2008) *Dying on the Inside – Examining Women's Deaths in Prison*. London: INQUEST.

Savill, R. (2006) 'Two-year nightmare of the family torn apart by 'abuse' case blunders', *Daily Telegraph* 19.10.06: 5.

Scrambler, G. and Scrambler, A. (eds), (1997) *Rethinking Prostitution: Purchasing Sex in the 1990s*. London: Routledge.

Scraton, P. (1990) 'Scientific knowledge or masculine discourses? Challenging patriarchy in criminology', in L. Gelsthorpe and A. Morris (eds) *Feminist Perspectives in Criminology*. Buckingham: Open University Press.

Scraton, P. and Moore, L. (2008) 'Women in a male jail', *Criminal Justice Matters*, 71: 32–3.

Shaw, C.R. and McKay, H.D. (1942) *Juvenile Delinquency and Urban Areas.* Chicago: University of Chicago Press.

Sheehan, R., McIvor, G. and Trotter, C. (2007) *What Works with Women Offenders.* Cullompton: Willan.

Sheley, J.F. (1995) *Criminology A Contemporary Handbook,* second edition. London: Wadsworth.

Sheehan, McIvor and Trotter (2007) *What Works with Women Offenders.* Cullompton: Willan.

Silvestri, M. and Crowther-Dowey, C. (2008) *Gender and Crime.* London: Sage.

Simmons, J. and Dodd, T. (2003) *Crime in England and Wales 2002/2003.* London: Home Office.

Simmonds, L. and Mawby, R.I. (2000) 'Addressing victims' needs: evaluation of Victim Support', paper given at British Criminology Conference, Leicester, July.

Simon, R.J. (1975) *Women and Crime.* Toronto: Lexington Books.

Simon, R.J. and Landis, J. (1991) *The Crimes Women Commit, The Punishments They Receive.* Canada: Lexington Books.

Simpson, S.S. and Elis, L. (1996) 'Theoretical perspectives on the corporate victimisation of women', in E. Szockyi and J.G. Fox (eds), *Corporate Victimisation of Women.* Boston: Northeastern University Press.

Simpson, S.S. and Gibbs, C. (2006) 'Making sense of intersections', in K. Heimer and C. Kruttschnitt (eds), *Gender and Crime Patterns in Victimisation and Offending.* London: New York University Press.

Slack, J. (2008) 'Go soft on the wives who kill in cold blood', *Daily Mail,* 29 July.

Slapper, G. and Tombs, S. (1999) *Corporate Crime.* London: Addison Wesley Longman.

Smart, C. (1976) *Women, Crime and Criminology: A Feminist Critique.* London: Routledge and Kegan Paul.

Smart, C. (2008) 'Criminological theory: its ideology and implications concerning women', in K. Evans and J. Jamieson (eds), *Gender and Crime: A Reader.* Maidenhead: McGraw Hill/Open University Press.

Smith, C. (2005) 'Gender and crime', in C. Hale, K. Hayward, A. Wahidin and E. Wincup (eds), *Criminology.* Oxford: Oxford University Press.

Smith, D.K. (2001) 'Superannuating the second sex: law, privatisation and retirement income', *Modern Law Review,* 64 (4): 519.

Smith, C. and Wincup, E. (2000) 'Breaking in: researching criminal justice institutions for women', in R. King and E. Wincup (eds), *Doing Research on Crime and Justice.* Oxford: Oxford University Press.

Smith, C. and Wincup, E. (2009) 'Gender and crime', in K. Hale, A. Hayward, E. Wahidin and E. Wincup (eds), *Criminology,* second edition. Oxford: Oxford University Press.

Spalek, B. (2006) *Crime Victims: Theory, Policy and Practice.* Basingstoke: Palgrave Macmillan.

Spalek, B. (2007) *Knowledgeable Consumers? The Impact of Corporate Fraud.* Briefing Paper 4 Harm and Society Foundation, Centre for Criminal Justice Studies King's College London.

Spalek, B. and King, S. (2007) *Farepak Victims Speak Out: An Exploration of the Harms Caused by the Collapse of Farepak.* University of Birmingham: Centre for Crime and Justice Studies.

Sparks, R. (1992) *Television and the Drama of Crime.* Buckingham: Open University Press.

Stanko, E.A. (1985) *Intimate Intrusions: Women's Experience of Male Violence.* London: Virago.

Stanko, E.A. (1988a) 'Hidden violence against women', in M. Maguire and J. Pointing (eds), *Victims of Crime: A New Deal?* Milton Keynes: Open University Press.

Stanko, E. (1988b) 'Fear of crime and the myth of the safe home: a feminist critique of criminology', in K. Yllo and M. Bograd (eds), *Feminist Perspectives on Wife Abuse.* London: Sage.

Stanko, E. (1990a) *Everyday Violence: How Women and Men Experience Sexual and Physical Danger.* London: Pandora.

Stanko, E. (1990b) 'When precaution is normal: a Feminist critique of crime prevention', in L. Gelsthorpe and A. Morris (eds), *Feminist Perspectives in Criminology.* Milton Keynes: Open University Press.

Stanko, E. (1993) 'Ordinary fear: women, violence and personal safety', in P. Bart and E. Moran (eds), *Violence Against Women: The Bloody Footprints.* London: Sage.

Stanko, E. (1995) 'Masculinity, femininity and criminology', *Criminal Justice Matters* 19.

Stanko, E. (1995b) 'Women, crime and fear', *Annals of the American Academy of Political and Social Science*, 539: 46.

Stanko, B. (2008) 'Typical violence, normal precaution: men, women and interpersonal violence in England, Wales, Scotland and the USA', in K. Evans and J. Jamieson (eds), *Gender and Crime: A Reader.* Maidenhead: Open University Press.

Stanko, E. and Hobdell, K. (1993) 'Assault on men: masculinity and male victimisation', *British Journal of Criminology*, 33 (3): 400–15.

Stanley, L. and Wise, S. (1993) *Breaking Out Again: Feminist Ontology and Epistemology.* London: Routledge.

Steffensmeier, D.J. (1983) 'Organization properties and sex-segregation in the underworld: building a sociological theory of Sex differences in crime', *Social Forces*, 61: 4.

Stewart, L. (2004) 'I am more angry at the system than at my rapist', *Daily Telegraph* 15.04.04: 21.

Sumner, M. (2006) 'Feminist Research', in V. Jupp (ed.), *The Sage Dictionary of Social Research Methods.* London: Sage.

Surette, R. (1998) *Media, Crime and Criminal Justice: Images and Realities*, second edition. Belmont: Wadsworth.

Surrat, H., Inciardi, J., Kurtz, S. and Kiley, M. (2004) 'Sex work and drug use in a subculture of violence', *Crime & Delinquency*, 50 (1): 43–59.

Sutton, R.M. and Farrall, S.D. (2005) 'Gender, socially desirable responding and the fear of crime: are women really more anxious about crime?', *British Journal of Criminology*, 45: 2.

Sutton, R.M., Robinson, B. and Farrall, S.D. (2010) 'Gender, fear of crime, and self-presentation: an experimental investigation', *Psychology, Crime & Law*, 1–3, iFirst.12–224.

Swasy, A. (1996) '"Rely on tampons and toxic shock syndrome": Procter and Gamble's responses', in M.D. Ermann and R.J. Lundman (eds), *Corporate and Governmental Deviance: Problems of Organisational Behaviour in Contemporary Society.* Oxford: Oxford University Press.

Szyockyi, E. and Fox, J.G. (1996) *Corporate Victimisation of Women.* Boston: Northeastern University Press.

Taylor, A. (1993) *Women Drug Users: An Ethnography of a Female Injecting Community.* Oxford: Clarendon.

The Telegraph (2009) 'Half men arrested for rape not prosecuted'.

Tombs, S. (1999) 'Health and Safety Crimes: (In)visibility and the Problems of Knowing', in P. Davies, P. Francis and V. Jupp (eds), *Invisible Crimes: Their Victims and Their Regulation.* Basingstoke: Macmillan.

Tombs, S. (2000) 'Official statistics and hidden crime: researching safety crimes', in V. Jupp, P. Davies and P. Francis (eds), *Doing Criminological Research.* London: Sage.

Tombs, S. and Whyte, D. (2007) *Safety Crimes.* Cullompton: Willan.

Turton, J. (2000) 'Maternal sexual abuse and its victims', *Childright,* 165: 17–18.

Upson, A. (2004) *Violence at Work: Findings from the 2002/2003 British Crime Survey.* London: Home Office.

US Department of State (2003) *Trafficking in Persons Report* http://www.state.gov/g/tip/rls/tiprpt/2003/21262.htm.

Victims' Advisory Panel (2004) *'Listening to Victims – The First Year of the Victims' Advisory Panel.* London: VAP.

Von Hentig, H. (1948) *The Criminal and his Victim.* New Haven, CT: Yale University Press.

Wahidin, A. (2004) *Older Women in the Criminal Justice System: Running Out of Time.* London: Jessica Kingsley.

Wahidin, A. and Powell, J. (2007) 'Old age, victims and crime', in P. Davies, P. Francis and C. Greer. (eds), *Victims, Crime and Society.* London: Sage.

Walby, S. and Allen, J. (2004) *Domestic Violence, Sexual Assault and Stalking: Findings From the British Crime Survey.* Home Office Research Study 276. London: Home Office.

Walklate, S. (1989) *Victimology: The Victim and The Criminal Justice Process.* London: Unwin Hyman.

Walklate, S. (1998) '"Excavating the fear of crime", fear, anxiety or trust?', *Theoretical Criminology,* 2 (4): 403–18.

Walklate, S. (2000) 'Researching victims', in R.D. King and E. Wincup (eds), *Doing Research on Crime and Justice.* Oxford: Oxford University Press.

Walklate, S. (2001) 'The victim's lobby', in M. Ryan, S. Savage, and D. Wall (eds), *Policy Networks in Criminal Justice.* Basingstoke: Palgrave.

Walklate, S. (2003) 'Can there be a feminist victimology?', in P. Davies, P. Francis and V. Jupp (eds), *Victimisation: Theory, Research and Policy.* London: Palgrave.

Walklate, S. (2004a) *Gender, Crime and Criminal Justice.* Cullompton: Willan.

Walklate, S. (2004b) 'Gender, crime and criminal justice', in J. Muncie and D. Wilson (eds), *Student Handbook of Criminal Justice and Criminology.* London: Cavendish.

Walklate, S. (2005) *Criminology: The Basics.* London: Routledge.

Walklate (2006) 'Community safety and victims: who is the victim of community safety?' in P. Squires (ed.), *Community Safety: Critical Perspectives on Policy and Practice.* Bristol: Policy Press.

Walklate, S. (2007a) 'Men, victims and crime', in P. Davies, P. Francis and C. Greer (eds), *Victims, Crime and Society.* London: Sage.

Walklate, S. (2007b) *Imagining the Victim of Crime.* Maidenhead: Open University Press.

Walsh, D. (1986) *Heavy Business: Commercial Burglary and Robbery.* London: Routledge and Kegan Paul.

Warr, M. (1984) 'Fear of victimization: why are women and the elderly more afraid?', *Social Science Quarterly,* 65 (3): 681–702.

Warr, M. and Stafford, M. (1983) 'Fear of victimization: a look at the proximate causes', *Social Problems,* 61 (4): 1033–43.

West, C. and Zimmerman, D.H. (1987) 'Going gender', *Gender and Society,* 1 (2): 125–51.

West, C. and Fenstermaker, S. (1995) 'Doing difference', *Gender and Society,* 9 (1): 8–37.

Watts, C. and Zimmerman, C. (2002) 'Violence against women: global scope and magnitude', *Lancet,* 359 (9313): 1232–7.

Whitehead, T. (2009a) 'Rise of "ladette" culture as 241 women arrested each day for violence', Telegraph.co.uk 1 May, accessed 15.01.2010.

Whitehead, T. (2009b) 'Number of 'ladette women' fined for drunk and disorderly behaviour 'rises by a third' Telegraph.co.uk 14 June accessed 15.01.2010.

Whitehead, E. (2001) *Witness Satisfaction: Findings from the Witness Satisfaction Survey 2000.* London: Home Office Research, Development and Statistics Directorate.

Winlow, S. and Hall, S. (2007) *Violent Night: Urban Leisure and Contemporary Culture.* Oxford: Berg.

Wittrock, U. (2005) *English Summary. Criminal Statistics 2005.* Sweden: National Council for Crime Prevention.

Wolfgang, M. (1958) *Patterns in Criminal Homicide.* Philadelphia: University of Pennsylvania Press.

Wolfgang, M. (1959) 'Suicide by means of victim precipitated homicide', *Journal of Clinical and Experimental Psychopathology and Quarterly Review of Psychiatry and Neurology,* 20: 335–49.

Women in Prison (2007) http://www.womeninprison.org.uk.

Women in Prison (2009) http://www.womeninprison.org.uk.

Women's Aid Federation of England and Wales (2004) *Women's Aid Briefing Paper Domestic Violence, Crime and Victims Bill January 2004.* London: Women's Aid.

Worrall, A. (1990) *Offending Women. Female Lawbreakers and the Criminal Justice System.* New York: Routledge.

Wykes, M. and Welsh, K. (2009) *Violence, Gender and Justice.* London: Sage.

Young, J. (1986) The failure of criminology: the need for a radical realism, in R. Matthews and J. Young (eds), *Confronting Crime.* London: Sage.

Zedner, L. (2003) 'Victims', in M. Maguire, R., Morgan and R. Reiner (eds), *The Oxford Handbook of Criminology,* third edition. Oxford: Oxford University Press.

Index